DATE D

*The Nature of*

# Chicago

# The Nature of
# *Chicago*

## ISABEL S. ABRAMS

CHICAGO
REVIEW
PRESS

**Library of Congress Cataloging-in-Publication Data**

Abrams, Isabel S.
   The nature of Chicago: a comprehensive guide to natural sites in
and around the city / Isabel S. Abrams.
     p.     cm.
   Includes bibliographical references and index.
   ISBN 1-55652-312-2
   1. Natural history—Illinois—Chicago—Guidebooks.  2. Science
museums—Illinois—Chicago—Guidebooks.  3. Chicago (Ill.)—Guidebooks.
I. Title.
QH105.I3A53  1997
508.773'11—dc21                                         96-51835
                                                   CIP

Published by Chicago Review Press, Incorporated
814 N. Franklin Street
Chicago, Illinois 60610
ISBN 1-55652-312-2
1 2 3 4 5
Printed in the United States of America

*To my loved ones,*
*caretakers of the environment,*
*and*
*all those who say, "You can do it, kid!"*

# Contents

**Introduction 1**

*1*

## Glaciers, Wild Onions, and Skyscrapers 7

The natural forces and natural resources that shaped Chicago's history.
Tours around the city and downtown with glimpses of the city's
architecture, plan, geology, waterways, and greenways.

*2*

## Lake Michigan Lookouts 27

The tale of Lake Chicago and Lake Michigan. How the water and shoreline
influence Chicago's weather and lifestyle. Tours of ancient beach ridges and
the beach scene, with harbors and shoreline features.

*3*

## Landforms and Landscapes 49

Glacial debris and plant communities that shaped Chicago scenery.
Tours to moraines, eskers, kames, and Fermilab.

*4*

## Skywatch 59

How Earth traveling in space, celestial bodies in the heavens, and clouds in
the sky influence the environment of Chicago. Tours to Adler Planetarium
and Astronomy Museum and to the Cernan Earth and Space Center.

*5*

## The Sea of Grass 67

The ecology and history of Illinois prairie. Tours of original and
restored prairies and oak savanna.

*6*

## Native Americans and Nature 79

The settlements, hunting grounds, and travels of Native Americans.
Trails in the city and artifacts near downtown. Tours to Native American
sites in the forest preserves, along the Illinois and Michigan Canal National
Heritage corridor, and to the Isle à La Cache Museum.

*7*

## The Forest and the Trees 89

Oaks and other trees in Chicago forests.
Tours to forest preserves and nature centers.

## 8
## Wonderful Wetlands 103

The plants and animals of wetlands and the services they provide to the urban environment. Tours to marshes, ponds, bogs, fens.

## 9
## River Runs 115

The history of Chicago waterways. Tours of the Chicago River, Des Plaines River, Calumet River, Sanitary and Ship Canal, and Illinois and Michigan National Heritage Corridor.

## 10
## Botanical Beauties 133

Tours to Lincoln Park, Grant Park, Jackson Park, and other Chicago-area parks, gardens, conservatories, and arboretums.

## 11
## Animal Encounters 157

Tours to the habitats of exotic and native beasts: birding spots, the Lincoln Park Zoo, Brookfield Zoo, and Shedd Aquarium.

## 12
## Museums on the Wild Side 173

Celestial bodies, beautiful flowers, endangered animals, dinosaur skeletons, precious stones, and other natural wonders in Chicago's museums.

## 13
## Outdoor Action 183

Places for biking, boating, fishing, golfing, hiking, horseback riding, skating, skiing, swimming, and tobogganing in Chicago and its suburbs.

## 14
## Celebrate Nature 205

Chicago's calendar of nature celebrations. Event hotlines.

## 15
## Nature Organizations 233

## Afterword 247

## Glossary 249

## Suggestions for Additional Reading 253

## Index 259

# Acknowledgments

M y deep appreciation to Wayne Schimpff, my guide to coral reefs, glaciers, prairies, forests, and other natural wonders in Chicago; Ed Lace, who brought Native Americans and the western frontier to life; Dr. Paul H. Knappenberger Jr., who connected earth and sky; Lee Botts, who helped me see the shore and deep water of Lake Michigan; Ralph Frese for the beauty of Chicago rivers; Char Giardiana for the excitement of the I & M Canal.

Special thanks to Henry Henderson and Susan Malech Hoerr for the urban action scene; Carol Fialkowski and Jean De Horn for the science side; Chet Ryndek for forest preserves; Micheline Brown for the park picture; Julie Sniderman for park history; Dan Purciarello for public gardens; Linda Wilson and Amy Ritter for underwater life; Linda C. Vance and Bob Munz for the sand ridges; Doug Anderson for the birds; and Ed Radatz for a global perspective.

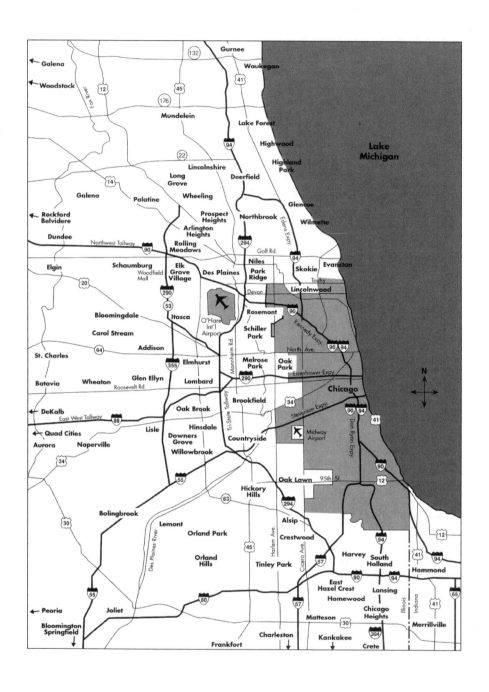

# Introduction

At first glance Chicago appears to be a bustling metropolis with little in the way of natural splendor. Look closer, though, and you will find wilderness as marvelous as the city's architecture coexisting with it. Chicago's beauty and its history were born in wildness and are preserved in the city's unique natural heritage.

Chicago is a wild place, not by virtue of its nightlife or crime, but because it shelters pristine landscapes, untamed plants and animals, and secluded retreats where greenery reigns. In a short drive from downtown you can visit forests and prairies that survive from the time of the glaciers or spend an afternoon exploring dunes, nature preserves, wetlands, or bogs. Break away from the pressures of urban life by strolling through wildflower gardens or biking through parks. If you prefer, surround yourself with exotic beasts and ancient life forms at the aquarium, zoos, and museums. All these sensory pleasures come from the wild side of Chicago.

Become acquainted with wilderness in the city and you will realize that natural resources and natural forces are the source of Chicago's vitality. The power of an ancient sea and moving ice shaped the land-forms around us. Rivers and Lake Michigan provide water and transportation. Strong winds clear pollution from the air. Surrounding land supplies food and minerals. These raw materials from the earth nurture Chicago's people and make their commerce prosper. Nature is the life-support system of the city.

Chicago reveals its natural wonders in every season. When the sun stays longer in the heavens and ice begins to thaw in February, Chicagoans look for one of the first signs of spring—skunk cabbage sprouting through snow in Catherine Chevalier Woods. In March and April blue and white wildflowers appear in the woodlands at Willow Springs. Robins and warblers arrive, and yellow crocus and red tulips bloom in gardens throughout the city. Garfield Park Conservatory puts on a spring show with red tulips, lavender hyacinths, and yellow daffodils.

In summer, bike, walk, or roller-blade along the lakefront or through Marquette Park. Summer is the perfect time to visit the zoos and explore wetlands, ponds, and rivers. Woodworth Prairie changes from week to week as black-eyed Susans, goldenrods, and many different grasses flower and disperse their seeds in late summer.

Short-lived autumn yellows Goose Lake Prairie and brings a cascade of color to the Morton Arboretum. Squirrels and chipmunks gather nuts and seeds in city parks. Falcons gather at Montrose Harbor and herons can be spotted at Paul H. Douglas Nature Sanctuary. The sunsets are crisp, the harvest moon appears, and the stars of Pegasus (the Horse) brighten the night sky.

Winter in Chicago seems endless and dreary when clouds cover the sun and the air freezes your breath. But sometimes snow blankets parks and streets, creating a wonderland of white. This is the season to visit the haunting beauty of the lakefront and see waves frozen into dramatic ice sculptures; to look at stars in the heavens that appear brighter than the lights of skyscrapers. Step into the Lincoln Park Conservatory for a breath of spring at the February Azalea Show, or into the Art Institute for a celebration of nature in art, away from the chill outside.

## How to Use This Book

*The Nature of Chicago* was written to help you discover Chicago's many natural treasures. Individual chapters are devoted to Lake Michigan, the landforms surrounding us, the sky above us, the prairies, Native Americans and their use of the land, forests, wetlands, rivers, parks and gardens, zoos and aquaria, and museums. The final three chapters list places to enjoy various outdoor sports and activities, special events, and organizations and clubs that celebrate nature. All the chapters include tours to destinations where you can see firsthand how nature has shaped and continues to share our city.

## About the Tours

Most of the tours described here will fascinate and educate everyone. Others are best suited to those who have a particular interest in the subject or who live in the area. Some of these sites are on protected or private land and may require that you make an appointment first. Where this is the case we have noted it. All of the tours have been rated to help you choose.

🍃🍃🍃 Three-leaf tours are worth a special trip for everyone—adults, children, and families. Information centers and facilities are nearby.

🍃🍃 Two-leaf tours represent excellent examples of a particular subject area or habitat. Many are off the beaten track and represent nature unfettered by gift shops and tourist centers. Most visitors will find them thoroughly worthwhile.

🍃 One-leaf trips are appropriate for visitors with a special interest in the subject or for a quick stop for those who are in the neighborhood already.

## Access for the Physically Challenged

Most forest preserves, parks, and museums are wheelchair accessible. However, a phone call to confirm this is recommended. Chicago has many accessible natural attractions in all areas of the city and suburbs.

## Getting There

For each tour, under "Getting there," distances are measured in miles from downtown Chicago.

Note: Signs on I-94 can be confusing. The signs say "west" when the highway actually goes north; and the signs say "east" when the highway actually goes south. In this guide, directions are given as north or south. (This becomes clear when you look at a map.) Just remember, I-94 "east" takes you toward Indiana and "west" takes you toward Wisconsin.

Obtain good maps. AAA (Chicago Motor Club) has a map of Chicago that lists city streets and a map of Cook County that lists places of interest (museums, etc.), suburban towns, beaches, forest preserves and picnic areas, parks, golf and country clubs, lakes, rivers and creeks, dams and locks.

Call the Chicago Transit Authority at (312) 836-7000 or toll free at (800) 972-7000 to request maps, routing advice, and fare information.

Caution: Phone numbers, locations, hours, and admission fees can change. Check before you travel to the tour site.

## Safety and Fun in Wild Places

🦐 Many of the places mentioned here are in secluded areas. Check with your hotel and/or local police about crime in the area before venturing out.

🦐 Be sure to dress appropriately for the weather and the terrain. Hiking boots or comfortable walking shoes are recommended, as are hats and gloves in the winter and sunscreen in the summer.

🦐 For long hikes, bring along a water canteen, a first-aid kit, and insect repellent. Sign a sheet at the nature center or tell someone what trail you are taking.

🦐 Be cautious where street traffic is heavy and near railroad tracks.

🦐 Lake Michigan can be dangerous. Swim in guarded areas only. Stay off the rocks and the ice at its edge.

🦐 Respect private property.

🦐 Build a fire only at designated sites and make sure that it is completely extinguished before you leave.

🦐 Allow birds and other wildlife to seek their own food. This helps keep the animals healthy and wild.

🦐 Stay on trails and boardwalks to protect yourself and the natural surroundings.

🦐 Leave only your footprints in the wilderness. Take equipment and garbage with you when you leave.

If you want to be up close and personal with nature, use your ears, eyes, nose, and hands. Be patient but watchful. Slow your pace and you will find things you never found before. Trail times are based on a leisurely pace of three miles an hour, allowing you to take the time to enjoy the panorama, see colorful insects, hear melodic birdsongs, and smell the fragrant wildflowers.

# 1

# Glaciers, Wild Onions, and Skyscrapers

*Urbis in Horto*—City in a Garden
—Chicago's motto

Chicago is a wild kind of town. Fierce winds bluster their way through skyscraper canyons. Birds migrate south from Canada, rest and feed on the shore of Lake Michigan, then soar above city streets on their journey south. Lions, tigers, and giraffes sun themselves in zoos; porpoises and whales swim near the downtown area.

The city may appear to be nothing more than cement, asphalt, and concrete, for lakefront offices have replaced the swamps that once smelled of wild onions. Homes, highways, and shopping malls have replaced the prairie grass that grew taller than a man on horseback. But take a closer look and you will find remnants of ancient grasslands and wetlands within the boundaries of this urban area. Endangered plants, Indian trails, and ancient waterways endure in this meeting place of land and water; this gathering place for millions of people. Chicago contains nature, just like the countryside. The city also interacts with the surrounding rural area.

According to historian William Cronon, city and country share a common past and have always shaped and reshaped one another. Thus, neither the urban environment nor the rural environment is as "natural" or "unnatural" as it appears. Chicago—like forest, prairie, or wetland—is an ecosystem. Its plants and animals interact with one

another and with the physical environment. Every human in this urban ecosystem breathes air, eats plants or animals, drinks water, and
makes a living with natural resources. Nature is the framework and
the life-support system for the city.

## Out of the Depths of a Coral Sea

Chicago is extremely flat because it stands on land that was once the
bottom of a warm shallow sea, called by geologists the Silurian Sea.
This sea existed four hundred million years ago and was so vast it covered the entire Mississippi Valley. Coral creatures, the ancestors of
jellyfish, sifted lime (calcium carbonate) from its salty water to con-
struct their skeletons. As generation after generation of coral animals
died, their skeletons hardened into limestone rock—the bedrock that
anchors Chicago's skyscrapers.

Ancient animals made the city's bedrock and ancient plants made
the fuel that energizes this modern city. These plants lived two hundred and fifty million years ago, in swamps that appeared as the coral
seas disappeared. Giant ferns dominated these warm, swampy forests.
As generations of plants died, they decomposed into peat and com-
pressed into rock. This black rock, with its fossils of the ancient
carboniferous forest, is mined as coal in southern Illinois. It is this
fossil fuel that lights and heats the buildings and runs the machinery of
Chicago.

## Glaciers Shape the Land

The coal-producing forests died off when the ice ages began, about a
million years ago, and ice sheets from the Arctic blanketed most of
North America. A glacier, or lake of ice, slid across Illinois, crushing
higher ground and deepening the basin of the inland sea. For more
than nine hundred thousand years, these glaciers advanced and retreated as the climate periodically cooled and warmed. Near the end
of the ice ages the entire Midwest was covered with a one-mile-thick
block of frozen water.

Huge amounts of debris were trapped in the ice until about eleven
thousand years ago, when the last ice age ended. Boulders, gravel, silt,
and clay dropped out of the melting edge and formed long ridges still
visible in Chicago's western suburbs. The melting glaciers also depos-

Sky and water frame this view of the Chicago skyline.

ited a sixty-foot-thick layer of clay, sand, and gravel on the land they crushed, leaving the flat terrain on which the city stands.

The glaciers melted and became what is known as the Great Lakes—the world's largest reservoir of fresh water. The ancient lake in this area, Lake Chicago, covered most of what is now Chicago's entire metropolitan area. The shore was miles inland, at Palos Park and La Grange. The lake periodically drained away through low spots, such as the one west of the city in the Palos region. In the course of time, Lake Chicago dropped sixty feet, leaving ancient beach ridges high and dry. One of these beach ridges, Ridge Avenue, is a main north and south commuter route. The "puddle" that Lake Chicago left behind is Lake Michigan—the third largest Great Lake and the sixth largest freshwater lake in the world.

## Prairie Territory

As land at the southern tip of Lake Michigan dried out, Illinois west of the lake became a prairie state. The cycle of seasons brought cold winters, dry summers, and spring and autumn rainstorms. The twenty to forty inches of rain that fell each year was too little rainfall to sustain forests but enough to sustain grasslands. Sun and rain nurtured the grass, and its roots went deep and wide in the soil.

When the first white explorers arrived in 1673, a "sea of grass" covered the flat terrain. It was a tallgrass prairie, with some grasses that grew almost as high as a covered wagon. Although it was dominated by grasses, it had a dazzling array of flowers as well. The soil was fertile, enriched by the grass and flowers that lived and died there.

For ten thousand years, hoofbeats made by thousands of buffalo rumbled across the grassy plains. Flocks of millions of passenger pigeons blocked out the sun, although individual birds were only about one foot long. Native Americans hunted these birds, as well as the large buffalo that grazed on the grasslands. Although Native Americans killed some buffalo, sixty million roamed the American prairie until they were slaughtered by white settlers with shotguns. By 1890, there were fewer than one thousand live buffalo. Not long after, the passenger pigeons became extinct. The only place you can see them now is at the Field Museum (see Chapter 12). Fortunately, a small group of buffalo—descendants of the original herd that roamed the grasslands—still grazes on the grounds of Fermilab (see Chapter 3), west of Chicago.

The midwestern population grew rapidly in the nineteenth and twentieth centuries. Settlers destroyed the prairie by using large plows to tear the deep roots of the grasses and turn the area into farmland. Farms eventually gave way to urban and suburban development. New roads, railroads, and expressways provided easy access to the countryside. Families fleeing the noise, dirt, danger, and crowds of the city built homes and planted lawns and gardens in the new suburbs. Few farms remain in and around Chicago; and less than 1 percent of Illinois is covered with prairie.

Small bits of prairie do survive in the Chicago area. You can see restored prairie in forest preserves, the Chicago Botanic Garden, and the Morton Arboretum; and a remnant of original prairie that may be ten thousand years old is located near 87th Street on South Harlem Avenue.

## Native Americans

Stone axes and arrowheads that were discovered in the Chicago area indicate that human beings arrived in this region about ten thousand years ago. It is not known why they came from the north after the glaciers retreated, but they hunted wild beasts and gathered roots and berries for about a thousand years, then mysteriously disappeared. About two thousand years later a new group of people settled on the grasslands. These early tribes hunted for food, but later generations farmed. Thus, three hundred years ago, when the first Europeans came to Illinois, they saw Native Americans planting corn, squash, and beans. These Native American farmers lived in villages on the banks of the Des Plaines River and their trails led to the heart of downtown Chicago. You can see the sites of their villages in the forest preserves and travel in their footsteps when you drive down diagonal city streets such as Archer and Milwaukee avenues.

## Chicago, a Native American Name

The name *Chicago* originated in a Native American language as "Chicagou," a word that seems to have meant "wild onion," "skunk," "polecat," or "stinking place." Perhaps this area was named "Chicagou" because wild onion, wild garlic, and skunk cabbage grew in the wetlands that were the hunting grounds of local Potawatomi people.

No one knows the exact origin of the city's name. Milo Quaife, who wrote a history of Chicago, found that a river near Cleveland was called "Chogage," and that the word *Chicagou* was common to several tribes, with meanings such as "big river," "long detour," "powerful odor," and "great building." That is why some historians translate *Chicago* as "strong," "great," or "powerful."

Throughout the years, Chicago has also acquired other names. It is called "Second City" because of its competition with New York City and because it was second in population toward the end of the nineteenth century. The twentieth-century poet Carl Sandburg dubbed it "Hog Butcher to the World" because, in the 1800s, the city prospered as cattle and hogs were driven to the slaughterhouses in the Union Stockyards located east of Halsted between 39th and 47th street. (All that remains of the Union Stockyards is an arch commemorating the site.) It was called the "I Will City" because of the citizens' determination to rebuild after the disastrous Chicago fire in 1871. It is known as the "Windy City," probably because New York newspaper editor Charles A. Dana wrote, "Pay no attention to the nonsensical claims of that windy city," in 1889, when several cities were competing for a world's fair. Thus, "Windy City" is a reference to Chicago's long-winded politicians, not its weather.

# Weather in the Windy City

Chicago winds can be strong, sometimes so strong that pedestrians on Michigan Avenue feel they are whisked down the sidewalks faster than cars move on the street. The strongest recorded gust occurred on March 8, 1991 and it was eighty-four miles an hour. On average, however, Chicago's winter winds are eleven miles an hour and summer breezes are eight miles an hour.

Winds from the west clear out pollution, sweeping it through skyscraper canyons toward Lake Michigan. Nevertheless, a layer of smog often mars the skyline and makes city dwellers rub their eyes and gasp for breath. The culprit behind these discomforts is ozone pollution, produced because so much fossil fuel (oil, gas, and coal) is burned to run automobiles and machinery, and to heat and light Chicago's buildings. In order to find out if the air is safe to breathe, Chicagoans call (312) 744-4365 for an air quality report, which gives the pollution index for such things as particulates, ozone, carbon monoxide, and ultraviolet radiation.

Chicago's atmosphere is also influenced by its real estate development. Asphalt streets, parking lots, homes, factories, and office buildings absorb heat from the sun and fossil fuel burning. In winter, this heat is slowly released into the cold night air. Thus Chicago, like all urban environments, is a "heat island," several degrees warmer than surrounding farms and natural areas.

Lake Michigan is so large that it moderates the city's weather. Like an ocean, it absorbs heat more quickly and releases it more slowly than the land. As a result, winter winds are warmed by Lake Michigan and sizzling summer temperatures drop near the lakefront. Nevertheless, the effects of Lake Michigan are felt throughout the urban area and the official Chicago temperature is measured inland from the lake, at O'Hare Airport.

Average winter temperatures are a high of thirty-two degrees Fahrenheit and a low of sixteen. Average summer temperatures are a high of eighty-two degrees Fahrenheit and a low of sixty-one. In summer, there are usually fourteen days above ninety and in winter there are usually twelve days below zero. These extremes force Chicagoans to be very adaptable.

Chicago's precipitation—rain, hail, and snow—averages thirty-six inches a year. Summer is rainiest (twelve inches); spring (ten inches)

Chicago's Stockyards Arch.

and fall (nine inches) are less rainy; winter averages five inches of precipitation, but that adds up to twenty-eight inches of snow over December, January, and February.

Most weather systems move from west to east, but weather fronts from the north and south also move through the area. When the fronts clash, they bring wind, clouds, rain, snowstorms, tornadoes, and dramatic changes in temperature including hot humid air from the Gulf of Mexico and arctic cold from Canada. No wonder Chicagoans delight in complaining about the weather.

## The Urban Plan

Chicago's design, with its open lakefront, urban parks, and encircling forest preserves, was largely the vision of architect and planner Daniel H. Burnham. He, along with Edward H. Bennett, authored the 1909 *Plan of Chicago*, which set the stage for what Chicago looks like today.

Burnham saw Chicago as a center of Midwest commerce that dominated an area as large as France. In order to promote Chicago's economic growth, in the early 1900s, he designed a highway system like a bicycle wheel—with a rim and spokes. Roads circling the city's rim connected one suburb to another. Roads arranged like spokes connected each suburb on the rim to the city center. The design worked well because the land was so flat, with no hills, ravines, or major rivers to interfere.

Many of the "spoke" roads originated as Indian trails. They became country roads when farmers carried their crops to Chicago markets. As the population grew, these diagonal roads that converged in the city center became paved streets. Now crowded with cars, they include Lincoln, Clybourn, Elston, Milwaukee, Ogden, Blue Island, Cottage Grove, and Archer avenues.

In the city, Burnham viewed Michigan Avenue as the main north-south street. Consequently, he promoted the widening of Michigan Avenue to attract department stores, hotels, and upscale shops that eventually led to the "Magnificent Mile" of today. Burnham viewed Congress Street, which was marshy land in the early 1800s, as the main east-west street. That is why he planned a civic center where Congress Circle (a major highway interchange) now exists, and a great railway passenger terminal where Chicago's Central Post Office arches over the Congress street traffic. Roosevelt Road, at the south end of downtown, is elevated over the railroad yards because of Burnham's suggestion.

Burnham's most important idea was that green spaces be provided so people could escape the tumult and asphalt of the urban environment. Grant Park and the entire lakefront park system are essentially what Burnham proposed. In addition, the extensive forest preserve system of Cook County that now encircles the city is largely the result of Burnham's vision.

# Names from the Wilderness

As you walk or drive through the city and read the street names, you hear echoes of the first pioneers and the original wilderness.

## North/South Streets

◗ LaSalle Street (140 W.) is named for the French explorer René-Robert Cavelier, Sieur de La Salle, who hoped to discover a passage from North America to the Orient somewhere south of the Great Lakes and who in 1682 established France's claim to the Mississippi Valley and Louisiana.

- Clark Street (100 W.) is named after George Rogers Clark, who in 1778 captured the British fort in Vincennes and gained the Northwest Territory for the United States.

- Dearborn Street (36 W.) is named after Fort Dearborn, built in 1803 to defend a strategic spot in the water route that connected the Great Lakes with the Mississippi River.

- State Street (the dividing line between east and west) is the end of State Road, a major Indian trail and stagecoach route across the prairie.

- Wabash Avenue (44 E.) is named after the Wabash River, in remembrance of Hoosier (Indiana) farmers who camped here when trading grain for store goods.

- Michigan Avenue (100 E.) is named after Lake Michigan (a Native American name), because it was the shoreline in 1833, when Chicago was incorporated.

## East/West Streets

- Ohio (600 N.), Ontario (640 N.), Erie (660 N.), Huron (700 N.), and Superior (730 N.) Streets are all Native American names.

- Hubbard Street (440 N.) is named after Gurdon S. Hubbard, a fur trader who in 1825 became superintendent of the Illinois rivers.

- Kinzie Street (400 N.) is named after John Kinzie, one of Chicago's early white settlers, who in 1812 was operating a trading post on the Chicago River.

## 🍂🍂 Nature in the Loop (2 hours)

Strictly speaking, the Loop is the area surrounded by the elevated train tracks—Wabash Avenue on the east, Van Buren Street on the south, Wells Street on the west, and Lake Street on the north. But most Chicagoans call the entire central business district "the Loop."

As you take this tour, you will discover how nature plays a vital role in the architecture and outdoor art of Chicago's downtown area. The skyscrapers you will see are anchored in bedrock that was once an ancient coral reef. The glass, concrete, and steel buildings and the asphalt streets are fabricated from the raw materials of nature: from limestone quarried in the area and from minerals found in sand, iron ore, and oil. The architecture is also influenced by Chicago weather. Buildings have flexible frameworks, strong walls, insulated glass, and braces that enable them to withstand fierce winds and great temperature swings.

🍂 Start your tour at State and Madison streets. This is the heart of the modern city, with State Street dividing east from west and Madison Street dividing north from south. State Street is a remnant of a major Native American trail that crossed the prairie. White men called it the Vincennes Trace (later Hubbard's Trace) and traveled it on horseback or by stagecoach from the Wabash River in Indiana to Danville and then to Chicago. Settlers put milestones on this trail and named it State Road. When railroads came to Chicago, State Road was abandoned. The State Street of today is only a small part of the original road that once brought Native Americans and farmers into the heart of downtown Chicago. In the 1830s, Chicago was a log cabin village that extended eight blocks west to Halsted Street and eight blocks north to Chicago Avenue. Beyond the tiny town lay farms and Native American settlements scattered across the prairie.

🍂 On the southeast corner of State and Madison you will see Carson Pirie Scott, one of Chicago's oldest commercial emporiums. The architect, Louis Sullivan, designed the store's elaborate wrought-iron entrance with its spectacular floral motifs. His designs here, and elsewhere throughout the city, were greatly inspired by nature. His horizontally elongated windows that catch the light have helped establish Chicago as a city that is famous for its architecture. This now valuable real estate was once swampy property that the first speculators sold for $6.42 an acre, mostly on credit.

🍂 Walk north on State Street one block to Washington Street, and then walk west to Dearborn. Here you will find Daley Plaza, on the northwest corner of Washington (100 N.) and Dearborn (50 W.). Dominating this open square is a sculpture called *Chicago Picasso*, created by the Spanish artist Pablo Picasso for the city. *Chicago Picasso* is made of steel that was oxidized by the environment to its brownish color. Is it a dog? A bird? A woman? You decide. When it was unveiled to great controversy and some ridicule in 1967, Mayor Daley said, "What is strange to us today will be familiar tomorrow." He was right.

❦ Walk west on Washington Street a couple of blocks to LaSalle, and then turn north. The State of Illinois Center, recently renamed the James R. Thompson Center, stands at 100 W. Randolph Street. On the open plaza in front you will find a twenty-nine-foot-tall abstract sculpture entitled *Monument à la Bête Debout* (Monument to a Standing Beast), by the French artist Jean Dubuffet. It is made of white plaster outlined in black.

On the second level, visit the Illinois Art Gallery to view cityscape paintings, ceramic wildlife sculpture, and jewelry made by Illinois artisans. The fourth floor boasts a painting entitled *American Buffalo*, by Roger Brown, that offers an imaginary view of the Chicago skyline from the prairie.

❦ Exit the building and head east to Dearborn Street. Then turn south to Monroe. The First National Bank is at 1 National Plaza, between Monroe (100 S.) and Madison. A large open plaza adjacent to the bank has a monolith entitled *The Four Seasons,* by the Russian artist Mark Chagall. Slowly walk around this seventy-foot-long and fourteen-foot-high mosaic studded with 250 colors of stone and glass chips. You will see fish, flowers, birds, and the four seasons. Chagall said, "The seasons represent human life, both physical and spiritual, at its different ages."

❦ Continue south on Dearborn Street two blocks, to the Dirkson Federal Building, at 219 S. Dearborn. Alexander Calder's *Flamingo* (a fifty-three-foot-high steel structure painted a vivid red) is on the west side in front of the Federal building. Calder named this work after the wetland bird "because it was sort of pink and has a long neck."

❦ Walk south on Dearborn Street and turn east onto Jackson Boulevard. The Monadnock Building stands at 53 W. Jackson. In 1893, this sixteen-story structure was the tallest office building in the world. It is widely recognized as the first skyscraper. In order to stabilize it on Chicago's muddy ground, architects designed a floating foundation of steel and concrete as an underground raft.

❦ Continue west along Jackson Boulevard to LaSalle Street and the Chicago Board of Trade at 141 W. Jackson. It is part of the Exchange Center, which includes the Chicago Board Options Exchange and the Midwest Stock Exchange. Much of Chicago's wealth comes from the raw materials of nature that are traded here.

The Chicago Board of Trade is a tremendous marketplace where wheat, soybeans, oats, rye, cotton, beef, and other commodities are bought and sold. Look forty-five stories up to see the statue of Ceres, the Roman goddess of grain, harvest, and plenty, by the American artist John Storrs. This is the world's busiest grain exchange and a place that harvests much of this country's wealth from farmland.

🐦 Continue north on the east side of LaSalle to the Rookery Building, at 209 S. LaSalle Street. It was named the Rookery because, when the lot was vacant, it became a gathering place for pigeons. The lobby is adorned with an intricate pattern of leaves and vines designed by Louis Sullivan.

🐦 Walk west on Adams Street and cross Franklin to reach the Sears Tower, at 233 S. Wacker Drive. This is one of the world's tallest buildings—110 stories and 1,454 feet tall. The building weighs 222,500 tons, so it is supported by 114 caissons sunk into bedrock as deep as the Statue of Liberty is tall. Be sure to see Alexander Calder's large mobile *Universe* suspended from the ceiling of the lobby. A flexible steel framework allows this skyscraper to sway about a foot in any direction as it withstands Chicago's winds. On a clear day from the Skydeck (103rd floor, open 9 A.M.–12 A.M.) you can see four states. Among the many offices is the national headquarters of Sears, Roebuck, and Company, a retail business that began by selling clothing and household goods to farmers and ranchers through its famous Sears catalog in 1891. Sears Tower has a daytime population of more than twelve thousand people, more than many Illinois farm towns.

## The Great Chicago Fire (October 8, 1871)

Legend has it that the fire began when a cow kicked over a lantern in the O'Leary's barn near De Koven Street (1100 S.) and Taylor Street. Winds spread the flames east and north. The fire jumped the Chicago River, headed downtown, and swept through the Near North Side all the way to the city line at Fullerton Avenue (2400 N.). Parents and children ran from deadly smoke and heat to safety at the lakefront while firefighters and other citizens fought to save their homes and workplaces. Using Lake Michigan water from the pumping station, they tirelessly poured it on the burning wooden buildings.

By the following morning, most of the buildings were debris and the great city of the Midwest was reduced to ashes. It is no wonder that Chicago's building code was immediately changed to demand fire-proofing, back doors, and fire escapes. Nor is it any surprise that the former wooden homes were replaced by stone and brick houses, or that office buildings were later constructed of steel and glass.

After the Chicago Fire, only two limestone buildings stood on the Near North Side. These buildings are the Water Tower, at 845 N. Michigan Avenue, and the Chicago Avenue Pumping Station across the street. They became city landmarks in 1972 and have become symbols of Chicago's "I will" spirit that rebuilt the city after the fire. The Chicago Water Tower was also recognized as the First American Water Landmark in 1969.

Surprisingly, the O'Leary home was never touched by flames because winds spread the fire north and left most of the Near West Side intact. Today, *Pillar of Fire,* a sculpture by Egon Weiner, stands near Jefferson and DeKoven Streets in the courtyard of the Chicago Fire Academy at 558 W. De Koven Street.

## 🍃🍃 Highway Gardens (1 to 2 hours)

Some of the best examples of Chicago's native trees, grasses, and plants can be seen while commuting along the city's highways, in a wonderful proof of how urban development and nature can support each other.

Edens Expressway was one of the first to be adorned with large-flowered prairie plants such as sylphium, prairie dock, compass plant, and black-eyed Susan. Prairie grasses, some very tall, include switchgrass, little bluestem, and Indian grass. Big bluestem, Illinois' state grass, grows more than six feet tall. In summer, it has a "turkey foot," or three-pronged seedhead, and in winter its dried leaves take on a maroon color. In autumn, Indian grass has orange, blue, and yellow seedheads.

Ten thousand trees absorb car exhaust and manage to live on the six-mile stretch of the Kennedy Expressway between downtown and the cutoff to Edens Expressway. They are almost all native trees, including several varieties of oak, hickories, and pines that form large groves. The Kennedy also provides seasonal delights for commuters, including purple prairie clover, lavender and deep purple coneflower in late spring; large purple-flowered blazing stars (liatris) in summer;

and purple asters and yellow goldenrod in autumn. Rattlesnake master, a tall plant that looks like a desert yucca, attracts wildlife and butterflies, including some that are endangered.

Wildflowers adorn the meeting place of the Eisenhower, Dan Ryan, and Kennedy expressways, called the Circle Interchange. Geraniums and other brightly colored blossoms greet commuters exiting east on the Ohio Street Bridge at Orleans Street.

Although Chicago's roads originated as paths through swampland, there are no wetland sites within the urban area. To view restored wetlands with white-flowered arrowhead, bright red cardinal flower, blue lobelia, and rose-colored swamp milkweed among cattails, travel highways northwest of Chicago, such as the one in Long Grove near Gilmer on Route 83 along the Elgin/O'Hare Expressway, and in Volo near Illinois 120 at U.S. 12.

The Stevenson Expressway, once the site of the Illinois and Michigan Canal, has limestone pattern bridges at LaGrange Road and Pulaski Road. In time, prairie plantings will extend from Joliet Road east to the city. The Illinois Department of Transportation (IDOT) plans to rehabilitate and replant the neglected factory areas along this expressway.

## A Glimpse of the South Side (2 to 3 hours)

The south side of Chicago has an abundance of parks with lagoons and meadows, such as Jackson Park, Douglas Park, and Washington Park (see Chapter 10). Also, the far south Calumet area contains wetlands rich in wildfowl tucked in between warehouses and factories (see Chapter 8).

● Calumet Avenue (325 E.) and 18th Street was the site of the Fort Dearborn Massacre. It was beachfront in 1812 when the United States was at war with Great Britain. Captain Nathan Heald evacuated the fort with his soldiers, civilian traders, their families, and two supply wagons. Suddenly, Indians appeared on the sand dunes and killed fifty-two men, women, and children. It is said that the bones of the victims remained on the dunes for several years before it was safe to collect and bury them.

● Old Stone Gate, at the intersection of Exchange Street (4200 S.) and Peoria Street (900 W.), is at the original entrance to the Union

Stockyards. The Union Stockyards consisted of 475 acres with slaughterhouses located east of Halsted between 39th and 47th streets. It was closed in 1971 but, before then, the stockyards processed lamb, beef, and pork and shipped them by rail or boat across the United States and around the world. These slaughterhouses were called "a very river of death" by Upton Sinclair in his 1906 novel *The Jungle*, whose description of the unsanitary conditions that prevailed there eventually led to federal meat inspection laws. Travel north on Halsted (800 W.) to the area of the Fulton Market (300 N.) where meatpackers and wholesalers do business today.

🌸 Hyde Park, on the south side of Chicago, is bounded by Hyde Park Boulevard and East 59th Street, and Cottage Grove Avenue and South Lake Shore Drive. The area was the site of the Columbian Exposition of 1873. The Museum of Science and Industry, with a lagoon and a wooded island, the statue of Columbia in Jackson Park, and the Midway Plaisance (the large thoroughfare connecting Jackson Park with Washington Park), are souvenirs of that great world's fair.

🌸 On the campus of the University of Chicago on Ellis Avenue (one block west of University Avenue) between 56th and 57th streets, you will see Henry Moore's statue, *Nuclear Energy*. It is on the site of Stagg Field, where scientists from the University of Chicago conducted the first self-sustaining nuclear chain reaction on December 2, 1942. Moore's sculpture commemorates the beginning of the Atomic Age.

## City Panoramas

An excellent way to see the whole scope of nature in Chicago is to get a great wide view of it. Here are some of the best places for a panoramic view.

Look down at the city from above. Take the elevator to the 103rd floor of the Sears Tower, 233 S. Wacker Drive. Enjoy a drink and look out at the city from the ninety-fifth floor of the John Hancock Center at 875 N. Michigan Avenue. Or dine at Cité, the revolving restaurant at Lake Point Tower, 505 N. Lake Shore Drive.

At ground level, see spectacular lakefront panoramas and cityscapes from Promontory Point, at 56th Street in Jackson Park, or from Montrose Point, 4400 N. in Lincoln Park, near Montrose Harbor on the lakefront.

The peninsula surrounding the Adler Planetarium on Solidarity Drive (1300 S.), and Navy Pier at Grand Avenue (500 N.), allow you to walk east of downtown for wonderful views of Lake Michigan and the north and south sides of Chicago.

## Timeline: Chicago

**400 million years ago.**
The climate is tropical and the warm Silurian Sea covers the entire Mississippi Valley.

**250 million years ago.**
The sea retreats and on the swampy shore, tree-sized ferns grow in a carboniferous forest.

**1 million years ago.**
Glaciers cover most of North America. They advance and withdraw as the climate cools and warms.

**12,000 years ago.**
Lake Michigan water level is sixty feet higher than today.

**11,000 years ago.**
Glaciers begin to melt. Lake Michigan is forty feet higher than today. The land has northern spruce forest and tundra.

**10,000 years ago.**
Prairies arrive in Illinois. Paleo-Indian hunters roam the plains.

**8,000 to 2,500 years ago.**
Archaic Period. Native Americans hunt and gather on the grasslands.

**8,000 years ago.**
Lake Michigan is twenty-five feet higher than today.

**4,500 to 2,500 years ago.**
Early Woodland people occupy the Chicago region. They plant small gardens, make stone carvings, build burial mounds, and probably trade with distant peoples.

**3,000 years ago.**
Pine forest replaces most spruce forest.

**2,400 years ago.**
Oak forest replaces most pine forest.

**1,000 years ago.**
Lake Michigan reaches present level.

**1,000 years ago.**
Native Americans (Mississippian people) build large villages, cemeteries, and farms in the upper Illinois River valley.

**1673.**
Native Americans guide French explorers Father Jacques Marquette and Louis Joliet to the Chicago portage, the low spot in the prairie and the vital link in the waterway between the Great Lakes and the Mississippi River.

**1682.**
René-Robert Cavelier Sieur de La Salle, a French explorer, emerges from the Kankakee marshes and finds the tallgrass prairies of Illinois.

**Early 1700s.**
The Fox nation forces a retreat by the French and the site of Chicago returns to wilderness.

**1776.**
The end of the Revolutionary War. Illinois Territory officially becomes part of the United States, but actually remains under British control.

**1779.**
Jean Baptist Point Du Sable, an Afro-French-Canadian trapper who was born in Santo Domingo, becomes the first nonnative American settler in Chicago.

**1787.**
The Northwest Ordinance, which prohibits slavery and encourages free popular education in the Northwest Territory, designates the Chicago region as a part of Wisconsin.

**1794.**
General Anthony Wayne defeats Native Americans at the battle of Fallen Timbers near Toledo, Ohio, ending two decades of warfare. The resulting Treaty of Greenville forces Native Americans to cede most of Ohio and parts of Indiana, Illinois, and Michigan to the United States.

**1803.**

Fort Dearborn is established to protect the Great Lakes and Mississippi waterway. The Louisiana Purchase transfers a vast tract of southern land from France to the United States.

**1812.**

During the War of 1812 Fort Dearborn is attacked by Native Americans (who sided with the British). Fleeing soldiers and their wives are slain and the fort is abandoned.

**1816.**

The Potawatomi tribe cedes a strip of land ten miles wide on either side of the mouth of the Chicago River that extends southwest to the headwaters of the Illinois River. This gives the United States control of the Chicago Portage route. Fort Dearborn is reestablished.

**1818.**

Illinois Territory is admitted to statehood.

**1825.**

The Erie Canal opens and settlers migrate to the Great Lakes region.

**1827.**

The route of a canal along the Chicago Portage is planned, along with the towns of Chicago and Ottawa in Illinois.

**1831.**

Cook County is established and Chicago becomes the county seat.

**1832.**

Chief Black Hawk's warriors cause white settlers of the Des Plaines and DuPage areas to flee to Chicago, where the population rises from one hundred to five hundred as a result.

**1837.**

The town of Chicago is incorporated.

**1848.**

The Illinois and Michigan Canal is dug across the Chicago Portage. This completes the waterway between the Mississippi River and the Great Lakes.

**1850s.**

Thirty thousand people live in Chicago.

**1856.**

Chicago is the chief railroad center in the United States.

**1860.**

The Republican National Convention in Chicago nominates Abraham Lincoln for president.

**1865.**

Chicago's Union Stockyards are established.

**1869.**

The West Park, South Park, and Lincoln Park commissions are established.

**1870.**

Three hundred thousand people live in Chicago, making it the country's fastest growing metropolis.

**1871.**

The Chicago Fire burns large sections of the city, destroying eighteen thousand buildings, leaving ninety thousand homeless and three hundred dead. Rebuilding begins immediately.

The Main and South branches of the Chicago River are reversed, sending sewage down the Des Plaines and Illinois rivers and protecting the purity of Lake Michigan drinking water.

**1890.**

Chicago's population reaches one million.

**1893.**

The World's Fair, called the Columbian Exposition, celebrates the four-hundredth anniversary of the discovery of America.

**1897.**

The Illinois-Michigan Canal is no longer profitable and traffic is virtually halted on the Joliet-Chicago section.

**1900.**

The Sanitary and Ship Canal is opened to solve city sewage problems.

**1903.**

Aaron Montgomery Ward, a millionaire merchant, wins his battle to preserve the lake side of Michigan Avenue as parkland for the city. Every building except the Art Institute of Chicago is torn down.

**1909.**

Daniel H. Burnham and Edward H. Bennett's Chicago Plan proposes city parks, forest preserves, and a public lakefront.

**1915.**

The Forest Preserve District of Cook County is organized.

**1934.**

Chicago's twenty-two separate park commissions are consolidated into the Chicago Park District.

**1942.**

The Atomic Age begins on December 2 with the world's first sustained nuclear reaction at the University of Chicago.

**1992.**

An underground tunnel collapses and Loop office buildings are flooded by Chicago River water.

**1995.**

More than five hundred people die in a July heat wave.

**1996.**

Chicago Wilderness, a partnership of organizations for protection, restoration, and stewardship of two hundred thousand acres of wild lands and native species in the Chicago metropolitan region, is established.

# 2

# Lake Michigan Lookouts

"The lakefront by right belongs to the people. It is a living thing, delighting man's eye and refreshing his spirit."
—Daniel H. Burnham (1846–1912), architect and city planner

Lake Michigan is the great natural treasure of Chicago. Its blue-green water stretches beyond the horizon, and along its shoreline beaches and parks extend from the northern suburbs past downtown to the southernmost part of the city. It is the third largest Great Lake and part of the world's largest freshwater ecosystem.

It is a body of water so huge that it moderates the climate of Chicago. By day, sunshine warms deeper water. When night falls, this warm water rises and heats the air. Although shivering Chicagoans may doubt it, this makes Chicago winters milder than those on the Great Plains. However, if the winds pick up moisture from the lake and carry it inland, they can produce "lake effect" snowfalls. In summer, the sun's heat causes water to evaporate from the lake's surface. As the water changes from a liquid to a gas, it absorbs heat and lowers the air temperature near the lake.

Lake Michigan is the city's front yard, a playground for residents and tourists. It is also a 307-mile-long, 118-mile-wide, and 300-foot-deep (925 feet at its deepest point) freshwater reservoir. Three million Chicagoans and more than ten million residents of other communities surrounding the lake rely on it for clean, pure drinking water. They use it to process food, chemicals, and other goods produced by industry. They tap it to clean streets, quench fires, treat wastes, and produce the electricity that powers the city. In other words, Lake Michigan is a lifeline for Chicago.

## The Inland Harbor

Surrounded by Michigan, Indiana, Illinois, and Wisconsin, Lake Michigan is the only one of the five Great Lakes completely within the boundary of the United States. Because it extends so far south, it is crucial to navigation in the nation's midsection. From the start, Lake Michigan was vital to North American travel. Native Americans paddled their canoes along its coastline long before Louis Joliet and Father Jacques Marquette arrived. After 1673, it became part of the main water route between New France (Canada) and the Mississippi River. French explorers and fur traders were followed by British and American travelers.

Port Chicagou was a fine natural harbor at the southeastern corner of Lake Michigan. However, large ships could not anchor there because a sandbar at the mouth of the Chicago River blocked its entrance. Engineers dug a channel through the sandbar and, in 1834, spring floods on the Des Plaines River completed the work. Torrents of river water swept through the channel and dredged it deep enough to admit the heaviest vessels. Soon after, piers were built at the river mouth and cargo ships carrying iron ore, coal, lumber, manufactured goods, and grain caused the village that was a trading post to develop into a major Great Lakes port.

After 1910 this commercial harbor was moved to Lake Calumet on the city's south side. As the port at Calumet Harbor grew, the downtown port gradually shut down. Nevertheless, European cargo vessels continue to traverse the Atlantic Ocean, pass through the St. Lawrence Seaway, and cross the Great Lakes to Chicago.

Lake Michigan is not only a great commercial asset but a recreational jewel. Twenty-four miles of public beaches and parks adorn the shore from Lincoln Park in the north to Calumet Park in the south. This lovely coast exists today because, in 1836, city fathers declared that Chicago's lakefront was public ground and should remain "forever open, clear and free." In spite of a century of pressure on the city to develop lakefront property, for the most part it remains parkland. Aaron Montgomery Ward, the famous mail-order millionaire, was one of the first to defend the open lakefront when, at the turn of the century, he prevented the construction of a civic center on the downtown shore. Later development was not blocked so successfully, resulting in intruders like water filtration plants, Soldier Field, Meigs Field, McCormick Place, and various high-rise office buildings, as well as expressway ramps and viaducts and Lake Shore Drive. Currently, Lake Shore Drive is being moved inland so that the Field Museum will no longer be separated from the Adler Planetarium and the Shedd Aquarium, and pedestrians will be able to stroll in parkland from the Art Institute to all three of these great museums.

## Shoring up the Shore

In order to shield Chicago's beaches and buildings from losing ground to Lake Michigan, piles of boulders, called riprap, and steel and wooden breakwaters extend from beaches into deeper water along the city's shoreline. However, the breakwaters are old and weak. If a severe storm causes them to collapse, Lake Michigan will engulf beaches, drown Lake Shore Drive, and flood major lakefront museums.

What should be done to avoid this catastrophe? Some say the breakwaters should be strengthened. But environmentalists believe the lake itself can cure Chicago's beach erosion problems. They ask that all breakwaters and other barriers be taken away. Then Lake Michigan currents will do what they do naturally: remove sand from the shore in winter and rebuild the beaches in spring and summer.

## The Changeable Lake

When clouds burst, Lake Michigan expands with rainfall. When the sun's heat evaporates surface water, the lake shrinks. For most of the year, upper layers of water, heated by the sun, tend to be warmer than lower layers. In late autumn, however, cooling air temperatures draw warmth from the water surface until the upper layer is actually cooler and therefore denser than the water below it. Then the phenomenon of turnover takes place: the cool upper water sinks to the lower part of the lake, and the warmer water below rises to the top. This dramatic event occurs once again in early spring, when surface water chilled by winter becomes colder and denser than the water below it and sinks to the bottom, being replaced by the less cold, deeper water.

Average water temperature varies greatly with depth, location, and degree of industrial activity nearby. The wind causes Lake Michigan to be generally warmer near the shore. In summer, lake temperature rarely reaches a maximum of seventy-five degrees Fahrenheit. In winter, lake temperature hovers around thirty-two. The surface never freezes completely, but ice floats on the surface and prevailing winds push it toward the southern shore.

Lake levels vary annually, rising or falling one to one and a half feet. The level is highest in midsummer, after the spring melt, and lowest in midwinter, when tributaries freeze. In 1987, a February storm with strong north winds that blew for twenty-four hours caused Lake Michigan to rise more than one foot and overflow onto Lake Shore Drive. Changes in atmospheric pressure can also cause water levels to fluctuate.

Over the long term, lake levels rise or fall depending on climate and precipitation. These fluctuations are not regular, as 150 years of tracking has shown, and there really is no such thing as a "normal" lake level. However, some people claim that the summer of 1988 was "normal" because lake levels dropped to the long-term average. The highest recorded lake levels occurred in 1985 and 1986, when they were six feet higher than they were at the lowest recorded level, in 1964.

## Aliens and Pollution

Lake Michigan's impact reaches far beyond the city. Its waters cover 22,278 square miles and drain 45,598 square miles of land. About five million Chicagoans and suburbanites and nine million other people inhabit its coastline. The lake also sustains many kinds of plants and animals in its aquatic and coastal environments. Unfortunately, shipping, industry, and settlements endanger many of these creatures.

Ships from distant ports sometimes carry alien invaders (nonnative species of plants and animals) in their ballast tanks or on their hulls, releasing them into the lake when tanks are emptied or ships dock. Because they have no natural enemies, these alien species can upset natural ecosystems, foul beaches, and cause great expense for industry.

Exotic (nonnative) animals have devastated the original Lake Michigan fisheries. The sea lamprey, an ocean fish, entered the Great Lakes, traveled through the Welland Canal, and, by the 1940s, developed a huge population in Lake Michigan. This fish attached itself to Lake

Michigan trout and other native fish and sucked out their bodily fluids. In the 1950s, Canada and the United States established the Great Lakes Fisheries Commision to deal with the problem. Twenty thousand chemicals were tested before two were found that killed sea lampreys. These were applied to lamprey spawning grounds in tributaries to the Great Lakes and have successfully controlled their population explosion for several decades. However, lampreys are starting to become resistant to these chemicals, so scientists are now searching for new biocontrol methods.

Alewives, exotic herrings from the Atlantic Ocean, eat the eggs and fry of native fish in Lake Michigan. Because the alewives have trouble adapting to lake turnovers, they die off in great numbers in fall and spring. In 1967, the time of the biggest die-off, Chicago beaches were covered with the bodies and stench of dead alewives.

Because of alien invaders, most of the fisheries in Lake Michigan are restocked each year with nonnative fishes. Coho and chinook salmon were introduced in 1965 and 1966 as forage fishes to control alewives. They feasted on the alewives and grew so large that a new sports fishery was established. After the alewives were under control, the salmon became smaller. The salmon are native to the northwestern United States, so they don't reproduce in Lake Michigan and must be restocked each year. Most important, they compete with native fish such as yellow perch, chub, and whitefish.

Other threats come from the spiny waterflea, a Chinese clam, the rough (a catfish), and the round goby. Zebra mussels (one-inch-long relatives of clams that came in ballast water from Europe) are costly, for they multiply rapidly and clog water intake pipes of power plants, drinking water facilities, and industrial plants. Even more serious is the risk that they will alter Lake Michigan ecosystems.

Pollution from people who inhabit the shoreline also threatens Lake Michigan. Municipal sewage causes algae blooms (seen as green scum) that choke off oxygen and poison fish and other aquatic creatures near the coast. Toxic chemicals from households, industries, and ships also pollute this vital water resource. When heavy rains flood Chicago's streets, the Chicago River and sewage outfall pipes located in deep water east of the beach pour untreated sewage into Lake Michigan. This sewage carries viruses, bacteria that cause cholera and typhoid, and other disease-causing organisms. Swimming areas are sometimes closed because of the health threat.

Pollutants carried by wind, gathered by rivers, and flowing out of industrial and municipal pipes contaminate water and lakebottom sediments. Sediment pollution is particularly bad in Waukegan Harbor, located north of Chicago, and in industrial areas, many on the south side. Sediment poisons do not remain buried because small animals eat them and they, in turn, are eaten by larger and larger fish. Because toxins accumulate in each step of the food chain, pregnant women and children are warned not to eat fish caught in Lake Michigan. Fortunately, modern water treatment plants make Lake Michigan water safe to drink.

## The Aquatic Habitat

Despite its problems, Lake Michigan is clean enough to be the habitat for a variety of aquatic plants and animals. Billions of algae, single-celled plantlike organisms, provide food for animals and give the lake its greenish color. Small shrimp and fish larvae graze on the algae. Together, they form plankton—tiny floating organisms—that drift on surface currents, providing nourishment for larger lake animals. Life beneath the surface includes attached communities of clams and crowds of crabs that crawl across the lake floor. Schools of fish, such as trout, perch, and salmon, swim and prey on one another in deeper water, but they mate and lay their eggs in shallow wetlands on the shoreline. Since these wetlands abound with food, birds that migrate between Canada and the Gulf Coast stop to rest and feed at Montrose Point, Jackson Park, and other places on the waterfront.

## Limestone Locales

The immense and powerful Lake Michigan we know today is, geologically speaking, a new and rather modest remnant of the truly vast waters that covered the Chicago area in ages past. Clues to these ancient features can be found today by people who know how and where to look. Coral reefs from the Silurian Sea (see Chapter 1) have been discovered throughout the Chicago region. Divers know that ancient reefs exist underwater, close to the shore between 9th and 59th streets and between 70th and 79th streets on the south side of Chicago. Engineers who dug under Addison Street (3600 N.) to build the Northwest Expressway found what is known as the Logan Square Reef.

**Lake Michigan Measurements**
(Courtesy: Lake Michigan Federation)

Length: 307 miles (494 kilometers)
Breadth: 118 miles (190 kilometers)
Average Depth: 279 feet (85 meters)
Maximum Depth: 925 feet (282 meters)
Water Surface Area: 22,278 square miles (57,750 km$^2$)
Drainage Basin Area: 45,598 square miles (118,100 km$^2$)
Shoreline length: 1,659 miles (2,670 km) including islands
Elevation: 581 feet (177 meters)
Outlet: Straits of Mackinac to Lake Huron
Retention/Replacement Time: 99 years
Surrounding Population: 14 million
Surrounding States: Michigan, Indiana, Illinois, Wisconsin

These reefs are made of limestone (calcium carbonate), the hardened skeletons of billions and billions of soft-bodied animals with mouths surrounded by tentacles, ancestors of modern jellyfish and sea anemones, who populated the salty Silurian four hundred million years ago. When the sea receded and the climate chilled, the coral creatures became extinct. You can hunt for their fossils in limestone quarries at Thornton, McCook, and elsewhere. Outcrops of the limestone reefs they created, like Stony Island, provided homesites for early settlers who preferred high ground to the marshy shore of Lake Michigan. A limestone quarry once existed near Rice (850 N.) and Western (2400 W.). During the Civil War, it was filled in as a garbage dump and now it is covered with buildings. Today you can see a limestone seawall built in the nineteenth century as you ride the Illinois Central railroad south between downtown and 43$^{rd}$ Street. When workers dug the Illinois and Michigan Canal, they took out limestone and sold it. Because it was available and cheap, builders used it instead of wood. Chicago's landmark Water Tower, at 845 N. Michigan Avenue, and many other old buildings in Chicago are made of limestone. The same is true for structures in nearby Lemont, Lockport, and Joliet. Salt springs fed by water that flows from underground limestone formations spurt from the surface in places such as Thorn Creek in Thornton, Illinois.

# Ancient Beach Ridges

When the Wisconsonian ice sheet—the last of the great ice sheets to blanket the Midwest—melted about fourteen thousand years ago, Lake Chicago, the immediate precursor to Lake Michigan, was born. Periodically, breaks occurred in the ridges around Lake Chicago and the lake receded as mile-wide rivers drained down the Illinois River. Three dramatic changes in lake level exposed beach ridges and sandbars that are still visible within the city and suburbs. Known as the Glenwood, Calumet, and Tolleston beach levels, they can be seen—or felt—if you drive ten or fifteen miles west from Lake Michigan along Devon Avenue (6400 N.) or South 111$^{th}$ Street. You won't see sand or cliffs, but you will go up and down. The streets rise on Lake Chicago's beach ridges and sandbars, and descend to its bottom and beaches. On South 111$^{th}$ Street, you will drive over the "swell and swale" left by glaciers and pass by Worth Island and Blue Island, which were surrounded by water millenia ago. Other east-west streets, such as Fullerton Avenue (2400 N.), Diversey Avenue (2800 N.), Belmont Avenue (3200 N.), or Irving Park Road (4000 N.), offer a less complete history of Lake Chicago.

Twelve thousand years ago, at the Glenwood beach level, glacial ice was still thawing and sixty feet of Lake Chicago's frigid water covered much of the Chicago region. The shoreline was miles inland, at LaGrange and Palos Park, located on the western border of today's city. Water covered the city as far west as Naragansett Avenue (6400 W.). Riis Park, at Fullerton Avenue (2400 N.) and Naragansett, stands on this ancient beach ridge. Similar ridges exist in the suburbs at LaGrange, Glenwood, Homewood, Wilmette, and Winnetka. A sandbar called the Oak Park spit extends from Oak Park to Forest Park and becomes a cliff in eastern Park Ridge. At the Glenwood level, Mt. Forest Island and Blue Island were real islands and the Des Plaines River flowed through a broad glacial valley to empty directly into Lake Chicago.

The Calumet beach level, forty feet higher than today, was reached about ten thousand years ago. As water receded, Mt. Forest Island became connected to Blue Island, and Worth Island emerged at what is now South 111$^{th}$ Street and Harlem Avenue (7200 W.). The Des Plaines River occupied the entire area where the Sanitary and Ship Canal, the Santa Fe Railroad, and Archer Avenue are today. The Calumet sandbar was on Western Avenue (2400 W.), north of Lincoln Avenue in Chicago and west of Ridge Avenue in Evanston.

The Tolleston beach level, reached eight thousand years ago, was twenty feet higher than the shore of Lake Michigan today. Much of the earlier lakebottom dried out at this time and became the Chicago Plain. This shoreline left ridges at Graceland Cemetery (4000 N. Clark) on the north side and Garfield Park (300 N. Central Park Boulevard) on the west side of Chicago, and in the southern suburbs of Hammond, Dolton, Riverdale, and Roseland. Steep cliffs sloped eastward at Michigan Avenue and South 111th Street.

Two thousand years after Lake Chicago reached the Tolleston level, when the lake was nearly its present size, a reversal known as the Nippersink Advance occurred. Lake Chicago began to rise again until it covered the Chicago area with a bay that extended to the Des Plaines River. A current flowed south in the bay and gradually built a sandbar that altered the flow of the area's two major rivers, the Chicago and the Des Plaines. After the Nippersink Advance, when the lake level fell again, the sandbar blocked the Des Plaines so it could no longer empty into the Chicago River. The Chicago River, east of the sandbar, now emptied into Lake Michigan, while the Des Plaines, west of the sandbar, reversed its path and flowed toward the Illinois River, the Mississippi, and the Gulf of Mexico.

It was only about one thousand years ago that Lake Chicago became pretty much the Lake Michigan we know today. Michigan Avenue was a beach extending all the way to Clark Street, and the land east of the avenue was dune or wetland for miles both north and south. At Lincoln Park, near North Pond, you can find plaques or markers that identify the position of ancient lake beaches. Look for them southeast of the Deming Place Bridge near Stockton Drive and near the sidewalk east of the center of North Pond.

## Navy Pier (1 to 2 hours)

Getting there: Located at 600 E. Grand Avenue and Lake Michigan. Park at the pier or take the CTA trains or bus.

Exploring Navy Pier is an excellent way to surround yourself with the power and beauty of Lake Michigan. Walk along this twenty-five-acre peninsula that extends three thousand feet from the shoreline to enjoy cool breezes and marvelous panoramas of the city skyline and boaters on the lake.

Originally built in 1916 as a port for commercial and Great Lakes excursion boats, Navy Pier later served as a Navy training facility and then a University of Illinois campus. It was renovated in the 1990s as a tourist attraction, so it now hosts concerts and many other events. Landward, you will see Olive Park, the Jardine Water Filtration Plant, and Ohio Street Beach. Take an aerobic walk or stroll on the promenade lined with old-fashioned street lights, comfortable benches, souvenir shops, restaurants, and rooftop terraces, or view the scenery from above on a ferris-wheel ride.

## The Illinois Lakefront Between Wisconsin and Indiana (2 to 4 hours)

For an overall picture of Chicago's unique beauty and diversity, take a leisurely morning or afternoon to drive the length of its lakefront.

Starting from the Wisconsin border in the north, you will go past Zion, with Illinois Beach State Park (see below), and mostly industrial Waukegan and North Chicago. Residential areas, many of them exclusive, dominate the north shore from Lake Bluff to Wilmette. Green Bay Road, once a Native American trail, and Sheridan Road will take you through these beautiful suburbs into Evanston, where you will pass a nineteenth-century lighthouse with a small dune restoration around it, and the lovely Northwestern University campus. Continue on Lake Shore Drive to view the "front yard" of the city.

Chicago's north side has many beaches hidden by apartment buildings. Lincoln Park is a green oasis with beaches, playing fields, boat harbors, a zoo, and a conservatory. The downtown area holds Grant Park, with Buckingham Fountain, Shedd Aquarium, the Field Museum of Natural History, and Adler Planetarium.

The south side lakefront begins with Burnham Park's yacht harbor and Northerly Island with Meigs Field. Plans are underway to transform the area into a park with prairie and wetlands. Continuing south, you will drive by Jackson Park, with beaches, a yacht harbor, and the Museum of Science and Industry. On the far south side, the lakefront is inaccessible to the Indiana border, blocked by Chicago's port and industrial facilities. However, a short distance beyond the border is the magnificent wilderness known as Indiana Dunes National Lakeshore (see below).

# Dune Lands

Sand dunes—giant hills of sand—start out as tiny ripples of sand on a beach. The dunes grow tall on the southern and eastern shore of Lake Michigan because of strong and steady winds. Gentle breezes blow the sand into ripples while rougher winds cause sand-grain collisions. A chain reaction begins as sand grains bounce into the air, land, and pry other grains loose. Prevailing winds push these colliding grains upward along the beach. Tiny ripples merge with bigger ones and form a mass of sand.

"The dunes are to the Midwest what the Grand Canyon is to Arizona. . . . They constitute a signature of time and eternity," wrote poet Carl Sandburg (1878–1967). You can see dunes at Indiana Dunes National Lakeshore, Illinois Beach State Park, and, on a more modest scale, at Lighthouse Park in Evanston.

In all these dune lands, you will view a changing landscape as you walk inland from the edge of the lake. Near the water, wet sand is smoothed and polished by waves. Away from the water, dry sand is battered and rippled by the wind. Storm waves as well as prevailing winds toss dry sand inland and pile it into dunes. These foredunes slope gently on the side facing Lake Michigan. On the opposite side of the ridge, they are steeper and more protected from the force of waves and wind. Inland from the beach, dunes have gentler slopes.

A sand dune on the Lake Michigan shore may move sixty feet in a year. Its speed slows if it is further from the lake or if a foredune or other obstacle shields it from the wind. The shape and size of the dune is determined not only by the force of the wind but by plant life growing on it.

Despite the blistering summer sun and violent winter storms, pioneer plants take root on the lake side of the foredune. Sun and wind evaporate water quickly so plants that live on the beach and foredunes have spreading or deep, probing roots, fleshy stems, and glossy or slim leaves to stay moisturized. They are dune builders, for sand accumulates against them. Marram grass holds the sand in place with underground roots and stems that may spread twenty feet in all directions. Cottonwood trees, with wide triangular leaves, have roots that reach deep to tap water. They are not smothered when buried in sand because new roots sprout from stems near the surface. Do the cottonwoods appear to be about ten feet tall? They are probably the tops of sixty-foot trees. On the opposite side of the dune, marram grass and cottonwoods mingle with other plants.

Sand dunes appear to be peaceful spots, but they are silent battlefields for predator and prey. Grasshoppers and snout beetles eat the greenery, but birds such as the killdeer or kingbird eat them. Robber flies search for velvet ants. Velvet ants, covered with fine hairs that protect them from heat or cold, lay their eggs in the burrows of digger wasps. The wasps compete with the kingbirds, for they both dine on robber flies.

Dr. Henry Cowles, a University of Chicago professor who is sometimes called the father of North American ecology, developed a major principle of ecology—succession—based on what he saw as he hiked across the Indiana sand dunes. He observed that there was a predictable succession of plant communities on the dunes, each one adapted to a particular environment. Grasses grew on the front of the beach where winds and waves were strong. Oak forests stood on more protected dunes. Each plant community or ecosystem was adapted to a particular physical environment. When the water, wind, or soil in that environment changed, there was succession—a corresponding change in the plant ecosystem. (The animal community also changes, because animals depend on the plant ecosystem.) Succession of plant ecosystems is clearly seen in dune lands.

## Indiana Dunes National Lakeshore (4 to 8 hours)

1100 N. Mineral Springs Road
Porter, IN 46304-1299
(219) 926-7561
Emergencies: (800) PARK-TIP

Getting there: Located in Porter, Indiana 41 miles east of Chicago. Take I-94 south to Indiana Route 49 north. Follow Route 49 north to U.S. 12. Go east 3 miles on U.S. 12 to the southwest corner of Kemil Road. For more travel information call (219) 926-7561, ext. 225, or the Chicago South Shore and South Bend Railroad. Call (219) 926-7561 or (219) 938-8221 for information and reservations.

Access: Call for special needs. Sand and snow chairs available.

Facilities: Beach house and pavilion, picnic grounds, Paul H. Douglas Center for Environmental Education.

Tours: Trails range from one-quarter mile to five and a half miles, easy to rugged.

Marram grass at Lighthouse Beach dune, Evanston.

Visit the country's first urban national park—a wilderness with beaches, wetlands, and forests—on the southern shore of Lake Michigan. This refuge harbors more than fourteen hundred plant and animal species on its fourteen thousand acres of land. During your safari on the sand dunes, you may spot endangered butterflies, migrating birds, and rare plants. Listen to rangers describe the flora and fauna. Attend the Spring Maple Sugar Time Festival, the Autumn Harvest Festival, and other events. Or take guided tours on Potawatomi Pathways, or to see wildflowers, autumn colors, Pinhook Bog, and other natural attractions.

Although it is surrounded by steel mills, factories, homes, and highways, this wild ecosystem exists because Senator Paul Douglas of Illinois defended it against industrial development and fought to designate it as a national lakeshore.

## 🍂🍂 West Beach Succession Trail (1 to 2 hours)

West Beach
Indiana Dunes National Lakeshore
1100 N. Mineral Springs Road
Porter, IN 46304-1299
(219) 926-7561
Emergencies: (800) PARK-TIP

Getting there: Located in Porter, Indiana 41 miles east of Chicago. Take I-94 to Indiana 51 north. Go east on U.S. 20 1 mile. Turn north onto County Line Road and go 2 miles to West Beach entrance and the visitor center.

Here you can climb a series of sand dunes with lovely vistas, pioneer plants, and a series of plant communities as you go from beachfront to inland environments. This trail is one mile long and strenuous, so do some stretching exercises to prepare for the climb. It is well worth the effort, for you will see what Dr. Henry Cowles called a "floral melting pot," and you will observe his principle of succession on this trail.

Start at the beach and follow the numbers on the wooden markers. Ignore the sign for the dune succession trail as you leave the parking lot. I didn't and, as a result, I climbed up more than one hundred stairs over the first dune instead of down. I also saw succession backward. Take your shoes off and walk along the shore just above the water's edge. Listen to the sands sing. The clear ringing sound you hear is not your imagination. It is the music composed by friction from your feet in harmony with quartz crystals, moisture, and pressure. Notice the sea rockets, low-growing annuals that withstand the constant wash of the waves.

Turn away from the water and walk toward the back of the beach to the foredunes, where sand piles up against clumps of marram grass. The small pond you see was made by wind that scoured the sand away until it revealed the water table. In this new habitat, Fowler's toads lay their eggs, hatch into tadpoles, and swim like fish until they grow legs. Birds drink the water and feed on algae—single-celled plantlike organisms that capture solar energy to make food. Rare flowers such as the horned bladderwort, which eats insects, and the Kalms lobelia grow along the pond edges.

Climb the wooden boardwalk to the sand dune's ridge. You will see a greater variety of plants on this side of the dune because it is shielded

Pioneer grasses give way to cottonwood and jack pine in this view of succession in the Indiana Dunes.

from the force of the wind. Notice that the marram grass now mingles with other grasses, trees, and flowers. Little bluestem grass has leaves with a bluish cast and seeds in the white fluff at the tips of its stalks. Sand cherry bushes have reddish trunks and leaves that turn red in autumn. Flowers such as the white sand cress or the yellow puccoon also live on this protected side of the dune.

Watch out for insects that feed on the plants, and for birds—such as the killdeers (with brown backs, white breasts, and two black collar stripes) and kingbirds (with gray backs and white breasts)—that eat the insects.

Notice that, farther back from the beach, stands of jack pine grow on the dunes. Although the soil is sandy, it is a bit more fertile than beach sand because it contains minerals from dune plants that died and decayed there, enabling the pines to take hold. Notice that these evergreen trees have scaly rough bark, leaves shaped like needles to prevent water loss, and one- to two-inch-long cones in bundles of two. The cones carry naked seeds—seeds that are not covered by a fruit or shell and are spread by the wind. Between the trees, you will find bearberry, a low woody creeper with underground runners and small evergreen leaves. Like the pine, the bearberry is a northern plant and a survivor of an ecosystem that thrived long ago when glaciers chilled the climate.

As you walk, look for a blowout—a huge bowl-shaped depression. A blowout forms when violent winds wear away low spots between the hills of sand or when people trample dune plants. Inside the blowout, life begins again with pioneer plants: marram grass and cottonwood. Notice their extensive root systems exposed on the sand ridge. In time, wind and birds may restart the process of succession by reseeding the blowout with sand cherry, willow, and red osier dogwood.

West of the stairs is a tree graveyard—the blackened remains of trees killed by fire, buried by a wandering dune, and later uncovered by the action of the wind.

Walk along the boardwalk and climb the stairs to see the last stage in succession: the more stable forest, often called a climax forest. Tall black oaks dominate the forest on these dunes. The oaks are accompanied by hickory, basswood, and ash trees, and together they form a canopy that shades sassafras, dogwood, and witch hazel shrubs.

Look for the level area where sand was mined out of gently rolling dunes. You can see signs of recovery—small mounds of sand where marram grass, little bluestem, and sand cherry have taken hold. Years from now, if this disturbed area passes through all the stages of succession, it will be covered with an oak forest.

The West Beach area also offers the Long Lake Trail Loop (1.5 miles) and West Beach Trail Loop (1.2 miles). Nearby, the Inland Marsh Trail (2.5 miles) takes you over the high ridges of the Tolleston dunes, formed ten thousand years ago, when Lake Michigan was twenty-five feet higher than today.

## 🍃 Paul H. Douglas Center and Miller Woods Trail (1 to 3 hours)

Indiana Dunes National Lakeshore
1100 N. Mineral Springs Road
Porter, IN 46304-1299
(219) 926-7561
Emergencies: (800) PARK-TIP

Getting there: Located in Porter, Indiana 41 miles east of Chicago. Take I-94 south to Indiana Route 49 north. Follow Route 49 north to

A blowout in the Indiana Dunes.

U.S. 12. Take U.S. 12 and turn north at Lake Street. Or take the Chicago South Shore and South Bend Railroad. Call (219) 926-7561 or (219) 938-8221 for information and reservations.

Examine duneland ponds or hike on short trails through Miller Woods, an oak savanna. Or participate in teachers' workshops, children's programs, or ecology studies at this environmental education center.

###  Bailly/Chellberg Trail (2 hours)
Indiana Dunes National Lakeshore
1100 N. Mineral Springs Road
Porter, IN 46304-1299
(219) 926-7561
Emergencies: (800) PARK-TIP

Getting there: Located in Porter, Indiana 41 miles east of Chicago. Take I-94 to Indiana Route 49 and go north to U.S. 12. Go west 1½ miles on U.S. 12, then turn left onto Mineral Springs Road. Or take the Chicago South Shore and South Bend Railroad. Call (219) 926-7561 or (219) 938-8221 for information and reservations.

On land that was occupied by Native Americans, a fur trader, and farmers, see the Bailly Homestead and beech-maple forest. The visitor center provides a guide for this two-mile trail. Exit the building to see a ravine being eroded by a stream that flows through glacial till (rock ground fine by glaciers). In 1822, Honore Gratien Joseph Bailly de Messein, a French Canadian, set up a fur-trading post at what is now the Bailly Homestead. Bailly lived with Ottawa and Potawatomi traders, and later built a tavern on the Detroit-Chicago Road (now U.S. 12). His homestead has a reconstructed fur-trading cabin and the Bailly family's living quarters.

What may have been a Native American trail takes you through abandoned farms and stumpland to the cemetery where the Baillys are buried. Continue to Chellberg Farm, where Swedish settlers arrived in 1872 to raise cows, chickens, wheat, and corn. Visit their barn, chicken house, pump house, corn crib, granary, farm house, and maple sugar house.

## Mt. Baldy Trail (1 hour)
Indiana Dunes National Lakeshore
1100 N. Mineral Springs Road
Porter, IN 46304-1299
(219) 926-7561
Emergencies: (800) PARK-TIP

Getting there: Located in Porter, Indiana 41 miles east of Chicago. Take I-94 south to Route 49 North. Follow Route 49 north to U.S. 12. Turn east on U.S. 12 and go 8 miles to the Mt. Baldy area.

Meet the challenge of climbing 703 feet to the top of the largest living sand dune in the Indiana Dunes National Lakeshore. View Lake Michigan and see oak trees buried by the sand as this dune slowly moves southward.

**Cowles Bog Area (3 to 4 hours)**
Indiana Dunes National Lakeshore
1100 N. Mineral Springs Road
Porter, IN 46304-1299
(219) 926-7561
Emergencies: (800) PARK-TIP

Getting there: Located in Porter, Indiana 41 miles east of Chicago. Take I-94 south to Indiana Route 49 north. Follow Route 49 north to U.S. 12. Travel west 1½ miles on U.S. 12, then turn right onto Mineral Springs Road.

Walk in the footsteps of Dr. Henry Cowles, who did his first plant ecology studies here. Hike four miles of trails to see unique flora and fauna in sedge prairie. Sedges look like grasses with square stems and grow in meadows where the water is rich in calcium and stays below the surface most of the year. Also visit wetland woods, interdunal ponds, marshes, and wooded sand dunes. A fen (not a bog), with plants that grow in alkaline soil, is a short distance from the trail.

 **Dorothy Buell Memorial Visitor Center**
Indiana Dunes National Lakeshore
1100 N. Mineral Springs Road
Porter, IN 46304-1299
(219) 926-7561
Emergencies: (800) PARK-TIP

Getting there: Located in Porter, Indiana 41 miles east of Chicago. Take I-94 south to Indiana Route 49 north. Follow Route 49 north to U.S. 12. Travel west on U.S. 12 to Kemil Road.

Obtain guide maps at the center for the heron rookery trail and other dune trails that range from one to six miles. Hike, horseback ride, or cross-country ski Ly-co-ki-we (Miami Indian for "sandy ground") Trail (½ to 4 hours). It crosses two ancient sand dune ridges separated by a wetland.

## ⚘⚘ Indiana Dunes State Park (4 to 8 hours)

1600 N. 25E
Chesterton, Indiana 46304
(219) 926-1952

Getting there: Located in Chesterton, Indiana 44 miles east of Chicago. Take I-94 east to Indiana Route 49 north exit and proceed to the entrance. Or take the Chicago South Shore and South Bend Railroad. Call (219) 926-7561 or (219) 938-8221 for information and reservations.

Swim at lovely beaches, camp near two-hundred-foot-high sand dunes, and hike through dune lands or eighteen hundred acres of forest that contain an amazing assortment of plants and wildlife. Choose from ten different trails that vary from a quarter mile to more than five miles and from easy to rugged.

## ⚘⚘⚘ Illinois Beach State Park (3 to 7 hours)

Wadsworth Road and the Lake Michigan shoreline
Zion, IL 60099
(847) 662-4811

Getting there: Located in Zion, 41 miles north of Chicago. Take Route 41 north to Wadsworth Road and go east 10 miles. The park extends 7 miles, from North Point Marina near the Wisconsin state border to Waukegan on the south. North and south sections of the park are separated at Shiloh Boulevard by the Commonwealth Edison Nuclear Power Plant and Power House.

At Illinois Beach State Park, you can walk the only remaining beach ridge shoreline in the state of Illinois. Trek across sand dunes and through wetlands and oak savanna to find more than 650 species of plants, including cactus, wetland sedges, and endangered and threatened wildflowers. Perhaps you will spot a peregrine falcon or come upon a coyote or opossum in this 4,160-acre park on the shore of Lake Michigan. Call to arrange a guided tour, or attend nature walks on Saturday and Sunday in spring and summer.

The Northern Unit, with its main entrance at 17th Street, was built as Camp Logan, a Union prisoner of war camp during the Civil War. In World Wars I and II, Camp Logan was an Army basic training center. After World War II, it was occupied by the Illinois National Guard.

The Northern Unit offers trails for cross-country skiing, biking, and hiking, and also swimming and fishing. The Southern Unit, with main entrance at Wadsworth, has a lodge, campground, and nature center as well as hiking and biking trails, swimming, and fishing ponds.

Because prevailing winds blow offshore—from the beach toward the lake—the sand dunes at Illinois Beach State Park have gentle slopes. Prickly pear cactus, a desert plant, inhabits higher, drier sand. In depressions between dunes, you will come upon wet prairies with grasses and sedges, and marshes with dense stands of cattail, blue joint grass, and prairie cordgrass. Notice that the sand ridges at the back of the shore are covered by grasses and dotted with black oak trees. Fragrant pine trees, brought a century ago, also grow here. Birds such as the peregrine falcon, as well as deer, foxes, and snakes, make their living in this sandy territory.

Take the .2 mile Beach Trail or the 2.2 mile Oak Trail to observe the succession of dune ecosystems from the beach to inland forests. Or walk the 1.7 mile Dead River Loop through forest and prairie. Dead River is not really a river but an elongated stream with abundant aquatic plants and fish, sealed off from the lake by sand dunes. However, when heavy rainfall causes it to rise, Dead River breaks through the sandbar and drains the surrounding marshes as it empties into Lake Michigan.

##  The Evanston Lakefront (2 to 3 hours)

Northwestern University
Campus tour: (847) 491-7271 (1½ hours)

Getting there: Evanston is just beyond the city limits, 13 miles from downtown. Take Lake Shore Drive and Sheridan Road north.

Take a free walking tour of the beautifully landscaped university campus, which is located on the shore of Lake Michigan with spectacular views of the Chicago skyline.

Lighthouse Landing Park
Sheridan Road at Central Avenue
Evanston, IL 60201
(847) 328-6961

Just north of the Northwestern campus is Grosse Point Lighthouse (open June through December; call first), which was built in the last century to keep boats from going aground during Lake Michigan storms. The building adjacent to the tower now houses the Evanston Art Center. East of the lighthouse is a small dunes restoration project you can roam on your own, and to the north is a wooded garden with a fish grotto designed by landscape planner Jens Jensen. Lighthouse Beach, operated by the City of Evanston, is a pleasant place to swim and relax in the summer months. There are public restrooms. An entrance fee of a few dollars is charged for the swimming beach during the summer season.

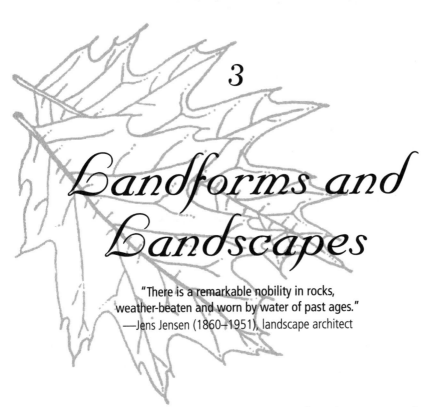

# 3

# Landforms and Landscapes

"There is a remarkable nobility in rocks,
weather-beaten and worn by water of past ages."
—Jens Jensen (1860–1951), landscape architect

More than four hundred million years of geologic events have shaped the land beneath and around Chicago. About one million years ago, after eons of warm, salty sea and swampy carboniferous forest had deposited their beds of limestone and coal, the Ice Ages brought glaciers—lakes of ice—deep into the Midwest, where they receded and retreated over millenia, scouring out new landforms and laying new sediments on top of old. In many parts of northern Illinois and Wisconsin, gravel, boulders, and clay dropped out of the melting glaciers and piled up in long hills called moraines. Rivers flowed in and on the thawing lakes of ice. Where a surface river tumbled into a huge crack, it deposited sediments that grew into a gravel hill, or kame (pronounced "came"). Where a river flowed deep inside the glacier, sediments formed a snakelike ridge, or esker.

Depressions or "kettles" formed by the heavy glaciers filled with meltwater and became ponds and small lakes. Higher ground dried out, but underground streams that flowed through rock sometimes surfaced slowly as a seep or more forcefully as a spring.

Groundwater became alkaline as it trickled through limestone and dissolved ancient calcium carbonate from the rock. This calcium-rich water came to the surface in natural springs and seeps. On the surface, where water evaporated, the calcium was often redeposited as tufa, a light crumbly rock. These alkaline, or marl, flats were so very flat that water could not flow off or out. As a result, few plants other than beaked spike rush, shrubby cinquefoil, or prairie dock survive in this highly alkaline and very soggy habitat.

Wind and water eroded exposed rocks and produced tiny particles of soil. Plants that could tolerate the harsh conditions took hold on the soil with their roots and, as generations of plants lived and died, they enriched the soil with humus—decayed plant material.

## Underground Chicago

In the layers of glacial clay, mud, and gravel beneath Chicago's Loop lie sewer pipes, telephone and electrical cables, and other city infrastructure. By 1914, workers had dug sixty-two miles of tunnels under the central business district on both sides of the Chicago River. An underground railroad carried tons of merchandise, coal, and ashes between the port and downtown businesses. Today, these tunnels built in glacial debris are subway train routes, parking garages, pedestrian arcades, and passageways between terminals at O'Hare Airport. In 1992, a retaining wall collapsed and torrents of Chicago River water flooded the tunnels and damaged Loop buildings.

Until the 1850s, when the city was raised from the glacial mud in a mammoth engineering project, vehicles got stuck and pedestrians had to wade in ankle-deep water, trying to avoid the rats that lived under sagging sidewalks. Two-story buildings were able to stand on foundations set in mud. But after the Chicago Fire, heavier structures were constructed that the swampy soil could not support. Engineers dug down through ten feet of fire rubbish and ten feet of gray lakebottom silt to a ten-foot-thick crust of firmer clay laid down when Lake Chicago drained away ten thousand years ago. This was where they put the foundations of three- to six-story buildings. The first Federal and County buildings and City Hall were still taller, so engineers went down to a thirty-foot-thick layer of wet gray clay. Unfortunately, this wasn't enough. The new buildings sank into the mud and had to be demolished.

Architects and engineers realised that, if they wanted to build tall structures, they had to dig much deeper for their foundations. So they drilled under the wet gray clay called hardpan (about twenty feet thick,

**Wild Symbols of Illinois**

Grass: Big Bluestem
Tree: White Oak
Flower: Wild Blue Violet
Animal: White-tailed Deer
Bird: Cardinal
Insect: Monarch Butterfly
Fish: Bluegill
Fossil: Tulley Monster
Mineral: Fluoride

containing dense water-bearing sand, silt, and boulders) to the ancient limestone beneath. This layer of bedrock, eighty to 120 feet below the surface, is the foundation on which Sears Tower, the John Hancock Building, and other skyscrapers now stand.

### Tribune Tower (½ hour)

435 N. Michigan Avenue
Chicago, IL 60611
(312) 222-3232

The Tribune Tower celebrates rocks throughout history. Walk around this building, where the Chicago Tribune is published, to see a rock collection embedded in the outside walls. These rocks come from the Pyramids of Egypt, the Great Wall of China, and other monuments from all parts of the world. You will also find stones from historic American sites and from every state.

## Ecosystem Origins

Five major ecosystems—arctic tundra, coniferous forest, tallgrass prairie, eastern deciduous forest, and northern hardwood forest—meet in the Chicago area. That is why this urban region at the southern tip of Lake Michigan is the habitat of a great number of Illinois' fifty thousand plant and animal species.

These ecosystems developed as groups of plants adapted to a particular combination of climate, landforms, water, and soil. Animals adapted to the climate and the plants. In time, small ecosystems—communities of plants and animals adapted to the immediate physical environment—developed into prairies, forests, and wetlands. Examples of all these ecosystems and of the glacial activity that created them can be seen on the following tours.

## 🍃 Tinley Creek Division of the Forest Preserve District of Cook County (1 to 3 hours)

13800 S. Harlem Avenue
Orland Park, IL 60462
(708) 385-7650
(708) 385-7654

Getting there: Located in Orland Park, 23 miles southwest of Chicago. Call to request a map of this vast preserve. Take I-94 south to I-80. Go west on I-80 and exit at Route 43 (Harlem Avenue) north. Go north on Harlem Avenue to Tinley Creek Woods (between 151st Street and 135th Street).

Visit a gravel hill left by glaciers, the ridge called the Tinley moraine. It contains Turtlehead, Arrowhead, and Ham Bone lakes; trails through woodlands; and deep ravines and gullies along Tinley Creek. The southern boundary of land the Potawatomi ceded to the United States is at Indian Boundary Line. You will also come upon prairie patches, a model airplane flying field, and Vollmer Road Wildlife Marsh (north of Vollmer Road, between Central Avenue and I-57), which harbors rare birds during migration season.

## 🍃🍃 Camp Sagawau (1 to 3 hours; by appointment only)

1255 W. 111th Street
Lemont, IL 60439
(630) 257-2045

Getting there: Located in Lemont, 27 miles southwest of Chicago. Take I-55 west from downtown to Route 83. Turn south on Route 83 and cross the Des Plaines River and Cal Sag Canal. Stay on Route 83 after it turns southeast. The entrance is 100 yards east of Archer Avenue on the north side of Route 83.

These thirty-five acres of oak savanna and five acres of prairie offer a walk along the rim of the only canyon in Cook County. A quarter mile long, twenty-five feet deep, and twenty-five to seventy-five feet wide, the canyon harbors many rare plants. Climb down to see the small creek that created this canyon by wearing away the Niagaran dolomite rock over which it flows. The rock, formed over four hundred million years ago, was covered by glaciers three times. The stream at the canyon bottom may be ankle deep or neck deep, depending on the time of year, and it contains fishes and frogs. Shaded by basswood, red oak, and sugar maple, the stream is also bedecked with wildflowers. Any time of year, you may watch birds or spot voles, opossum, and other small mammals.

Note: In order to protect the rare plants in this nature preserve, you must call for reservations and tour with a naturalist. Canyon hikes are offered on many weekends, and in spring, bird hikes reveal eastern bluebirds, indigo buntings, and many other birds. There are also fossil hikes and prairie tours. In October, come for the Salamander Safari— a census of amphibians and reptiles in the preserve. From January to March, the camp offers Nature Ski—cross-country ski tours paced for the enjoyment of nature, accompanied by a naturalist, for adults and children over twelve.

On winter weekends, the preserve offers cross-country ski instruction for adults and children fourth grade and up. The January Ski Fest offers fun and games including the Cross-Country Slide and Glide Party, moonlight skiing, and two-for-one rentals.

## Black Partridge Woods Nature Preserve (1 to 2 hours)
Lemont, IL 60439
Contact:
Forest Preserve District of Cook County
(708) 771-1330

Getting there: Located in Lemont, 27 miles southwest of Chicago. Take I-55 west and exit on Lemont Road south. Go south on Lemont Road to 111th Street (Bluff Road). Go west on Bluff Road 1 mile to the entrance.

This eighty-acre preserve, named after Black Partridge, a chief of the Potawatomi Indians, is on a moraine with river bluffs, ravine forests, spring-fed streams, and the largest stand of square-stemmed blue ash in the area. This is where spring is announced with the fragrance of skunk cabbage.

## 🍂 Bluff Springs Fen Nature Preserve (1 to 2 hours)

Elgin, IL 60120
Contact:
Nature Conservancy
8 South Michigan Avenue, Suite 900
Chicago, IL 60603
(312) 346-8166

Getting there: Located in Elgin, 38 miles northwest of Chicago. Take I-90 west and exit at Route 31 south. Go south on Route 31 and turn east across the third bridge over the Fox River, at Chicago Street. Immediately after crossing the bridge, turn south (right) onto Villa Street. Continue southeast on Villa to Liberty. Turn south on Liberty and drive 0.8 mile to Bluff City Boulevard. Then turn east on Bluff City Boulevard and go 0.6 mile to the preserve, located near the Bluff City Cemetery.

This ninety-one-acre geologist's delight has a kame—a gravel hill with exposed bedrock and a thin layer of soil. Conditions are often bone dry due to well-drained soil and the slope of the hill, so the gravel prairie near the top has unusual wildflowers. Tufa can be seen near the marl flats surrounding alkaline seeps. A nearby fen is less alkaline and boasts a variety of plants. The preserve also encompasses a sedge meadow (sedges are plants with square stems that look like grass), marsh (wetland dominated by reeds and grasses), mesic black soil prairie (grassland with good drainage), and a bur oak savanna (scattered bur oak trees surrounded by prairie plants). In these habitats you may come upon rare animals and breeding areas for birds such as willow flycatchers and woodcocks.

Begin the trail in oak savanna—dominated by bur oak and Hill's oak, and containing endangered plants. Go past a sedge meadow with small orange and brown butterflies called skippers and cross a creek where bottom-dwelling mottled sculpin spread their fins like wings. On the left branch of the trail near the creek, you will find tufa rock. Climb the kame to see drought-resistant plants, including endangered milkweed in the gravel prairie at the top. A panorama of tallgrass prairie, fen, and savanna awaits you at the summit.

Descend the kame to view a marl flat, tufa rock, and a spring run. Surrounding them is a fen with six species of orchids, including the rare snake-mouth orchid, grass pink, and white lady's slipper. Follow the trail out of the wetlands, past a transplanted hill prairie, and through woodlands to reach the south end of the kame.

## 🍃 Cap Sauers Holdings Nature Preserve (1 hour)

Between McCarthy Road (north),
104th Avenue (east),
and Calumet-Sag Road/Route 83 (south)
Hickory Hills, IL 60457
Contact:
Forest Preserve District of Cook County
(708) 771-1330

Getting there: Located in Hickory Hills, 18 miles southwest of Chicago. Take I-55 south and exit south at Route 12/20. Go south on Route 12/20, which becomes Route 45, to McCarthy Road. Turn west on McCarthy Road 1.5 miles.

On 1,520 acres of the Valparaiso Moraine and an esker, you will behold upland forests, savanna, sedge meadows, and prairies that are undergoing restoration. Be sure to take the Esker Trail, entrance located south of Route 83 and west of 104th Avenue. For more sites to visit in the Cap Sauers Preserve, obtain a map from the Forest Preserve District of Cook County.

## 🍃 Shoe Factory Road Prairie Nature Preserve (1 hour; by appointment only)

Hoffman Estates, IL
Contact:
Forest Preserve District of Cook County
(708) 771-1330

Getting there: Located in Hoffman Estates, 30 miles northwest of Chicago. Take I-90 west and exit at Barrington Road south to Highway 72 (Higgins Road). Go west on Highway 72 a short distance to Shoe Factory Road. Turn left on Shoe Factory Road and go 2.6 miles to the preserve.

This nine-acre preserve has a kame with a high-grade dry gravel prairie perched on its crest.

## 🍃 Trout Park Nature Preserve (1 hour)

Elgin, IL 60120
Contact:
City of Elgin
150 Dexter Court
Elgin, IL 60120
(708) 695-6500

Getting there: Located in Elgin, 38 miles northwest of Chicago. Take I-90 west and exit at Highway 25 (Dundee Road) south. Go south on Dundee Road 1 block to Trout Park Boulevard. Go west 1 block on Trout Park Boulevard to Trout Park.

Visit bluffs, ravines, seeps, springs, and undisturbed woodlands. This is the southernmost place in the United States with a native white cedar remnant, and it has much interesting flora and fauna of the Fox River Valley.

## 🍃🍃 Fermilab (2 to 3 hours)

P.O. Box 500
Batavia, IL 60510-0500
(630)-840-3351

Getting there: Located in Batavia, 36 miles northwest of Chicago. Take the East/West Tollway (I-88) west and exit north at Farnsworth/Kirk Road. Travel north on Farnsworth/Kirk Road to Pine Street and turn east to the entrance.
Hours: Daily, 6 A.M.–8 P.M. Wilson Hall self-guided tour, daily, 8:30 A.M.–4:30 P.M.
Admission: Free.

If you want to know what rocks, soil, air, water, and living things are made of, Fermilab is the place to go back to basic matter. View displays and films on elementary particles. Also see Native American arrowheads and tools, and grounds with massive sculptures, restored prairie, and a farm with live buffalo.

Drive through the "gate," a metal sculpture entitled *Broken Symmetry*, and along the road that winds through prairie to the A-shaped building that dominates this plain. Park here, then enter the building. Ask for the map and brochure with a self-guided tour at the information desk.

The buffalo herd at Fermilab. *Photo courtesy of Fermilab Visual Media Services.*

Meet quarks, leptons, and bosons, "fundamental particles at the very heart of matter," on the fifteenth floor. The film *Fermilab's Pursuit of the Fundamental* explains the search for elementary particles and what happened during the "Big Bang," the start of the universe.

Look out the east window to see the circular cooling ponds above the buried Main Ring accelerator. This is where the Tevatron, the world's most powerful particle accelerator, enables scientists to search for elementary particles. From the north window you can see the buffalo herd. The west window offers a view of the Lederman Science Education Center and the prairie. Displays show Illinois rocks and Native American tools.

Return to the first floor, where a Foucault pendulum hangs from a thin cable attached to the ceiling. It demonstrates the earth's rotation. On the sundeck, look for *Mobius Strip,* by Robert Wilson, a stainless-steel visualization of infinity.

Exit the parking area, turn right at the first road, and drive past the industrial area, circling around to the buffalo farm. At first, these huge beasts appear to be statues, but you will see them slowly chewing their cud. Leave the farm to see the stately *Proton Pagoda* sculpture.

Take the Margaret Pearson Interpretive Trail, where markers guide you along wood-chip trails on half-mile and 1.2-mile loops. This area consists of 325 hectares of restored tallgrass prairie, a habitat for foxes, beaver, and other small mammals. In spring and autumn, the prairie provides food for flocks of Canada geese. In winter, the dried grass is bronzed by the sun and capped with snow.

# 4

## Skywatch

*"We are rooted in the earth and, at the same time, the cosmos."*
—Vaclev Havel (1936– ), playwright and president of the Czech Republic

The sky is a wondrous place, not only because it is beautiful, but because it is where Earth was born and the space in which it travels. When you look at the moon, the sun and other stars, and the planets in the big sky that frames the city, you understand the vastness of nature. You come to know Chicago's full address: a city in the state of Illinois, in the country called the United States of America, located on the continent of North America, on a planet called Earth (the third planet from a star called the sun and one of nine planets) in the Solar System, part of a galaxy (with billions of stars) known as the Milky Way, located in one corner of the universe.

## The Sky Calendar

Perhaps you have forgotten that your personal calendar is based on events in the heavens. A day is one rotation of Earth on its axis. A month is one rotation of the moon around Earth. (This cycle causes the phases of the moon.) A year is the time it takes for Earth to orbit the sun. A week has seven days, named after the sun (Sunday), the moon (Monday), and the names of five planets in other languages: Mercury (Tuesday), Venus (Wednesday), Mars (Thursday), Jupiter (Friday), and Saturn (Saturday).

# Stars and Earth

Stars played an important role in the creation of Earth and its life-forms. Carbon, oxygen, nitrogen, and hydrogen—all the elements that human beings and all other living things are made of—were formed inside stars. These stars have nuclear reactions in their cores, and those that are much more massive than the sun accumulate the heavier elements, including iron. When a massive star reaches the end of its life, it explodes and becomes a supernova. This explosion, in which the star casts off its outer layers, ejects its elements into interstellar space. The elements mix with other gases and dust particles out there, and eventually form new stars. The sun is a second- or third- or fourth-generation star, formed from elements created inside earlier stars. It may seem strange, but Earth and every living and nonliving thing on it consist of elements manufactured inside stars. Can you believe that the entire population of Chicago, all its life-forms, its land, and Lake Michigan originated as stardust?

Earth's position in relation to its star, the sun, has a profound effect on Chicago's environment. Although you may feel that you are standing still in the city, the planet you live on spins and speeds through space. As Earth makes its yearly journey around the sun and receives varying amounts of heat and light, seasons change. Chicago experiences the cold of winter, the blossoming of spring, the fruits of summer, and the colors of autumn. Animals mate, give birth, migrate, and hibernate in rhythm with the seasons.

Like a top spinning in space, Earth turns on its axis. The spin causes Chicago winds and weather systems to move from west to east, and it establishes the twenty-four-hour cycle of daytime and nighttime. As day turns into night, sunlight diminishes and temperatures drop, and this affects all plants and animals. Dawn arrives in Chicago when it is on the side of Earth facing the sun ("the sun comes up"). Evening begins when the city is on the side of Earth away from the sun ("the sun goes down"). The people of Chicago wake and sleep; animals hunt and relax; and flowers open and close in this daily, or circadian, rhythm in harmony with the spin of Earth in space.

Like every star in the sky, the sun is a nuclear reactor that produces tremendous amounts of energy. Some of this energy spreads out through space to heat and light Earth.

## The Weather

Sunshine drives weather systems because its heat churns Earth's atmosphere and oceans, setting them in motion. Rays from the sun hit Earth and bounce back into the atmosphere, which acts like a greenhouse and traps the heat rays. Earth's tilt and its yearly trip through space cause the sun to shine most directly on the equator all year round, so air, land, and water near the equator receive much more heat than the regions near the North Pole and South Pole. Heat spreads through the atmosphere and oceans, but it doesn't simply flow from the equator to the North or South Pole. As Earth rotates on its axis, winds and ocean currents veer east or west.

Chicago is a windy city because of sunshine. The uneven heating of different parts of Earth sets the atmosphere and oceans in motion. This causes weather systems from Canada and the Gulf of Mexico to clash in the region and stirs up waves and currents on Lake Michigan. The sun's heat also affects Chicago's water cycle. On a hot day, water evaporates, moving from the surface of Lake Michigan into the atmosphere. Air humidity rises and the water condenses, forming clouds high above the lake. When Chicago receives less sunshine and the temperature drops, water falls from the clouds as rain, hail, or snow.

Chicago is in the Northern Hemisphere, so prevailing winds come from the west. If you want to predict the weather, examine the clouds in the western sky.

Cirrus clouds are curling white wisps of ice crystals at altitudes of twenty to forty thousand feet. They are often located at the edge of a distant storm. Cirrostratus clouds cause a halo around the sun that warns of rain. Cumulus clouds, which consist of dense water droplets in billowing white towers from eight to forty-five thousand feet high, are present in sun-filled skies. Cumulonimbus clouds become dark, grow to sixty thousand feet in altitude, and bring thunderstorms, heavy rain, and, sometimes, hail. Stratus clouds are below eight thousand feet, flat like ceilings, and cause fog and drizzle. Nimbostratus clouds block the sun and produce steady rain and snow. Sunshine influences the formation and movement of clouds, as well as rainfall and snowfall.

## Plants and Sunbeams

Sunlight supplies the energy for photosynthesis, the process in which green plants capture solar energy and make food. Since animals, including humans, cannot make their own food, they eat plants (or animals that eat plants) to obtain the energy for life. In other words, both animals and plants depend on sunbeams to stay alive.

Vegetation in Chicago differs from that in a desert, rainforest, or other ecosystem, mainly because the plants in each place are adapted to a particular combination of hours of sunlight, climate, and moisture. All of these environmental factors are controlled by sunshine. The sun shines most directly near the equator, providing equal days and nights, a warm humid climate, and rain all year. That is why rainforest trees and coral reefs are found between the tropic of Cancer and the tropic of Capricorn. Evergreen forests and tundra plants—shrubs and lichens that withstand severe cold, winds, and drought—live in the Arctic. Lack of sunshine results in freezing temperatures, snow, and darkness. That is why plants grow slowly and most animal life is in the ocean (which is warmer than the air) near the North and South Poles.

The prairie—dominated by grasses, decorated by wildflowers, and inhabited by many birds, insects, and small mammals—is the main ecosystem of the Chicago area. All the plants and animals of the prairie must adapt to arctic cold, snow and darkness in winter, warming temperatures and rain in spring, and tropical heat and drought in summer. In the woodlands of the forest preserves, diminishing sunshine causes many trees to change color and lose their leaves in autumn.

## The Night Sky

The best sky-viewing sites are along the lakeshore because no buildings or trees block the view and bright lights are behind you. However, any open area, such as a park, allows you to see a nice chunk of the sky.

In the dark sky, you can view the Milky Way, our galaxy. You can also see the thousands of stars that are visible to the naked eye. Different constellations or star patterns are visible in each season. The winter sky has the most bright stars. They are in the constellation Orion (the Hunter), Taurus (the Bull), and Gemini (the Twins). The brightest star of all, Sirius, is in one of the hunting dogs that accompanies Orion across the sky. The spring constellation is Leo (the Lion). The summer sky has a triangle of three bright stars: Vega in the Lyre, Denab in the tail of Cygnus (the Swan), and Altair in the Eagle. In autumn, you see the great square of Pegasus (the Horse). The Big Dipper, an easy star pattern, is up all year round.

You can distinguish between stars and planets because planets move through constellations of stars. Mercury, Venus, Earth, Mars, Jupiter, Saturn, Uranus, and Pluto are the planets that orbit the sun in our solar system. The word *planet* means "wanderer" in Greek, and early cultures thought it was the gods that moved in the heavens.

## Storms on the Sun

Sunspots, storms on the surface of the sun, are related to the sun's magnetic field. The number of sunspots increases and decreases over an eleven-year cycle and seem to be linked with solar flares. During a solar flare (an event that must be viewed through a telescope with filters to protect your eyes), gas erupts on the surface of the sun and pieces of the sun are ejected into space. Known as the solar wind, this eruption creates a strong stream of charged particles such as protons and electrons. These charged particles travel ninety-three million miles through space and strike Earth's atmosphere near the North and South Poles. This causes atoms and molecules in the air to glow and form red, green, blue, and white moving patterns of light in the night sky. In the Northern Hemisphere, this dazzling display is known as the aurora borealis, or northern lights. Because of Earth's magnetic field, the aurora is brightest during winter in the arctic. However, Chicago is far north, so you can occasionally see these colorful fireworks in the dark sky above Chicago. The next sunspot maximum will be 2001, a year when many solar flares are likely. Go to the lakefront then and you may see the brilliant colors of the aurora borealis light the night sky of Chicago.

## The Moon

The moon lights the evening sky with light reflected from the sun. (Notice how the position of the moon changes between dusk and dawn.) The moon influences Earth by pulling the oceans toward it. This gravitational pull establishes the tides along coastlines. As Earth rotates, the coasts facing the moon have high tide. The coasts away from the moon have low tide. Each month, as the moon orbits Earth, it goes through phases, changing from crescent to half moon to full moon and waning again. Mating and other cycles in the lives of some animals are tied to the lunar cycle, but it is not clear if they are influenced by the moon's gravity or by moonlight.

## Special Sky Events

Many events in the heavens can be seen from Chicago. The lakefront or an open field or park with few city lights makes viewing easier. A lunar eclipse happens when the sun comes between the moon and Earth. During a solar eclipse, the sky darkens at midday because the moon comes between Earth and the sun. (Warning: You must look at the sun through proper filters so your eyes are not harmed.) A comet— a frozen mound of ice and dirt—moves slowly across the sky from night to night. Shooting stars or meteors look like stars that take only seconds to shoot across the sky. They are not stars but pieces of rock, some the size of a grain of sand. As they speed through Earth's atmosphere, they heat up when they collide with molecules of air and become very bright for a few seconds as they shoot through the sky. Around August 12, meteor showers are frequent above Chicago. Because of building and street lights, you will see about five shooting stars an hour in the city. Where the sky is much darker, you will see forty or fifty an hour. Many human-made satellites that report weather and study nature on Earth also orbit above Chicago. At least a dozen are bright enough to see with the unaided eye.

### Adler Planetarium and Astronomy Museum (2 to 5 hours)

1300 S. Lake Shore Drive
Chicago, IL 60605
(312) 322-0304

Hours: Daily, 9 A.M.–4:30 P.M.; Friday, 9 A.M.–9 P.M. View the night sky through a telescope Fridays at 8 P.M.
Admission: Fee. Tuesdays are free.
Access: Wheelchair accessible.
Facilities: Planetarium. Telescope. Restaurant. Shop.

A visit to the Adler is truly out of this world, for you will explore the the moon, planets, the sun, and distant stars. You will also discover how celestial bodies influence Earth's weather, tides, seasons, and the lives of plants and animals. Begin with the Sky Show in the auditorium that presents the latest discoveries of NASA (National Aeronautics and Space Administration). Then lean back and look up in the Sky Dome

Adler Planetarium and Astronomy Museum.

as the planetarium flashes constellations, celestial events, and photos taken by telescopes that orbit in outer space. On clear Friday nights at 8 P.M., peek at stars and planets through the Doane telescope (located behind the main building). Later, you can peer at photos of Chicago's night sky, taken through the telescope that evening.

Exhibits reveal the connection between astronomy and religion, and show how the sky serves as a clock, calendar, and compass. The Race to the Moon display contains mementoes of astronauts. You won't have to wear a spacesuit to travel through the Solar System. Simply walk along the wall and journey to the sun, Mercury, Venus, Earth, Moon, Mars, Jupiter, Saturn, Uranus, and Pluto. Be on the lookout for a raging storm on Jupiter, snowballs in the rings of Saturn, and the methane clouds of Neptune. Transport booths give your weight and weather reports on Jupiter, the sun, Mars, and the moon.

View the sun's surface through a telescope. At Universe in Your Hands, see the armillary sphere, the astrolabe, and other Islamic and European inventions and uncover connections between religion, rulers, and astronomy. Time on Your Hands demonstrates how to use your left hand, palm up, as a sundial. Find out about galaxies, supernova explosions, and black holes. Navigation exhibits present instruments that take advantage of heavenly bodies to find the right direction on Earth. Light, Spectra, Action gives you the chance to examine invisible and white light. Perhaps you will solve the puzzles of how rainbows happen or why the sky is blue.

Come for Sun Fests—celebrations of the seasonal equinoxes and solstices. Activities vary, so you may hear music, watch sun dances, make your own pocket sundial, or listen to Native American sky legends. Weather permitting, you can safely look at the surface of the sun through a telescope.

Also come for comet viewing, eclipses, and other outer-space events. Attend workshops on telescopes and lectures by astronomers and astronauts. Bring children to Sky Shows and adventures with the sun, seasons, and stars. The museum's renovation promises many more heavenly happenings.

## Cernan Earth and Space Center (2 hours)

Triton College
2000 5th Avenue
River Grove, IL 60171
(708) 583-3100
(708) 456-0300, ext. 3372
for field trips and special events

Getting there: Located in River Forest, 11 miles west of Chicago. From Chicago, take the Eisenhower Expressway west to 1st Street. Turn north on 1st Street to North Avenue, then turn west to 5th Avenue.
Hours: Show times: Thursday, 9 P.M., Friday, 9 and 10 P.M.
Admission: Fee.

The Cernan Earth and Space Center presents films for preschool to second graders on the cause of day and night, the importance of the sun, constellations, planets, star clusters, and the moon. Films for grades three and up cover subjects such as the northern lights, planets, constellations, seasons, galaxies, and the formation of Earth and its environmental dangers. Call for the laser light show schedule. A monthly skywatch, Saturdays at 7:30 P.M., offers the latest discoveries in astronomy and space science and, if weather permits, a view of the night sky through the telescope.

# 5

# The Sea of Grass

"A great part of the (Northwest) territory is miserably poor, especially that near
Lakes Michigan and Erie, and that upon the Mississippi and Illinois consists of
extensive plains which have not had . . . a single bush on them for ages.
The districts . . . will never contain a sufficient number of inhabitants to
entitle them to membership in the confederacy."
—James Monroe, in a note to Thomas Jefferson, 1786

Before Chicago existed, most of Illinois was covered with tall grasses
and wildflowers. In this "sea of grass," big bluestem, Indian grass,
prairie dock, and compass plant grew as tall as a man on horseback;
switchgrass was chest high; and little bluestem, northern dropseed,
purple coneflower, and prairie cinquefoil were waist high. Fields of
flowers—yellow goldenrod, white aster, and purple gentian—bloomed
through the seasons in a profusion of color.

It was a lush, sunny grassland. Flocks of birds gathered seed while
hordes of grasshoppers chewed on leaves. Swarms of bees sipped flower
nectar. Tens of thousands of prairie dogs and buffalo grazed on the
greenery. Hawks and eagles soared through the sky, scanning the ground
for mice and rabbits while earthbound foxes, wolves, and bobcats
hunted larger animals.

Each spring, melted snow and rain formed shallow lakes on the prairie. New shoots sprouted and, by midsummer, the grass was tall with
roots deep in the soil. In autumn, the leaves yellowed and withered
with the first frost. But the roots survived underground. Year after year
the grass grew and died, adding its minerals to the soil.

Native Americans sustained themselves on the bounty of the prairie. Women and children harvested leaves, fruits, herbs, and tubers

for cooking and healing. Warriors shot birds and small mammals for meat, and they hunted deer and buffalo, not only for food, but to obtain leather for their clothing and shelters.

The French explorers who came upon the rolling landscape without trees named it "prairie," their word for meadow. European immigrants, who were accustomed to forests, thought the Illinois Territory was barren.

More than two hundred species inhabit this domain of perennial grasses mixed with herbaceous (nonwoody) plants. Most important are the grass family (Graminaeae), which includes Indian grass and turkey foot; the pea family (Leguminosae), which has nodules on its roots containing bacteria that fertilize the soil; and the sunflower family (Compositae), which is represented by flowers such as asters and black-eyed Susan.

The tallest grasses are the ten-foot-high Indian grass and big bluestem. Their roots reach seven feet down in the soil, and underground stems, called rhizomes, help them spread. Many of the grasses are three to six feet tall. Northern prairie dropseed grows two feet high. It has seeds that smell like buttered popcorn and leaves that dry into corkscrews. The flowers of all the grasses tend to be small and not very colorful, for wind rather than insects or birds pollinates the flowers. Breezes carry pollen, a yellow dust, from the stamen (the male part of the flower) to the pistil (the female part of the flower), and this starts seed formation. Later, the wind disperses the seeds through the air.

Broad-leaved plants, called forbs, have larger flowers than grasses. The fragrance and color of these blossoms attract the insects and birds that pollinate them and disperse their seeds. Different colors sweep over the prairie as each kind of flower blooms in its season. The rainbow of color begins in early spring with pastel shooting stars and violets. It continues in summer with brightly colored black-eyed Susan and the flaming spikes of blazing star; and it ends in autumn with goldenrod and New England asters among the bronzed leaves of prairie cordgrass and bluestem.

Most forbs and grasses are perennials. Because they have deep roots and underground stems, these prairie plants survive for decades and even centuries.

Illinois prairie grasses.

## Chicago-Area Prairies

The original prairies are ten thousand years old, for they followed the melting glaciers. The swells and swales (ups and downs) of the landscape established different habitats, each with its typical species of wildflowers and grasses. Butterflies drink their flower nectar; caterpillars and grasshoppers munch on their leaves. The air is filled with the chirps and trills of songbirds that feed on the insects. A rustling sound signals that a vole or shrew is searching for fruits or seeds.

The greatest biodiversity occurs on relatively flat but well-drained mesic prairie—grassland that is moderately wet. This is the domain of tallgrass prairie, where big bluestem, Indian grass, and false indigo tower above the prairie cinquefoil and prairie rose. It is also the domain of oak savanna, where fire-resistant oak trees are scattered among the grasses. Here and there, these trees spread their branches and provide a shady oasis from the relentless sun on the grassland.

In undisturbed prairie, you will see prairie dock with broad heart-shaped leaves and rattlesnake master with bristly, long, thin leaves. Compass plants orient the flat surfaces of their leaves to the rising and setting sun. Some say that pioneers who were lost in the vast grassland used the compass plant to find their way.

Prairies are now a rare sight because farmers plowed the land and animals trampled and overgrazed it. Nevertheless, remnants of virgin (pristine) prairies do exist along railroad rights-of-way, in pioneer cemeteries, on South Kedzie Avenue within city limits, and in Chicago suburbs. Restored prairies grow in parks and forest preserves.

Rocky or gravel-covered hills have dry prairies where prairie smoke, pasque flowers, and some tallgrass prairie plants bloom despite the shallow soil and exposed bedrock. Most gravel prairies are gone, but Spring Hill Farm Fen, Bluff Spring Fen, and Shoe Factory Road Prairies have fragments. Dolomite prairies live on outcrops of dolomite rock such as those on the Des Plaines River, southwest of Chicago. The soil is extremely alkaline, yet false pennyroyal, rock jasmine, marbleseed, and nodding wild onion mingle with little bluestem. Shrub prairies have chokeberry and low-bush blueberry among the grasses.

Sand prairies contain deep-rooted bunch grasses that resist the wind, and forbs with narrow small leaves and silvery hairs that conserve water. Prickly pear cactus, a desert plant with flat stems, spines (modified leaves), and yellow anemone-like flowers, grow low to the sand. Spring blossoms with sand phlox and bird's-foot violet. Summer brings orange butterfly weed and the drone of grasshoppers to this sandy grassland.

Hill prairies grow on steep slopes covered with loess—soil made of clay and very fine sand. This is the domain of little bluestem and strange animals such as the six-lined racerunner, a lizard; the plains scorpion; and flies that resemble wasps.

Wet prairies reside in low spots, where they withstand spring floods and summer and autumn drought. Cordgrass lives here along with sedges (triangular-stemmed plants that resemble grasses). These sedges often form mats or hummocks, where red-winged blackbirds and marsh wrens settle, and frogs croak at sunset. Alkaline fen prairies—wet prairies that occur only near limestone bluffs or moraines—contain many rare plants. Prairie potholes, depressions with cattails and reeds, attract muskrats and mink as well as ducks and herons.

Around the world, prairies go by many names. The Midwest, for example, has eastern prairies, true prairies, or tallgrass prairies; the high plains have short-grass or mixed-grass prairies. In Russia these grasslands are called steppes; in South America they are called pampas. They are known as veld in South Africa, basalt plains in Australia, and tussock grasslands in New Zealand.

Why is prairie, rather than forest, the main ecosystem of Illinois? Because grasses, with their deep roots, can withstand the state's extreme temperatures: over ninety degrees Fahrenheit in the summer and below zero in the winter. Grasses also manage nicely with twenty to forty inches of average rainfall each year. Summer droughts, periodic fires, and grazing animals also seem to prevent trees from crossing the border of the grassland.

Until white settlers began to control the prairie, lightning lit fires every year, and easterly winds quickly spread the flames. Native Americans started other fires to trap buffalo. Fires on the prairie consumed dried leaves and fertilized the soil with their minerals. The blazes killed most tree seedlings, but did little harm to oak trees or native grasses and even caused some seeds to germinate. Fires sustained the prairie and oak savanna by holding back the forest.

## Assault by Agriculture

The assault on Illinois prairies began with barges that traveled down the Erie Canal and steamships that crossed the Great Lakes. They were filled with New England farmers and European immigrants coming to stake their claims on the rich prairie soil.

The settlers devastated the prairie with their barbed-wire fences and plows. The fences were built to confine herds of cattle, which overgrazed and trampled the native grasses. Special plows, often pulled by ten oxen, tore at the deep grass roots. Sodbusting was backbreaking work, so some settlers, who had paid $1.25 per acre for the land, paid even more to sodbusters who cut two-foot-wide furrows in the soil. Most of the Illinois prairie was destroyed between 1830 and 1870, when most of it had been converted into cropland. The "sea of grass" was conquered by the plow.

Population boomed in Illinois territory when the railroads came and farmers could easily send their crops and livestock to eastern markets. By the time of the Civil War, prairies were virtually gone. Of the twenty-two million acres of prairie that existed before the settlers, only twenty-three hundred acres remain. Bits of original grassland still exist at Goose Lake Prairie, along railroad rights-of-way, and in pioneer cemeteries. Restored prairie can be seen at Somme Prairie, Morton Arboretum, and in Chicago parks, forest preserves, and suburbs where brush is cleared and grasses and wildflowers are planted. Nevertheless, Illinois is mostly farmland, and its corn and soybeans make fortunes at the Chicago Board of Trade.

## Ashburn Prairie (½ to 1 hour)
Kedzie Avenue (3200 W.) and South 67th Street
Chicago, IL 60617

Imagine a prairie ten thousand years old, with some of the first grasses and wildflowers to cover the area after the last glaciers retreated. This one was saved from bulldozers and real estate development by people in the community who realized it was a rare natural treasure. In 1993, school and community volunteers and the Chicago Park District began the rescue operation of this one-and-one-half-acre tallgrass prairie before builders could destroy it. They used large tractorlike machines called tree spades to dig out plugs of prairie sod that were six feet in diameter and eight feet deep. This was necessary because the grass roots were more than six feet deep. Grasses and flowers were lifted from the soil and these prairie plugs were loaded on trucks, shipped down Kedzie Avenue, and replanted where you can see them now.

## Goose Lake Prairie State Natural Area (3 to 5 hours)
5010 N. Jugtown Road
Morris, IL 60450
(815) 942-2899

Getting there: Located in Morris, 60 miles southwest of Chicago. Take I-55 south and exit at Lorenzo Road. Go 7 miles west on Lorenzo Road, turn north (right) onto Jugtown Road, and continue to the park entrance. Or take I-80 and exit south on Route 47 to Pine Bluff Road. Turn left (east) on Pine Bluff Road to Jugtown Road. Turn north (left) to the park entrance.

Hours: March to November, daily, 10 A.M.–4 P.M.; December to February, weekdays, 10 A.M.–4 P.M.

Facilities: Trails. Visitor Center.

Visit Illinois scenery that was common 150 years ago. Typical tallgrass prairie covers more than half of the area's twenty-five hundred acres. Take the Tallgrass Nature Trail to see eight- to twelve-foot-high cordgrass, big bluestem, Indian grass, and switch grass, and forbs that bloom and paint the prairie with changing colors through the seasons. Marsh Loop Trail passes near ponds and marshes. Go by a glacial pond and a log cabin dating from 1834, believed to have been a station on the underground railroad for slaves fleeing the South. Prairie View Trail climbs a strip mine spoil mound for a panorama of reclaimed mine area, prairie potholes, and prairie marsh. You will also have a view of Dresden Bluffs (at the junction of the Kankakee and Des Plaines rivers), the Dresden Nuclear Power Plant, and the General Electric Midwest Fuel Recovery Plant.

## 🍃 Gensburg-Markham Prairie Nature Preserve (1 to 3 hours)
Markham, IL 60426
(312) 583-4050

Getting there: Located in Markham, 22 miles southwest of Chicago. Take I-57 to Exit 348 and Highway 6 (159th Street). Take 159th Street east 1 mile to Whipple Avenue, then turn and go north 2 blocks to the nature preserve.

A beach ridge of ancient Lake Chicago runs through this sixteen-acre preserve. It contains a range of ecosystems, from mesic to sand prairie and sedge meadow. The sand prairie contains rare plants such as grape fern, sundrop, narrow-leaved sundew, and grass pink orchid, along with nodding wild onion, cream wild indigo, prairie coreopsis, and prairie alum root. Birders may spot short-billed marsh wrens and swamp and Henslow's sparrow, for they nest here.

## 🍃 Glenbrook North High School Prairie Nature Preserve (½ hour)

2300 Shermer Road
Northbrook, IL 60062
(847) 272-6400, ext. 274

Getting there: Located in Northbrook, 25 miles north of Chicago. Take I-94 (Edens Expressway) north and exit at Willow Road west. Go west on Willow Road to Pfingsten Road. The prairie is on the northwest corner of the Glenbrook North High School campus.

This gently rolling moraine is covered with one and a half acres of mesic black-soil prairie, where sky-blue aster blooms amid northern dropseed grass. Wetter areas contain cordgrass and bluejoint grass.

## 🍃 Santa Fe Prairie: Palos Restoration Project (1 to 2 hours)

Palos Hills, IL 60465
(708) 771-1330

Getting there: Located in the Palos Hills area, 19 miles southwest of Chicago. Take I-55 south and exit at Route 45 south. Go south on Route 45, then turn east to the tracks that border the Des Plaines River. The prairie is on Santa Fe Railroad land near the river.

This ten-acre plot is part of the Illinois and Michigan National Heritage Corridor. On mesic prairie and wet, calcium-rich, and gravel soils, you can test your ability to identify more than two hundred native plants.

## 🍃 Somme Prairie Nature Preserve

Northbrook, IL 60062
(708) 771-1330

Getting there: Located in Northbrook, 25 miles north of Chicago. Take I-94 (Edens Expressway) north. Exit at Dundee Road (Route 68) west, and travel west to Waukegan Road (Route 43).

On seventy acres, you can wander through marsh, wet prairie, mesic prairie, and oak savanna. Leadplant, prairie gentian, hoary puccoon, and prairie phlox are some of its interesting flora.

### 🍃 Wolf Road Prairie Nature Preserve (1 to 3 hours)

Westchester, IL 60153
(708) 771-1330

Getting there: Located in Westchester, 14 miles southwest of Chicago. Take the Eisenhower Expressway (I-290) west and exit south on Route 45 (Route 12/20 or LaGrange Road). Go south on Route 45 to Westchester Street. Turn west on Westchester Street (31st Street) and drive to Wolf Road.

Original tallgrass and uncommon forbs such as Indian paintbrush, bottle gentian, and Indian plantain thrive on these forty-four acres. You will also see a marsh and a small savanna. Listen for frogs and look for fox snakes and woodchucks while you walk the trail.

### 🍃 Braidwood Dunes and Savanna Nature Preserve (1 to 3 hours)

Braidwood, IL 60408
Contact:
Forest Preserve District of Will County
22606 S. Cherry Hill Road
Joliet, IL 60433
(815) 727-8700

Getting there: Located in Braidwood, about 60 miles southwest of Chicago. Take Highway 55 south and exit on Route 113. Go southeast on Route 113 to Highway 53.
Hours: Weekends only.

Sand prairies, sand savanna, sedge meadow, and marsh thrive on 259 acres, an area with rich fauna. There are thirty species of birds, reptiles such as the six-lined racerunner, bullsnake, and western slender glass lizard, and amphibians such as the tiger salamander and western chorus frog.

## 🌿🌿 Woodworth Prairie (1 to 3 hours)

Niles, IL 60714
(847) 965-3488
(312) 996-8673 all year

Getting there: Located in Niles, 16 miles northwest of Chicago. Take I-94 north to Dempster Street and exit west. Go west on Dempster Street to Milwaukee Avenue. Turn north on Milwaukee Avenue to the entrance, on the east side of Milwaukee Avenue just north of Golf Road.

This five-acre tract is one of the best examples of virgin high mesic prairie—tallgrass prairie with big bluestem, Indian grass, and other high grasses adorned with a tremendous variety of flowers and butterflies.

## 🌿 Grant Creek Prairie Nature Preserve (1 to 3 hours)

Wilmington, IL 60481
Contact:
Site Superintendent
Des Plaines Fish and Wildlife Area
24621 N. River Road
Wilmington, IL 60481
(815) 423-5326

Getting there: Located in Wilmington, about 55 miles southwest of Chicago. Take I-55 south and exit at Route 241 near Wilmington. Go east on the frontage road of I-55, then turn north 0.8 mile to the east side of I-55, north of River Road.

These seventy-eight acres of high-quality wet prairie have blue jointgrass and tussock sedge. Mesic prairie contains false wild indigo and tall coreopsis. Listen for grasshopper sparrows and sedge wrens. Fox snakes, green snakes, and coyotes also roam this area.

## Lockport Prairie Nature Preserve (2 to 5 hours)

Lockport, IL 60441
Contact:
Forest Preserve District of Will County
22606 S. Cherry Hill Road
Joliet, IL 60433
(815) 727-8700

Getting there: Located in Lockport, 33 miles southwest of Chicago. Take I-55 south and exit south on Highway 53. Highway 53 becomes Highway 7. Go south on Highway 7 1 mile to Division Street. Turn east on Division Street and go ¼ mile to the nature preserve, entrances on both sides of the road.

On 254 acres bordering the Des Plaines River, you will see calamint, slender sandwort, and other unusual plants on dolomite (a calcium-rich rock) prairie. Visit a fen and marshes with shorebirds, birds of prey, and wetland mammals such as opossums.

## Wilmington Shrub Prairie Nature Preserve (1 to 3 hours)

Braidwood, IL 60408
Contact:
Illinois Department of Natural Resources
Natural Heritage Biologist
100 First National Bank Plaza, Suite 10
Chicago Heights, IL 60441
(708) 709-3300

Getting there: Located in Braidwood, about 60 miles southwest of Chicago. Take Highway 55 south and exit on Route 113. Take Route 113 east 3 miles to a county road. Turn north on the road and go 1.5 miles to the preserve, entrance on the west side. Follow a path ½ mile to the preserve.

Shrub prairie with hardhack, bristly blackberry, and running pine inhabits this area. On its 146 acres, you will also find many interesting plants on habitats such as sand prairie, wet prairie, sand savanna (with scattered trees), sedge meadow, and marsh.

##  Midewin National Tallgrass Prairie (2 to 4 hours)

Joliet, IL 60436
Contact:
Open Lands Project
(312) 427-4256

Getting there: Located in Joliet, 40 miles southwest of Chicago. Take I-55 to the junction of Route 53. Turn south on Route 53 past Joliet to the Joliet Army Ammunition Plant on the east side and the Des Plaines Conservation Area on the west side of the highway.

*Midewin* is a Potawatomi word for healing, and this prairie will heal the Joliet Arsenal (a former military site). Located near the junction of the Des Plaines, Kankakee, and Illinois rivers, an area that serves as habitat for sixteen state endangered and threatened plants and animals and as a nesting area for birds of the Midwestern grasslands, the Midewin National Tallgrass Prairie will consist of forty thousand acres. The Joliet Arsenal, once a three-thousand-acre munitions production area, will be converted into two industrial parks and a landfill. Adjacent land will have a National Veterans Cemetery and a nineteen-thousand-acre prairie. Because the land is near the Des Plaines Conservation Area and twenty-two other natural areas, Midewin National Tallgrass Prairie will link all into a huge preserve ideal for hiking, camping, hunting, and environmental education.

# 6

## *Native Americans and Nature*

"Sell a country! Why not sell the air, the clouds and the great sea, as well as the earth? Did not the Great Spirit make them all for the use of his children?"
—Tecumseh, Shawnee Chief, Council at Vincennes, 1810

Toward the end of the Ice Ages, small groups of hunters camped on bluffs overlooking the Illinois and Des Plaines rivers. These paleo-Indian people, whose stone spear tips were found at Calumet Beach on Chicago's south side, lived ten thousand years ago and more. They hunted the hairy ancestors of modern elephants—mammoths that foraged in the prairie and mastodons that browsed the forests.

The early nomads were followed by the Archaic Indians, hunters and gatherers who established a culture eight thousand years ago that lasted more than five thousand years. While digging the foundation for the Equitable Building, at Michigan Avenue and the Chicago River, workers found their spear points.

Early Woodland people occupied the Chicago region between forty-five hundred and twenty-five hundred years ago. They planted small gardens with sunflowers and squash, made stone carvings of people and birds, and built burial mounds. They owned objects made of copper from the north and alligator teeth from the Gulf coast, which indicate that they traded with distant peoples.

About A.D. 1000, Mississippian people established large villages with sunken earth lodges and nearby cemeteries in the upper Illinois River valley. When archeologists examined their garbage pits, they found corncobs, clamshells, and the bones of fish, snakes, birds, squirrels, deer, and bison—a silent testimony to the diversity of animals in the Chicago region. These Native Americans planted the "three sisters"— corn, beans, and squash (including pumpkin)—and tobacco and tomatoes. Thus a typical meal consisted of vegetable stew with squash, and corn bread sweetened with maple sap they obtained each spring by tapping trees in the forest.

## Europeans Meet Native Americans

Long before the white man came, Miami lived side by side with Ottawa, Chippewa, Sauk, Fox, and other peoples along the Des Plaines River and other Illinois rivers. Each was an independent group. Their trails connected Chicagou with the great fishing and hunting grounds of the Huron and the Kaskaskia, and with ancient trade centers on the Wabash River in Indiana. In the early 1700s, the Miami were forced out of the Chicago region by the Potawatomi. Raids by the Iroquois forced the Potawatomi, along with the Chippewa from Wisconsin and the Ottawa from Michigan, into the Chicago area. Potawatomi, Chippewa, and Ottawa formed an alliance and lived here until the Treaty of Chicago in 1833.

At first, Native Americans traded with white men and acted as guides. Later, they were caught up in battles to retain their ancient lands. In 1730, Native Americans and the French were defeated near Starved Rock (near Utica, west of Chicago) and the British took over. After the British were defeated in the Revolutionary War, the United States of America staked its claim to the Northwest Territory, which included Illinois Territory. Native Americans rejected the claim and began to raid the farms and wagon trains of white pioneers heading west.

U.S. General "Mad" Anthony Wayne defeated the Native Americans who controlled the Illinois prairie at the battle of Fallen Timbers in 1794. Motivated by promises of British support, warriors from the Northwest Indian Confederation—including Miami, Potawatomi, Shawnee, Delaware, Ottawa, Chippewa, and Iroquois people—fought from behind a barricade of fallen trees. However, they lost the battle and the Treaty of Greenville forced them to cede most of Ohio and parts of Indiana, Illinois, and Michigan to the United States. Native Americans abandoned their homelands at Chicago, Peoria, and the mouth of the Illinois River. From then on, white settlers traveled without fear of attack on the Chicago-Illinois waterway.

In 1816, the Potawatomi ceded a strip of land ten miles wide on either side of the mouth of the Chicago River. That strip extended from what is now Chicago southwest to the headwaters of the Illinois River. In 1832, Chief Black Hawk's warriors attacked white farmers in the Des Plaines and DuPage areas. The farmers fled to Chicago and increased the population from one hundred to five hundred. In 1833, Potawatomi, Ottawa, and Chippewa (Ojibway) people were forced to leave the Chicago region and live on a reservation at Council Bluffs, Iowa.

## Wilderness and Property Rights

For thousands of years, Native Americans roamed Illinois territory. They believed that everyone was entitled to share it, for the wilderness was free and could not be owned by individuals. The British said Indians were merely tenants of the soil, and the land belonged to the King of England. (This was intended to prevent the French from taking over Illinois Territory. However, the Indians did not believe the king owned the land.) The United States colonial government adopted the British view of land ownership. Thus began battles about private property rights (versus wetland conservation and saving endangered species) and protection of public wilderness (versus ranching, lumber, mining, and real estate interests) that continue today.

## Indian Villages

More than two thousand years ago, Native Americans lived on sandbars where Rosehill Cemetery (5800 N. Ravenswood) and Graceland Cemetery (4000 N. Clark) are now. Native American settlements also existed in many forest preserves. Ottawa Trail Woods, on Harlem Avenue just north of 47th Street, had a village where Chief Shabbona presided over Potawatomi, Chippewa, and Ottawa people. Whistler's Woods, at Halsted and South 134th Street in Riverdale, was the site of a freshwater spring and a Native American village.

## Wigwams of Bark, Wattle, and Daub

Burnt pieces of daub, or clay, indicate that many if not most Native American homes in the Chicago area were built by hammering posts in the ground several inches apart until they formed a circle. Sticks and vines, woven between the posts, formed a wall that was plastered with clay from the marshland. Tipis—portable homes of animal hides—were more typical of Plains Indians. However, many early pictures of Fort Dearborn show tipis.

A Potawatomi wigwam was portable, so families could move in winter and summer. It was a bark-covered structure with an entrance on one side, storage pits in the floor, a fire in the center, and a smoke hole on top. The roof was made of bark or grass mats, and sometimes an elk or buffalo hide. One or two families shared the wigwam. Women and children slept along the edges, with the father protecting the entranceway.

Food was preserved by drying, smoking, and cooling. Native Americans chilled wild turkey and raccoon meat in three-foot-deep storage pits. They preserved fish and venison by drying, salting, or smoking it over a fire. And they hung beans, pumpkin, and corn out to dry. Salt was needed to preserve foods, so Native Americans traveled to salt springs such as those at the Indiana Dunes and in Thornton, Illinois.

## Commuter Roads

Road names containing the word "ridge" and streets that follow high ground were once probably Indian trails. Milwaukee, Ogden, Archer, and Elston avenues and Northwest Highway were also Indian trails.

The Vincennes Trace was a well-traveled trail between Watseka, Illinois and downtown Chicago. The trail followed the eastern border of Illinois and went along a sand ridge through Calumet City and continued along Vincennes Avenue on the eastern edge of Blue Island to State Street, which led to downtown Chicago.

The Ottawa Woods Trail began at the Chicago Portage National Heritage Site on the west side of Harlem Avenue, south of 47th Street (see Chapter 9), where Native American guides led Father Jacques Marquette and Louis Joliet. The trail continued on high ground through Ottawa Trail Woods and along Ogden Avenue. It passed 35th Street and Cicero Avenue, continued on the bank of the South Branch of the Chicago River, and ended at Clark Street, near the Lincoln Park Zoo.

Indian trails often crossed fords—shallow spots in a river. In the Chicago region, trails went across Riverside Ford, Stony Ford (at Joliet Road), Laughton's Ford in Ottawa Trail Woods, and Summit's Ford (at Laramie and Route 55, around 55th Street).

# The Great Hunting and Fishing Grounds

Native Americans followed trails along the Chicago and Des Plaines rivers and in the Skokie marsh, where fish were plentiful. They hunted flocks of ducks and geese and other wetland birds, as well as wild turkey for meat. They also killed beaver, otter, and raccoon for their furs. On the prairie, Native Americans hunted buffalo. In the forests, they aimed their arrows at deer and fox.

## 🍃 Trail Trees (½ to 1 hour)

Trails were marked with bent trees that still exist in the northern suburbs. They can be found in Wilmette, Winnetka, and Turnbull Woods, on the nature trail of the Chicago Botanic Garden in Glencoe.

## 🍃🍃🍃 Ottawa Trail Woods (1 to 3 hours)

West side of Harlem Avenue (7200 W.), north of 47th Street
Chicago, IL 60638

This place was once a village where Shabbona, chief of the Potawatomi, lived, along a well-traveled Native American trail (see above). It is also the site of one of the last trading posts east of the Mississippi River. A monument in the woods commemorates the Laughton Brothers Trading Post, where Indians traded their furs from 1828 to 1834. After that, it became a general store, where blacksmith tools, dried fruits, and other items were sold to pioneers.

# River Portages

Native Americans used several low spots in the prairie to portage or carry their canoes from one river to another. A monument marks the historic Chicago Portage at Harlem Avenue (7200 W.), south of 47th Street. (See Chapter 9). There were also other portages between the Des Plaines and the Chicago rivers. One of them was near 107th and Central in Chicago Ridge, which some historians think was the portage that Marquette and Joliet crossed in 1673. Others were located at Central Street (5000 W.) and the Chicago River and north of the city, near Glenview.

## The Green Bay Trail

Green Bay, Wisconsin and Chicago, Illinois were centers of Native American trade, so Green Bay Trail was well traveled long before Chicago or Green Bay were "discovered" by the French in the seventeenth century. The trail paralleled the Lake Michigan shore and was never more than twelve miles away from its water. It passed through dense pine forests and muddy wetlands such as the Skokie marsh, a major hunting and fishing ground.

The English captured Green Bay from the French, and by 1783 it was officially American territory. Nevertheless, Green Bay remained a British outpost until the War of 1812. By 1826, however, mail carriers tracked wild game and camped on streambanks in the Green Bay area during their five-hundred-mile round trips. The small towns that first appeared on the Lake Michigan shore had harbors for shipping, so farmers used the Green Bay Trail only for local travel. Today, Green Bay Road is a paved route that extends from the heart of Chicago, through northern suburbs, to Milwaukee and Green Bay, Wisconsin.

The Green Bay Trail consisted of two paths or branches. One started at the north end of the Michigan Avenue Bridge and went north along the North Branch of the Chicago River from Rush Street to Chicago Avenue, past Clark Street and North Avenue to Grosse Pointe in Wilmette (where it was closest to Lake Michigan), and then headed northwest past Waukegan, Illinois, and Kenosha and Racine, Wisconsin.

The other path started from the fork of the Chicago River, ran between the North Branch and the Des Plaines for about fifteen miles, then crossed the Des Plaines River and Gurnee Ford before it met the first path and continued north to Green Bay.

### 🍃 Indian Boundary Division of the Forest Preserve (1 to 3 hours)

Forest Preserve District of Cook County
536 N. Harlem Avenue
River Forest, IL 60305
(708) 771-1069

About twenty-three hundred Native Americans lived in the Indian Boundary area until the 1829 Treaty of Prairie du Chien forced them to leave. Historic sites include Robinson Woods, located near Bryn Mawr Avenue (5600 N.), and East River Road (adjacent to the Des Plaines River). Its woods were named after Alexander Robinson, chief of the Potawatomi, who helped the family of John Kinzie and Captain and Mrs. Heald escape the attack at Fort Dearborn. The Alexander Robinson homesite is an unmarked grassy clearing in the forest. You will also find an Indian cemetery at East River Road and Lawrence Avenue (4800 N.). Evans Field on Thatcher Avenue, just north of North Avenue (1600 N.), was once a burial ground and Indian village. Indian Boundary Line, north of Fullerton Avenue (2400 N.) and west of Thatcher Woods, is the northern edge of land the Potawatomi ceded to white people.

Note: Obtain a map to identify sites along the Des Plaines River from Touhy Avenue (7200 N.) to Madison Street in northwest suburban Chicago.

## 🍃 Chicago Portage Canoe Trail

This is the historic Des Plaines River route that Native American guides showed Father Jacques Marquette and Louis Joliet. See Chapter 13 for more details.

## 🍃 Isle à La Cache Museum (1 to 2 hours)

501 E. Romeo Road
Romeoville, IL 60441
(815) 886-1467

Getting there: Located in Romeoville, 31 miles southwest of Chicago. Take I-55 south. Exit south on Joliet Road and go to Romeo Road (135th Street). Turn east (left) to the museum.
Hours: 10 A.M.–4 P.M. Closed Monday.
Admission: Free.

Like a time capsule, this small museum contains mementoes of Native Americans and French voyageurs who hunted and traded furs in Illinois territory before the American Revolution. Listen to splashing water, birdcalls, and other sounds of the wilderness as you look at Native American artifacts such as a birchbark canoe, wigwam, clothing, and bone scrapers. View French voyageur mementoes such as a contract, a diary, personal articles, and trade objects and learn about "soft brown gold," other furs, and why beavers disappeared.

School groups may call to arrange a program led by guides who are dressed like French voyageurs or Native Americans. In June, Rendezvous: French and Indian Trade Fair takes you back to the sixteenth century, with canoe races, tomahawk throws, and musket shoots.

###  Native American sites on the Illinois and Michigan Canal National Heritage Corridor (3 hours to 1 week)

For maps and other information, contact:

National Park Service
U.S. Department of the Interior
(815) 740-2047

Illinois and Michigan Canal
Visitor Center
Gaylord Building
Lockport, IL 60441
(815) 838-4830

I & M Canal State Trail
Gebhard Woods State Park
William G. Stratton State Park
P.O. Box 272
Morris, IL 60450
(815) 942-0796

Channahon State Park
P.O. Box 54
Channahon, IL 60410
(815) 467-4271

Kankakee River State Park
P.O. Box 37
Bourbonnais, IL 60914
(815) 933-1383

Buffalo Rock State Park
and Effigy Tumuli
P.O. Box 39
Ottawa, IL 61350
(815) 433-2220

See Chapter 9 for other canal attractions.

Native American villages, burial mounds, artwork, and artifacts can be found along much of the hundred-mile-long corridor in northern Illinois that extends from Chicago to LaSalle and Peru at the Illinois River.

For five thousand years, humans continuously inhabited the sandstone butte that overlooks the Illinois River near the town of Utica. In 1682, LaSalle constructed Fort St. Louis on this butte to induce the Illinois Indians to remain in their village. Called Le Rocher ("the rock") by the French, it is now named Starved Rock because of a siege that supposedly took place in 1769 (in the aftermath of Pontiac's uprising) that caused a group of Native Americans to starve to death.

Across from Starved Rock is Old Kaskaskia Village (much of it underwater behind the Illinois waterway lock and dam). Nearby sites are of archeological importance but there is little visual evidence of their history. These places include the Zimmerman site, which housed Native American settlements for a millenium. The Kaskaskia people hunted bison and planted maize, beans, and squash, using hoes made of the shoulderblades of bison and elk. They lived in loaf-shaped wigwams covered with reed mats when Father Marquette arrived in 1673. There were 460 cabins in the village before the Iroquois raid in 1680.

Visit the grave of Shabbona, Chief of the Potawatomi, at Evergreen Cemetery in Morris. Look for burial mounds in Higinbotham Woods Earthwork in Joliet's city park. Fisher Site, on the south bank of the Des Plaines River opposite Dresden Heights, has depressions left by burial mounds and earth lodges. Briscoe Burial Mounds can be found on the north side of the Des Plaines River valley, just west of the Interstate 55 crossing near Channahon. The Channahon area and Hickory Creek section are prehistoric sites.

At Buffalo Rock State Park, the bluffs that line the Illinois River near Ottawa (two miles west on Dee Bennett Road) contain earth art, also called "effigy tumuli." Molded of clay by unknown artists, five sculptures—snake, turtle, catfish, frog, and water strider (an insect)—represent animals native to Illinois.

For more information about Native American history, art, and artifacts, contact:

Native American Education Service
2838 W. Peterson
Chicago, IL 60659
(773) 761-5000

# 7

# *The Forest and the Trees*

"I enter some glade in the woods, perchance where a few weeds and dry leaves alone lift themselves above the surface of the snow, and it is as if I had come to an open window. I see out and around myself. . . ."

—Henry David Thoreau (1817–1862)

Since forests require more water than prairies, most Illinois forests—ecosystems dominated by trees—cling to waterways. Cottonwood and willow trees put their roots into stream banks while spruce and pine trees prevail on river bluffs and sand dunes. The deciduous forests are most common in Illinois. Maple, oak, basswood, and other deciduous trees glow orange, red, and gold in autumn before they lose their broad flat leaves. They flower in spring and then bear seeds inside the fruits that ripen in summer.

Evergreen forests are now rare in Illinois because the climate is warmer than it used to be. Evergreens, such as pine or spruce, grow needle-like leaves that hold fast and remain green through the winter. The larch or tamarack is an exception, for it yellows and drops its needles. The evergreens do not bear flowers or fruits. They are known as gymnosperms or conifers because they bear cones with "naked" or exposed seeds.

## Forest Succession

A warming climate, diminishing rainfall, and other environmental changes caused a succession of forest ecosystems to dominate the

Chicago region. After the glaciers left, an open spruce forest covered much of northern Illinois. When year-round temperatures rose, succession proceeded when the pine forest ecosystem took over. Most of the pines were cut to supply lumber to the fast-growing city of Chicago. However, a few pine groves still stand on ridges and sand dunes near Lake Michigan, and in White Pines State Park, west of Oregon, Illinois. The pine trees themselves also contributed to their demise, for their forests became so dense that pine seedlings were shut out from the sun. Where the young pines could not grow, hardwood trees invaded the woodlands.

Today, oaks, hickories, beech, maple, and other hardwood trees prosper in what is called the climax forest, the most stable forest ecosystem in northern Illinois. However, succession will start again if environmental stresses such as pollution, violent storms, logging or other human impacts, or climate changes harm the climax forest. Depending on the environmental change, oak-hickory forest might die off, and the next stage in succession might be desert, grassland, or a different forest ecosystem.

## Asian Relatives

Common Illinois trees such as the magnolia, sassafras, and maple are related to trees in Asia rather than Europe. Why? Because climate change killed the European forest. One hundred million years ago, when the climate was warm, these trees thrived in forests throughout Asia, Europe, and North America. When the climate cooled, the North American and Asian forests survived by migrating south. Wind, water, birds, and other animals spread the tree seeds and those that sprouted in warmer, more southerly locations started new forests. In Europe, however, the high peaks of the Alps blocked seed dispersal, so the forest died of the cold. That is why Illinois magnolia, sassafras, and maple trees have only Asian cousins.

## Woodland Locations

Soil type and soil moisture determine the mix of trees in Illinois forests. Cottonwoods adapt to the sand soil of the dunes bordering Lake Michigan because they have deep roots that tap water. Pines require soil with a bit more humus, or decaying plant material. Some trees adapt to clay soils that hold so much water that their roots stay wet.

Typical northern Illinois hardwood forest as seen at the Morton Arboretum near Chicago.

Others survive only in clay and sand mixtures or in mineral-rich soil. Bottomland forest, where silver maple, cottonwood, and green ash often grow, thrives in moist, fertile soil along riverbanks and island rims. Trees that keep their roots wet, such as elm, hackberry, and basswood, do well in the clay soil of floodplains. Oaks and hickories require soil with more sand, so they take the higher, drier ground in upland forests.

## Prairie Groves

When Illinois settlers arrived, large prairie groves—forests surrounded by grassland—offered shelter from sun and wind that swept across the prairie. These groves had pawpaw, sassafras, and poison ivy growing in the shade of oak and hickory or maple and basswood trees. The home-steaders chose these shady woodlands and gave them names such as Morton Grove, Downers Grove, and Buffalo Grove. With population growth, these prairie woodlands changed into country towns, then sub-urbs. However, some prairie woodlands still exist in the area.

## Forest Ecology

Like a tall apartment building, a forest has many levels, each with a different environment and different tenants. At the top or canopy, tree leaves receive sunlight and new shoots sprout. Birds perch and turn their heads from side to side to catch insects on the wing. On lower branches, nuthatches peck at the bark in search of insect grubs. Mosses and lichens grow on tree trunks. Even dead trees are habitats for mice and other small mammals. Bacteria and fungi that feed on dead wood find nourishment and shelter on a fallen tree while they recycle nutri-ents back into the soil. Clearly, a leafless trunk or a hollow log is a vital part of the forest.

Shade-loving plants such as shrubs, ferns, herbs, and wildflowers are part of the understory. From this sheltered place beneath the trees, warblers and wrens sing out. Insects and snails nibble leaves and spi-ders spin webs on the greenery. On the forest floor, snakes and lizards crawl in search of insects. Squirrels and chipmunks gather nuts and packrats pile up mounds of sticks. Tree seedlings take root and mush-rooms grow on the moist soil covered with leaf litter. Even beneath the soil there is life. Tree roots gather water, woodchucks hide, and earthworms burrow below ground level.

## Oaks and the Understory

Oaks are the dominant trees in many Illinois forests and savannas (grass-lands with scattered trees). An oak sprouts from a seed called an acorn and spreads its branches out as far as it spreads its roots underground. This stable shape keeps the oak upright during violent storms. The corky bark that shields it against fire also contributes to the oak's long life span. Bur oak has thick, furrowed bark and leaves that are narrow near the stem and end with wide rounded lobes (fingerlike projections on the leaf margin). Red oak has leaves with more pointed lobes. White oak, the Illinois state tree, has valuable wood and reaches a height of sixty to one hundred feet. Its leaves, with fingerlike lobes, are silvery when young.

# Deciduous Tree I.D.

In a deciduous forest, try to identify common broad-leaved trees such as oak, maple, crabapple, hickory, hawthorn, and buckthorn.

Box elder has tulip-shaped leaves.

Ash has compound leaves. These are split into leaflets opposite one another on the stem. The bark has diamond patterns.

Walnut leaves are similar to ash but with smaller leaflets.

Cherry has few low branches.

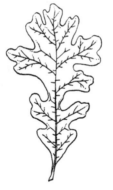

Oak has lobed leaves and branches that spread out in all directions.

Shagbark hickory has bark that looks as if it is peeling.

Maple has lobed palm-shaped leaves.

Basswood has heart-shaped leaves and two trunks.

Cottonwood has palm-shaped leaves, wrinkled bark, and seeds with cottony fluff to carry them on the wind.

The forest understory has many shade-tolerant plants such as mint, with a square stem and fragrant leaves; knotweed, with tiny flowers on long spikes; and burdock, with leaves like elephant ears and reddish stems that grow in a circle. Because poison ivy has irritating oils, "Leaves of three, let it be." If you come upon a low-growing plant or vine that has a reddish stem where three leaves meet, don't touch it, even in winter.

Wherever you see multiflora rosebushes or blue chickory flowers, the area has been disturbed by human activity. In forest openings, prairie plants take root. Look for clusters of tiny starlike flowers that grow on snakeroot, a prairie plant with fluid that poisons the milk of grazing cows. In wetter areas, you may see wild ginger, a native plant with roots used as a spice. Sniff the air for the pungent odor of skunk cabbage. Conservationists say that spring arrives in Chicago when skunk cabbage blooms in late February.

## Observing a Forest in Winter

Don snowshoes, boots, or skis for a trip through any deciduous forest. In winter, when leaves are gone and the paths are more open, you can see the silhouettes of trees and the topography of the land. Notice that each kind of tree has its own branching pattern. The same is true for shrubs. Examine a twig for small air holes, the scars of fallen leaves, and buds that will produce new leaves in spring. Look for last year's birds' nests in the treetops. Find animal tracks in the snow. Listen to your feet crush leaves that enrich the forest's soil and spur its growth.

### North Park Village Nature Center (1 to 3 hours)

5801 N. Pulaski Road
Chicago, IL 60646
(773) 744-5472

Hours: Daily, 10 A.M.–4 P.M. Closed New Year's Day, Easter, Thanksgiving, and Christmas.

Do you and your family take pleasure in nature walks, star watching, and animal tracking? Do you yearn for wildlife encounters? Then choose from a wide range of programs run by the City of Chicago Department of the Environment at North Park Village Nature Center. If you prefer to work outdoors, the nature center staff and volunteer stewardship network will welcome your help in maintaining this preserve. Come for the Spring Maple Sugar Festival to see how maple trees are tapped to make maple syrup. Do crafts and walk on snowy trails at night during the Winter Solstice Festival.

Escape the surrounding city any time of year. Follow easy trails that pass through woodlands with many maples, a rare oak savanna, and a marsh. This forty-six-acre nature preserve also has a historic grove of trees and Bluebird Prairie. In the nature center, you will find live animals and displays of Native American tools. Try your skills at identifying animal skulls and animal tracks. In the children's activity room, compare your armspread with the wingspread of the great blue heron.

## 🌲🌲🌲 The Grove National Historic Landmark (1 to 3 hours)

1421 Milwaukee Avenue
Glenview, IL 60025
(847) 299-6096

Getting there: Located in Glenview, 20 miles northwest of Chicago. Take I-94 (Edens Expressway) north and exit at Lake Street west. Go west on Lake Street to Milwaukee Avenue and turn south to the entrance on the east (left) side of the street.
Hours: Monday–Friday, 8 A.M.–4:30 P.M. Saturday–Sunday, 9 A.M.– 5 P.M.
Access: Some trails for persons with handicaps.
Facilities: Interpretive center. Historic home. Natural history library. Science classroom with animal displays for children.

Hike through an ancient prairie grove on this eighty-five-acre national historic landmark. It was once the farm of a pioneer family, so visit Kennicott House to see furnishings and gardens of the 1850s. Stop at the interpretive center to view legless lizards, freshwater eels, and other animals. Outdoors, you will find a tipi and a log cabin, and trails that circle a pond and go through the prairie grove that has existed since the time the glaciers retreated.

Come for nature walks, birding, workshops, and lectures. Or bring your children for animal activities and outdoor adventures. Make reservations for group tours. If your family includes four-to six-year-olds, visit the ponds and forest and listen to tales of Native Americans during Wonder Days. In April, come for the Earth Day environmental exhibits and music. In July, attend Civil War Living History Days, when authentic Union and Confederate troop encampments, cannons and guns, skirmishes and military drills make the Civil War come alive. In October, enjoy the folk music, nature walks, and pioneer craft demonstrations at the Grove Folk Fest; or take a hayride at the Pumpkin Trail.

## River Trail Nature Center (1 to 3 hours)

3120 N. Milwaukee Avenue
Northbrook, IL 60062
(847) 824-8360

Getting there: Located in Northbrook, 25 miles northwest of Chicago. Take I-94 (Edens Expressway) north to the Lake Avenue west exit. Drive west on Lake Avenue to Milwaukee Avenue and turn north. The entrance is on the west (left) side of the street.

Hours: Summer: weekdays, 8 A.M.–5 P.M., weekends, 8 A.M.–5:30 P.M. Winter: closes at dusk. Exhibit building opens at 9 A.M. and closes ½ hour earlier than the grounds. Closed Fridays. Grounds closed Thanksgiving, Christmas Day, and New Year's Day.

Walk trails, ride bikes, watch birds, or search for Native American artifacts at this forest preserve. Located on the Des Plaines River, a Native American canoe route, it offers a maple forest, a wetland with waterfowl, and a vernal pond (a depression that contains water and aquatic life in spring).

Sunday programs cover a wide range of topics including autumn color walks, family scavenger hunts, winter bark and bud identification, and discussions of fungi, animals, and plants of the forest. Children's progams include stories, crafts, and outdoor activities. Enjoy the March Sugar Maple Festival, with demonstrations on how sap is collected from maple trees to make pure maple syrup; or the October Fall Honey and Harvest Festival, with trail walks and crafts.

Enter the nature center to look at a bee colony, bones and skulls, and live birds, reptiles, and other animals. See a diorama about Chicago's first permanent resident, Jean Baptiste Pointe DuSable. Don't miss the exhibit on Native American tools or the weather station.

Outside the building, you can read tree rings and savor the fragrant herb garden. Walk around the building to view landscape gardens with prairie grasses, woodland flowers, and a Native American garden with corn, pumpkin, and squash where raccoons and woodchucks dine. Take the opportunity to get close to predators by visiting the red fox, a red-tailed hawk, and a great horned owl. Don't miss Bee City or the Fisherman's Forecast Station.

Walk to the Des Plaines River to watch mallard ducks. The Green Bay Trail follows the river here. The marker at Kruse's Hole indicates that this spot once had a whirlpool, and a sandbar that was used as a cattle crossing.

Follow two walking trails (one and a half miles) through the forest and wetlands. The Des Plaines River Trail, with biking, walking, and horseback riding, passes through this area. The trail now stretches from River Forest to the Lake-Cook county line, and there are plans for an extension in Lake County.

## Crabtree Nature Center (1 to 3 hours)
Palatine Road, one mile west of Barrington Road
Barrington, IL 60010
(847) 381-6592

Getting there: Located in Barrington, 36 miles northwest of Chicago. Take I-94 (Edens Expressway) north and exit at Willow Road west. Willow Road becomes Palatine Road. The nature center is 1 mile west of Barrington Road on the north side of Palatine Road.
Hours: Summer: weekdays, 8 A.M.–5 P.M., weekends, 8 A.M.–5:30 P.M. Winter: closes at dusk. Exhibit building opens at 9 A.M. and closes ½ hour earlier than the grounds. Closed Fridays. Grounds closed Thanksgiving, Christmas Day, and New Year's Day.

In the quiet atmosphere of these rolling hills, meander through one thousand acres of wetlands and restored prairie and forest. Come for field trips, discussions with naturalists, or children's activities, and check with the center for Migratory Bird Day and other events.

Exhibits in the nature center reveal the Biography of a Boulder, Ice-Shaped Land, and the consequences of replacing nature's "giant rain barrel." See native animals and an Illinois prairie painting. Discover the secrets of bat and butterfly migration and find out which feathered flyers are the swift and long-distance travelers.

Outside, look for an osage orange tree, used by Native Americans to make arrows and by pioneer farmers as livestock fences. Nearby, shagbark hickory and bur oak stand tall, and predatory birds look hungry.

Stroll down the path to the wetland, a battleground between oak-hickory forest and tallgrass prairie. Or follow Bur Edge Trail through forests and wetlands.

At Crabtree Lake, sit in the duckblind and see enormous flocks of Canada geese, ducks, and other birds. Boards with silhouettes of birds at rest and in flight can assist you in identifying the waterfowl. A sign at Phantom Prairie claims it is "Not for the meek," but don't be deterred. You can walk a short distance along its edge to see what the pioneers saw—a broad vista of tall grasses dotted with trees.

## Little Red School House Nature Center (1 to 3 hours)

9800 S. Willow Springs Road
Willow Springs, IL 60480
(708) 839-6897

Getting there: Located in Willow Springs, 19 miles southwest of Chicago. Take I-55 south and exit at Willow Springs Road. Go south to the schoolhouse.

Hours: March to October: weekdays, 8 A.M.–5 P.M., weekends, 8 A.M.–5:30 P.M. Winter: closes ½ hour earlier. Exhibit building opens at 9 A.M. and closes ½ hour earlier than the grounds; closed Fridays. Everything closed Thanksgiving, Christmas Day, and New Year's Day.

Come to the Little Red Schoolhouse, where a raccoon with a black mask over its eyes and other native animals greet you. Outdoors, you can amble through fourteen thousand acres of lovely gardens, woodlands, savanna, and wetlands in the heart of the Palos Preserve. Call for the schedule of family activities such as daytime field trips and bird walks and nighttime starwatching.

The Little Red School House was built in 1886 and later moved to this site. It contains intriguing exhibits such as "Stick 'em up," with a sock and hitchhiking seeds; a fungus that grows like a shelf; fossil ferns and horsetails; guilty ragweed and innocent goldenrod; and Indian arrowheads. In the garden that surrounds the building, you will feel small next to the Jerusalem artichoke and other giant plants. Look for the small pool where a carp swims laps with a painted turtle. The nearby farm garden can make you hungry for the spinach, radishes, and peas that grow among colorful flowers. Close by, you will find caged owls and a red-tailed hawk.

Stop at the "gravestones" with "Obituary Earth" before you wander down the path to Long John Slough. The trail takes about one hour and borders a lake with tree stumps and ducks in the water, then goes inland through forest. On the twenty-minute-long White Oak Trail, the magnificent Illinois state tree awaits you.

## 🍂🍂 Thatcher Woods and Hal Tyrrell Trailside Museum (1 to 2 hours)

738 Thatcher Avenue
River Forest, IL 60305
(708) 366-6530

Getting there: Located in River Forest, 11 miles west of Chicago. Take I-290 (Eisenhower Expressway) west and exit north at First Avenue. Go north on First. On the east side, the forest preserve borders the Des Plaines River. Thatcher Woods is between Chicago Avenue and North Avenue. Take Chicago Avenue east to Thatcher Avenue to see the museum.
Hours: Museum, daily 10 A.M.–4 P.M. Closed Thursdays.

"Wildlife accepted daily 8 to 4," says the sign at Cook County's Wildlife Rehabilitation Center. Call (708) 366-6530 if you need help for an orphaned or injured native animal. Also come for prairie and wetland walks and cycle tours through the forest with a naturalist as a guide.

At the center, visit a lively opossum, a fluffy rabbit, and a coiled-up snake. Listen to bluejays prattle and watch turtles lift their heads out of water for a breath of air. If you wonder whether predators suffer from heartburn, see the Bird Pellets exhibit. The Trailside Archeology display presents arrowheads and other Native American artifacts. Find out why "Wrappus discardi" and other nonnative items ruin the woodlands.

Outside, follow the path south to predators: a grey fox, hawks, and owls. To gain a glimpse into the workings of forests, be sure to see the exhibit that asks, "Is that tree dead?"

Hike where Native Americans hunted long ago: along the Des Plaines River through Thatcher Woods, or through the sunlit savannas of Thomas Jefferson Woods (between Lake Street and Washington Boulevard) and G.A.R. Woods (south of Washington Boulevard).

## 🍃🍃🍃 Sand Ridge Nature Center (1 to 3 hours)

15890 Paxton Avenue
South Holland, IL 60473
(708) 868-0606

Getting there: Located in South Holland, 21 miles south of Chicago. Take I-94 (the Dan Ryan Expressway) south to the 159th Street exit. Go east on 159th Street to Paxton Avenue and turn north to the entrance.

Hours: March to October: weekdays, 8 A.M.–5 P.M.; weekends, 8 A.M.–5:30 P.M. Winter: closes ½ hour earlier. Exhibit building opens at 9 A.M. and closes ½ hour earlier than the grounds; closed Fridays. Everything closed Thanksgiving, Christmas Day, and New Year's Day.

Stand on a six-thousand-year-old sand ridge left behind when Lake Chicago began to shrink. See pioneer demonstrations in historic log cabins. Or search for Franklin's ground squirrel and other endangered species on 235 acres of prairie, wetlands, and woodlands. Celebrate Earth Day in April with nature hikes, a walk-a-thon, and booths set up by conservation organizations. On Archeology Awareness Day in September, take a taste of Native American foods and history. On Settler's Day in November, see a Revolutionary War encampment set up by the Northwest Territorial Alliance, and watch people in costumes of the early 1800s demonstrate pioneer living.

In December, come to Christmas Past in the log cabins on the premises, where there are strings of cranberries and popcorn, and where chestnuts roast on an open fire.

If you want to know trees, learn how to use keys, examine tree rings, and go on field trips in a program called Totally Trees. Come for the demonstrations on natural dyes, candle making, basket weaving, and bread baking. Bring the children to Nature Tales programs, with walks and crafts such as making a dreamcatcher, a tree stump garden, or an owl hand puppet. Children may also attend Eye-Opener programs in which they examine environmental issues such as recycling and preservation of natural areas, go into the field, and make animal track T-shirts or other crafts.

The nature center has a map that reveals bird migration routes and some of Chicago's environmental connections to the rest of the world.

Log cabins at Sand Ridge Nature Center.

The Bullsnake Buffet, Life of Nishnabek, and other displays provide a bit of Chicago history and introduce you to some of its native animals.

Behind the building, walk through a butterfly garden with plants that caterpillars eat. (The monarch butterfly relishes milkweed, but the frittelaria prefers snapdragons.) Continue down the path to log cabins where pioneer demonstrations are often held.

Amble along lovely trails and ponder the mysteries of forest, sand ridge, and wetland ecosystems. The Redwing Trail (half an hour) takes you to oak forest and Redwing Pond. You will also visit dry upland forest with white oaks (the Illinois state tree). The Lost Beach Trail (an hour and a half) goes through forests on an ancient beach ridge and sand dune. Dogwood Trail (about forty minutes) offers several kinds of forests and wetlands with waterfowl. Keep your feet dry on the boardwalk as you trek through the marsh. See blue flag iris bloom in spring;

rose mallow and cardinal flower in late summer. Pines Trail (ten minutes) winds through the pine plantation, oak forest, and a restored prairie with many wildflowers.

To locate other woodland sites, contact:

The Forest Preserve District of Cook County
536 N. Harlem Avenue
River Forest, IL 60305
(312) 261-8400
(708) 366-9420
(800) 870-3666
(708) 771-1190 TDD

The Forest Preserve District of DuPage County
P.O. Box 2339
Glen Ellyn, IL 60138
(630) 790-4900

Lake County Forest Preserves
2000 N. Milwaukee Avenue
Libertyville, IL 60048
(847) 367-6640
(847) 367-3675 TTY/TDD

Forest Preserve District of Will County
(815) 727-8700

# 8

# *Wonderful Wetlands*

"The marsh . . . holds, beside mosquitoes and stagnation, melody, the mystery
of unknown waters, and the sweetness of Nature undisturbed by man."
—Charles William Beebe (1877–1962), naturalist

## Out of the Swamp

Wetlands—the meeting places of land and water—contain an amazing array of fascinating plants and animals. Nevertheless, movies and books often portray them as sinister places where strange beasts lurk and criminals hide. In the past, wetlands were viewed as wastelands. That is why marshes and swamps were drained to make way for farms, asphalt roads, and urban development in the Chicago area.

At the beginning of the nineteenth century, low, wet grassland surrounded Fort Dearborn, which stood on the north bank of the Chicago River overlooking Lake Michigan. Soldiers and civilians who lived nearby preferred to travel by canoe. But even when Chicago became a town, citizens avoided the marsh, where horses and carriages got stuck in the mud and people were bitten by swarms of mosquitoes. In the 1840s, they tried to improve transportation by constructing wooden plank roads across the swampy land. The toll was twenty-five cents to ride on the Southwestern Plank Road that bridged the "nine-mile swamp" between Riverside and Chicago. The Lake Shore Road was five miles long and ran from what is now North Avenue and Clark Street to Green Bay Road.

Another plank road extended north from Blue Island along Western Avenue to the southwest corner of Chicago, and then followed Blue Island Avenue thirteen miles into the heart of the city. But the plank roads failed because the prairie flooded and the roads could not be securely anchored in the muddy soil of the marshland.

In the 1850s, the citizens of Chicago lifted the city from the mud. They used earth fill to raise the grade of the land about fifteen feet above normal lake level to stop flooding and improve the city's streets. The problem was not solved, however, because taller and heavier structures were continually designed and built after the Chicago Fire. New federal and county buildings and City Hall sank up to eighteen inches in the mud and had to be torn down. Engineers and architects struggled to find new ways to support the skyscrapers, bridges, and tunnels you now see throughout Chicago.

## Wetlands at Your Service

Today, the urban environment is much drier than it used to be, but wetland plants still live in some city parks and on riverbanks. Marshes, swamps, bogs, and fens exist in the surrounding countryside. These wetlands are also havens of biodiversity, with many valuable, rare, and endangered plants and animals.

Native Americans and early settlers used wetland plants such as cattails for weaving baskets, chicory roots for a coffee substitute, and rosehips to supply vitamin C. They made elderberry tea to reduce fever; wintergreen tea to relieve rheumatism; and crushed boneset leaves to relieve bee stings, poison ivy rashes, and the pain of broken bones.

Wet, grassy ecosystems filter pollution from water and produce more plant material per acre than farmland. They provide abundant food and cover, so they serve as mating places and nurseries for fish and other aquatic animals and are favored resting and nesting spots for migrating birds. In addition, wetlands shield inland areas from the force of storms on Lake Michigan. They absorb the energy of violent winds and waves and store rain that would otherwise flood the city. No wonder, then, that wetland protection and restoration has become a priority, not only in the Chicago area, but throughout the entire nation.

# Marsh Matters

Marshes are the domain of water-loving plants such as grasses, cattails, bulrushes, reeds (with round stems), and sedges (with triangular stems), that grow on the edges of ponds, lakes, and rivers. Some marsh plants float. Others are submerged or rooted on the bottom with their leaves above the surface. Disturbed marshes are usually dominated by cattails and have little plant diversity, whereas undisturbed marshes contain a variety of grasslike perennials, some of which are quite tall, and attractive wildflowers including spotted Joe-Pye-weed, tufted loosestrife, swamp milkweed, and blue flag iris.

Because food is plentiful in these grassy wetlands, green frogs hunt insects each night. Herons spear fish and muskrats build their houses of cattails in the water. Even in winter, the snowy owl, weasel, and mink drink and hunt in the marshes around Chicago.

Swamps differ from marshes in that swamps have scattered trees. Red maple, yellow birch, pin oak, bur oak, and white swamp oak can be seen in swampy areas near Chicago. Swamps are the habitat of beavers, the engineers of the wetland world. They eat twigs and leaves and gnaw at trunks and branches. When they cut down trees and dam the waterways with their lodges, beavers change the course of streams and rivers.

##  Cowles Wetland (½ hour)

Ridge Park
9625 S. Longwood Drive
Chicago, IL 60643
(312) 747-6639

Take pleasure in a wetland at a city park. On a ridge where groundwater seeps to the surface, you will find a wet woods. Stand in the shade of swamp white oak and look for colorful bluejays and butterflies. Perhaps a raccoon will cross your path.

Cowles Wetland was saved from the fate of becoming a parking lot when local residents fought for its preservation. The were helped by the Chicago Park District, who sent the "Tree Gang," a group of foresters, who hacked their way into the woodland. When the foresters cleared the grapevines, they planted seedlings of white oak—the Illinois state tree. Today, white oak and swamp white oak spread their branches and stand tall in this restored urban wetland.

# Lagoons

Bring your pole and bait for fishing and your binoculars for bird watching at the lagoons in Chicago's parks. These tree-, grass-, and stone-edged waterways can be found in Columbus, Douglas, Hurley, Ridge, Riis, Sherman, Garfield, Auburn, Marquette, and many other parks. Waterfowl flock near the lagoons because the Illinois Department of Conservation stocks them with fish. The Washington Park lagoon has been adopted by a community group that will beautify the park by restoring it to the natural wetland it was in the past.

##  Skokie Lagoons (1 to 3 hours)

Between Tower Road and Dundee Road east of I-94 (Edens Expressway)
Winnetka and Glencoe, IL
Contact:
Forest Preserve District of Cook County
(708) 771-1330

Getting there: Located in Winnetka and Glencoe, about 20 miles north of Chicago. Take Edens Expressway (Route 41)—the signs say "west" but the highway heads north. Exit Edens Expressway at Tower Road. Go east on Tower to Forestway Drive. Turn north (left) on Forestway Drive to the lagoons.

Seven ponds adorn this six-hundred-acre flood-control area and wildlife refuge. The waterways, surrounded by lovely woods, invite canoeing, walking, bird watching, fishing, and picnics. White settlers tried repeatedly and unsuccessfully to drain this area because they wanted to farm its fertile soils. In the 1930s it was finally made into a recreational area. After World War II, suburban development damaged the Skokie Lagoons by sending eroded soil and partly treated sewage into the water. Aquatic plants died off and carp and bullhead took over from native fish such as bluegill.

In the 1980s, amid controversy, restoration began. A ditch was dug to stop pollution by taking waste water directly from Clavey Road to the Chicago River. Ponds were dredged to remove bottom sediment. In 1992, a fish stun and eradication campaign began. After native fish were stunned with electrical shocks and removed to a nearby lake, poison was added to the water to kill rough (nonnative) fish. When the water was safe again, the lagoons were restocked with native bass, bluegill, and catfish.

The renovation increased water visibility from one-half foot to seven feet, and aquatic plants, reptiles, amphibians, insects, and shorebirds now abound in this wetland habitat. Improvement continues with plantings of native prairie grasses and with the removal of buckthorn to give oak seedlings room.

## Bogs

A bog is a wetland that trembles and quakes because its vegetation floats in mats on the water's surface. The water is so acidic that the bog contains specially adapted plants, including moss and trees that float and plants that eat insects.

Soft sphagnum moss looks like solid ground, but it floats on the surface of a pond. Thus, if you dare to step onto the bog, it bends and trembles beneath your feet and you may sink into deep water. The name "bog" comes from a Celtic word that means "something soft that bends or sinks." A bog is sometimes called a quaking bog or trembling wetland. Perhaps you heard about the bogey-man as a child. Bogey-man stories originated in Europe, where criminals hid in bogs because most people avoided that quaking, dangerous ground.

A bog develops where a pond lacks drainage. Decaying plant material acidifies the trapped water until it holds little oxygen and few bacteria of decay. As a result, dead plants decay increasingly slowly and plant debris accumulates as peat. Sphagnum moss, also known as peat moss, thrives in the acidic water and spreads across the surface. The moss forms floating mats where tamarack (larch) trees take root. Over time, shrubs and other vegetation become part of the bog ecosystem.

Sphagnum moss is a fascinating plant. It is green, leafy, and stemless, and it absorbs eighteen times its weight in water. No wonder sphagnum moss was used by Native Americans as diapers for their babies. Because it is acidic, the moss was used as an antiseptic in World War I. Also known as peat or peat moss, it can be burned as a fuel or mixed with soil to encourage the growth of potted plants and garden flowers.

The bog's water comes from rainfall and surface runoff, so it is poor in nitrogen, potassium, calcium, and other minerals. Plants have difficulty absorbing nitrogen from the acidic water. Carnivorous plants solve this problem by obtaining nitrogen from animal protein. The pitcher plant lures insects with its red color, traps them in the smooth tunnel of its flower, and digests them. The sundew holds ants on its rosette of sticky leaves and digests them within fifteen minutes.

This is also the habitat of poison sumac (a plant that causes a rash), cranberry and blueberry bushes, ferns, and wild orchids. Because vegetation is abundant in a bog, mosquitoes and other insects abound. Deer, muskrats, weasels, raccoons, red foxes, and other small animals find food and shelter. Waterfowl and wading birds stop by as they migrate north to their summer nesting areas. Crossbills crack tamarack cones with their teeth and songbirds sing to keep other birds out of their territory. When night falls, frogs croak at their mates and bats fly silently through the air, stalking insects. A visit to a bog brings the pleasures of unusual plants, native wildlife, and picturesque scenery.

##  Volo Bog State Natural Area (2 to 4 hours)

28478 W. Brandenburg Road
Ingleside, IL 60041
(815) 344-1294

Getting there: Located in Volo, 46 miles northwest of Chicago. Take I-94 north to Route 60. Follow Route 60 west to Highway 12 (Route 59). Take Highway 12 north 2 miles to Brandenburg Road. Go west on Brandenburg Road about 1 mile to Volo Bog State Natural Area.
Hours: September to May, 8 A.M.–4 P.M.; June to August, 8 A.M.–8 P.M. Visitor's Center open Thursday to Sunday, 9 A.M.–3 P.M.
Facilities: Interpretive Center. Library.
Tours: Saturday and Sunday, 11 A.M. and 1 P.M. Group tours by reservation. Half-mile and 2.75-mile trail with boardwalks in wet areas.

Visit the only quaking bog in Illinois, where you can keep your feet dry on a boardwalk and view all stages of bog succession. Look closely and you will find unusual plants such as insect-eating pitcher plants and state-endangered orchids called rose pogonias. Since the bog is part of a 160-acre nature preserve, you can also walk trails through marsh, sedge meadow, forest, and savanna. Any time of year, the scenery is lovely and the birds and wildlife are plentiful.

Come for adult programs that include wetland ecology, bird walks, animal tracking, and bats. Arrange a group tour. Or volunteer for habitat restoration and other special projects. Children are invited for bog discovery, animal tracking, bird watching, and insect safaris. Families

Volo Bog.

enjoy the Winterfest, with snow sculpting and cross-country skiing; and the April Eco-fest, when environmental groups set up booths and bird walks and tours are given.

In order to see the bog, obtain a trail map from the visitor's center. A half-mile loop takes you through each stage of bog succession (hikers only). A nearly three-mile trail goes through woods, wetlands, field, and prairie.

Warning: You will encounter hazardous terrain and poisonous shrubs along the way. The plants you see are on a floating mat of roots and moss only a few inches thick. Beneath that mat is water and muck. Remain on the boardwalk.

Volo Bog is a ten-foot-deep lake that covers half an acre with acidic water. Forty feet of muck and decaying vegetation lie beneath the "eye," or center, and sphagnum moss and duckweed float on the open water. In concentric rings around the eye you will find later stages in bog succession. There is graminoid bog, with marsh shieldfern, bottlebrush sedge, and sensitive fern; and low shrub bog, with willow, alder, poison sumac, and leatherleaf. Forested bog has tamarack trees. The roots of tamaracks intertwine with sphagnum moss to form hummocks, small mounds that provide support for marsh marigolds, highbush blueberry, and other plants that grow above the waterline. Next in succession is the tall shrub bog, with winterberry holly, poison sumac, and red osier dogwood.

As you stroll through the bog, listen for red-winged blackbirds and watch the green-backed heron searching for frogs and fish. You may also spot weasels, red foxes, or white-tailed deer. A felled tree trunk may be the work of a beaver. Before you slap a mosquito, think about the fact that the females bite to get blood before they lay their eggs in the water. About seventeen hundred little brown bats live here and each one can eat three thousand mosquitoes and other insects each night.

A marsh surrounds the bog. It has blue flag iris and ferns among the reeds, sedges, and cattails. The adjacent sedge meadow has stinging nettle, a plant with small hairs that release irritating formic acid when touched. Jewelweed, which also grows here, was used by pioneers to releave the sting. In the upland forest you will see bur oak, shagbark hickory, white oak, and red oak. Look for white lichens, green moss, and liverworts growing on tree bark. Watch for the white stems of Indian Pipe, which obtains nourishment from a fungus growing around its roots.

## Fine Fens

A fen occurs where alkaline groundwater (water containing dissolved calcium carbonate) continually seeps up through the soil, and peat accumulates due to slow decay of plant materials. Panic grass, Ohio goldenrod, swamp thistle, and fringed gentian are restricted to fens, but you will also come upon prairie grass, sedges, prairie dock, shrubby cinquefoil, and orchids in this alkaline wetland.

# Seeps and Springs

A seep saturates the soil around it with its usually alkaline groundwater, which spreads over the soil surface or runs in small streams through it. A marl flat is a highly alkaline seep with tufa (a light crumbly rock) and few plants except beaked spike rush, skunk cabbage, and sedges. A spring is also continuously fed by groundwater, but it exits the soil with more force.

Sedge meadows are found where the water is rich in calcium and stays below the surface most of the year. In this wetland, tussock sedge mingles with marsh fern, and small brown and orange butterflies, called skippers, come to feed.

## 🍃🍃 Bluff Springs Fen Nature Preserve

This preserve has unusual landforms as well as fen habitat. (See Chapter 3.)

## 🍃🍃 Des Plaines River Wetland Demonstration Project
Wadsworth, IL 60083
(312) 922-0777

Getting there: Located in Wadsworth, 44 miles north of Chicago and 4 miles south of the Wisconsin border. Follow the Edens Expressway (Route 41) north and exit east on Wadsworth Road to the wetland.

Hike or bike through restored marshes that are rich in aquatic animals and endangered birds, where scientists do research. Or meander through lovely tallgrass prairie, sedge meadows, and oak groves. Not long ago, this place was an ecological mess. It had been drained for farming and grazing, then mined for sand and gravel and poisoned by a polluted river. Most native plants and wildlife died off as a result.

In 1983, the situation changed when the Lake County Forest Preserves and Open Lands Project established Wetlands Research, Inc. Its mission was to learn how to restore the nation's rivers with the use of wetlands, and it began by dividing the area into two sections. One section was for restoration and the other (with water diverted from the Des Plaines River) was for active experiments. In this living laboratory, researchers now investigate how wetlands can improve water quality, reduce flooding, and provide habitat for wildlife.

## 🍃 William W. Powers Conservation Area (½ to 3 hours)

12949 S. Avenue O
Chicago, IL 60633
(312) 646-3270

Getting there: Located at Wolf Lake, in the southeastern part of Chicago, along the Indiana border. Take I-94 south. Exit at 130th Street and go east to Brainard Avenue. Drive south on Brainard to 134th Street. Then turn east to Avenue O. Take Avenue O north to 129th Street. The entrance is on the east side.

Tucked away in the midst of an industrial region, this wetland area is divided by dikes and has six miles of shoreline for birding and bank fishing.

## 🍃 Cranberry Slough Nature Preserve (½ to 2 hours)

Southwest corner of 95th Street at La Grange Road
Palos Hills, IL 60465
Contact:
Forest Preserve District of Cook County
(708) 771-1330

Getting there: Located in Palos Hills, 19 miles southwest of Chicago. Take I-55 south and exit at I-45. Go south on I-45 to the southwest corner of 95th Street (Highway 12/20). The slough is ½ mile south of 95th and ¼ mile west of La Grange Road (U.S. 95). It is accessible only by foot.

Enjoy birding and hiking on 372 acres of flat land and rolling hills that were once part of Mount Forest Island. This area may have been one of the first dry spots that plants colonized when Lake Chicago's water level fell and wetlands appeared on the newly exposed land. Bring your binoculars to Cranberry Slough, a refuge for egrets, herons, ducks, swallows, and gulls, where blue jointgrass and sedges grow. See vernal ponds—wet and full of life in spring—and sedge meadow and marshes where you may spot beaver and other wildlife. Then hike through prairie, savanna, and oak-hickory woodlands on higher, drier ground.

A wetland in the heart of an industrial area.

## 🍃 Spring Lake Nature Preserve
## (½ to 2 hours; by appointment only)

Barrington, IL 60010
Contact:
Forest Preserve District of Cook County
(708) 771-1330

Getting there: Located in Barrington, 36 miles northwest of Chicago. Take I-90 west to Route 53 north. Go north on Route 53 (which is also Route 12) to County Line Road (Lake/Cook Road). Turn west on County Line Road 3.4 miles to the entrance, on the south side of the road.

On 560 acres, you will find woodlands, prairie, marsh, fen, sedge meadow, and two glacial lakes.

## 🍃 Thornton-Lansing Road Nature Preserve (½ to 2 hours)
Cottage Grove Avenue and 183rd Street
Glenwood, IL 60425
Contact:
Forest Preserve District of Cook County
(708) 771-1330

Getting there: Located in Glenwood, 24 miles south of Chicago. Take I-94 south and exit west on Glenwood-Lansing Road. Turn west on Glenwood-Lansing Road to Cottage Grove Avenue. Turn north on Cottage Grove Avenue and go one mile to 183rd Street.

These 440 acres contain samples of vegetation that covered the southern section of the Chicago Lake plain. Unique marsh and bog plants grow in sandy low spots while pin oaks inhabit higher ground.

Note: Other wetlands can be found near Lake Michigan (Chapter 2), in prairies (Chapter 5), and in forests (Chapter 7). To find more swamps, marshes, bogs, and fens near you, contact forest preserve districts in Cook, Lake, DuPage, and other counties; and park districts in Chicago and suburbs.

# 9

## River Runs

"I've known rivers.
I've known rivers ancient as the world and older than
the flow of human blood in human veins.
My soul has grown deep like the rivers."
—Langston Hughes (1902–1967)

## Urban Streams

Three rivers flow through Chicago: the Calumet in the south; the Des Plaines in the west; and the Chicago River in the central and downtown area. The Des Plaines runs through many forest preserves where Native American villages once existed. A favorite of canoeists, it is a green oasis in the urban environment. The Chicago River flows past developed neighborhoods with homes, parks, and factories along the North and South branches, factories near Wolf Point, and high-rise offices and apartment buildings in the downtown area. Travelled by tourists and other boaters, it offers intimate views of the city's world-famous architecture. The Calumet moves through port areas with heavy industry. Carrying barges loaded with cargo, it serves Great Lakes freighters and mineral processing and manufacturing facilities. All three rivers are muddy and polluted, with too few fish and too many algae, but efforts are being made to clean their water and replant their banks. Then lovers of nature as well as real estate developers and heavy industry can use and enjoy these cleaner, more scenic urban streams.

## River History

All of Chicago's rivers were born ten thousand years ago, as streams flowing out of melting glaciers and meandering through grasslands.

More than one thousand years ago, Native Americans swam and fished in these prairie streams. Muskrats built homes of cattails that grew in marshes on their edges. Beavers constructed homes of twigs and branches from the woodlands, often changing the rivers' flow with their dams. When the fur trappers arrived in this area, about 320 years ago, they hunted beaver for their "soft brown gold" so extensively that even today few of these furry animals are seen on Chicago's rivers.

When the prairie flooded, Native Americans paddled canoes through the low spot that later became known as the Chicago Portage into the Chicago River and Lake Michigan. In drier seasons, they lifted their canoes out of the Des Plaines River and walked knee-deep in mud as they portaged their canoes eight miles to the Chicago River. Then they paddled down the river to villages and trading centers on the southern shore of Lake Michigan.

In 1673, Native Americans guided Louis Joliet, a French-Canadian fur trader, and Father Jacques Marquette, a Jesuit priest, through the Chicago Portage. The French explorers had started their journey in New France (now Canada), crossed the Great Lakes, and sailed down the Mississippi to the mouth of the Arkansas River when they decided to turn back. By that time, however, they were convinced that the Mississippi emptied into the Gulf of Mexico. They had sailed north to the mouth of the Illinois River when their guides took them through the shortcut to Lake Michigan.

After paddling up the Des Plaines, they carried their canoes across the Chicago Portage to the Chicago River and continued on to Lake Michigan. Joliet and Marquette immediately realized that this portage made it possible to travel from Montreal to New Orleans by water, via the Great Lakes and the Mississippi River. They had discovered the key to French control of North America.

The historic trip of Marquette and Joliet also led to the first white settlement in the marshland at the mouth of the Chicago River—the place Native Americans called "Chicagou."

## 🍂🍂🍂 The Chicago Portage (½ to 1 hour)

Harlem Avenue (7200 W.), south of 47th Street
Chicago, IL 60638

Chicago's history began here, at this low spot in the prairie that is now a National Heritage site.

Rebechini's *Chicago Portage: The Waterway West.*

A sculpture called *Chicago Portage: The Waterway West,* by Rebechini (1989), commemorates the first time the portage was traversed by French explorers. The monument stands in a large grassy plaza with three larger-than-life figures: a Native American guide, Louis Joliet, and Father Jacques Marquette, who look northward toward Chicago. The wavelike base of the sculpture symbolizes the importance of this place in the transcontinental waterway.

Be sure to stroll down the broad grassy path to the left of the monument until you reach the water's edge. This is the low spot that transformed the Illinois prairie, and it is all that is left of the Chicago Portage.

Continue your visit at Ottawa Trail Woods, where you will find the Laughton Brothers fur trading post and a ford used by Native Americans. Stay on the west side of Harlem Avenue and go north of 47th Street. (See Chapter 6.) To travel where Marquette and Joliet did, along the Des Plaines River, follow the Chicago Portage Canoe Trail. (See Chapter 13.)

## The Great Divide

A drainage divide on Chicago's West Side separates the waters that flow eastward into Lake Michigan from those that flow westward to the Mississippi. Water west of it runs into the Des Plaines River and down to the Illinois and Mississippi rivers to the Gulf of Mexico. Water east of it flows into the Chicago River, through Lake Michigan, the Great Lakes, and the St. Lawrence River to the Atlantic Ocean. Marquette and Joliet crossed this drainage divide as they made their way through the Chicago Portage.

## Control of the Midwest and the Mississippi

Not long after the Chicago Portage was discovered, René-Robert Cavelier, Sieur de La Salle (whose name graces the main street of Chicago's financial center) used this waterway to spread French influence through the Mississippi Valley. However, by the late 1700s, the French had retreated and thirteen British colonies had become the United States of America. River travel was unsafe for white men because Native Americans were fighting to retain their ancestral lands.

Defeat at the 1794 battle at Fallen Timbers, near Toledo, Ohio forced Native Americans to cede the mouth of the Chicago River to the U.S. government. From then on, white settlers no longer lived in fear of Indian raids on Illinois rivers.

Chicago's river connections took on added importance when Thomas Jefferson made the Louisiana Purchase in 1803. To defend the Chicago Portage and the western frontier, Fort Dearborn was constructed on the south bank of the Chicago River at Michigan Avenue (which was then the shoreline of Lake Michigan).

## Chicago, Wisconsin? Or Chicago, Illinois?

Chicago is in Illinois (rather than Wisconsin) because the U.S. Congress decided that the canal to be built across the Chicago Portage should be administered by only one state. Plans for the Illinois and Michigan Canal were developed in the early 1800s, when Illinois Territory was applying for statehood. The original boundaries of what would become the twenty-first state were quite different from ours today. Eight hundred square miles of what is now northern Illinois—including Chicago and most of Cook County—were designated to be in Wisconsin. That meant Illinois would have only four miles of Lake Michigan shoreline.

The map changed, probably because Nathaniel Pope, Illinois's territorial delegate in Washington, lobbied to have what would become the Port of Chicago included in the new state's boundaries. Thus, in 1818, the border was moved north and Chicago, with its long and lovely Lake Michigan shoreline, landed in the state of Illinois.

## River Trade

In 1833, the U.S. Army cut a channel through a sandbar that blocked the Chicago River's mouth. This opened the natural harbor on Lake Michigan, making Chicago a Great Lakes port and the Chicago River a major route to the western frontier. In 1848, when the Illinois and Michigan Canal was completed, the canal and the Chicago River were the prime waterway for bulk cargo. Grain, lumber, and iron ore were loaded onto Great Lakes freighters heading east, and manufactured goods and farm implements were loaded onto canal barges heading west. The Port of Chicago soon handled more cargo than London, New York, San Francisco, and New Orleans put together.

River trade diminished in the 1850s as Chicago developed into the rail center of the United States. Railroads carried meat from Chicago stockyards and grain from Illinois farmland to buyers in New York and other cities on the east coast. This profitable trade with the East caused Illinois to turn away from Mississippi River commerce and markets in the South.

Did the switch from river to rail cause Illinois to turn away from the South in the Civil War? Some historians claim that, if the Mississippi River had been the only path to a coast, the economic welfare and the political decisions of Illinois would have been bound to the southern coast and the slave states. Railroads tied the prosperity of Illinois with the east coast, and that may have been one reason why Illinois soldiers fought for the Union from 1861 to 1865.

## River in the City

Before fur traders and white settlers built log cabins and a fort in the area, the Chicago River was a slow-moving stream that constantly changed its path as it flowed through the prairie. Now the river is tamed and confined to narrow channels that are bordered by urban roads, buildings, parks, and gardens.

The North Branch originates in Park City, near Waukegan, and has two major tributaries, the West Fork and the Skokie River. The source of the South Branch was near Kedzie and 31$^{st}$ Street. The Main Branch begins where the North Branch and South Branch meet at Wolf Point and originally flowed east about a mile, emptying into Lake Michigan.

## 🍂🍂 Main Branch Walk (2 to 3 hours)

Along the Chicago River in downtown Chicago, from the Michigan Avenue Bridge east to the Lake Michigan shoreline and west to Wolf Point.

See the birthplace of Chicago—the site of Fort Dearborn and the log cabins of the early settlers. View some of the the city's world-famous architecture on the one-mile-long Main Branch of the Chicago River.

The Michigan Avenue Bridge was built in 1920 to provide a beautiful gateway to the recently widened North Michigan Avenue. When the bridge opened, so much business was taken from the bustling Rush Street Bridge and dock area (farther west on the river) that it was no longer profitable and faded away. Be sure to look at the sculptures by James Earle Fraser and Henry Hering (1928) on the bridge supports. They are entitled Defense, Regeneration, The Pioneers, and The Discoverers, commemorating important events in Chicago's history.

This junction between the Chicago River and what used to be the Lake Michigan shoreline is where Chicago originated as a trading post in the wilderness. In 1772, Jean Baptist Point DuSable, a fur trapper, set up business and became Chicago's first permanent resident. Look for the brass plaque that pays a tribute to this Afro-French-Canadian settler. It can be found on the plaza of the Equitable Building, 401 N. Michigan Avenue, overlooking the Chicago River.

In 1803, the year that President Thomas Jefferson negotiated the Louisiana Purchase, Fort Dearborn was constructed to protect the Chicago Portage and the strategic water route to the western frontier. Look for a plaque at the south end of the Michigan Avenue bridge. Signs in the sidewalk on the corners of Michigan Avenue and Wacker Drive outline the perimeter of Fort Dearborn, which had a fence surrounding two barracks and two blockhouses.

The Kinzie mansion stood on the north bank of the river and faced the fort. It was owned by the family of John Kinzie, an early Chicago trader. As you view the modern buildings and traffic-clogged roads, visualize the large house, dairy, bakehouse, and stables owned by the Kinzies. Picture the garden, Lombardy poplars, and two immense cottonwood trees on their property, and the stunted pines and dwarf willow trees that grew on the sand dunes east of the mansion.

In the early 1800s, if you walked west, you would not find any houses on the south riverbank between Fort Dearborn and "the point"—the junction of the North, South, and Main forks of the Chicago River. The south side of the point had a tavern known as Old Geese plus the log cabins of Alexander Robinson, chief of the the Potawatomis, and Billy Caldwell, another Native American. In the late 1820s, the point became known as Wolf Point. The story goes that Elijah Wentworth, who also operated a tavern here, killed a wolf in his meat house and that is how the tavern and the promontory of land got their names. At that time, Wolf Point was a frontier town where Native Americans, British, and French caroused. After Chicago officially became a city, life at Wolf Point calmed down and shipping docks, rail lines, and warehouses moved into this area. Today, the North Branch is a working river bordered by factories, warehouses, and storage yards.

In the first decades of the nineteenth century, anyone who traveled on horseback between Wolf Point and Fort Dearborn was likely to be up to his stirrups in water. All the roads were so bad that most people traveled by canoe. At that time, the Chicago River did not flow directly east to Lake Michigan because it was blocked by a sandbar. It made a sharp turn to the south at this junction of Michigan Avenue and Wacker Drive and emptied into the lake through a narrow channel between Lake Street and Madison.

East of the Michigan Avenue Bridge, you will pass cafes and shops and a stream of water that shoots across the river once an hour in the late morning and early afternoon. Beyond this point, the river empties into Lake Michigan. In 1833, this area became the main harbor when the U.S. Army cut a channel through the sandbar that blocked the river's mouth. The Chicago River Lock, near this point (but hard to see) was completed in 1938. It is six hundred feet long, eighty feet wide, and twenty-three feet deep, with gates at each end. When the river rises or the lake level drops, these locks prevent river water from accidentally polluting Lake Michigan—the source of the city's drinking water. The lock system also assists boats in navigating through the channel from Lake Michigan, which is two feet higher than the river. The locks remain closed except to allow boats through or, in extreme circumstances, to pour sewage overflow into Lake Michigan. Most of the time, this water is not polluted, so you may see people fishing for bass.

Reverse direction and walk west on the south bank to see some of Chicago's famous buildings, built with fortunes made from natural resources. The Wrigley Building on the northeast corner of Michigan Avenue (a white "wedding cake" lit up at night) is named after a man who made his fortune on gum from a rainforest plant. The nearby Sun-Times Building prints one of Chicago's major newspapers on mashed tree trunks. Pause at the Dearborn Street Bridge, where Chicago's first movable bridge was built. Today, you may see jetskiers or a boat carrying commuters from the Northwestern train station to Michigan Avenue. There are many drawbridges along the Main Branch of the Chicago River. When they rise to allow boats to pass, street traffic stops.

Around the 1870s, three tunnels were dug to relieve street traffic by allowing pedestrians and horse-driven carriages to cross below the river. The tunnels were located under LaSalle Street on the Main Branch and under Washington and Van Buren streets on the South Branch. In 1871, when the Chicago Fire destroyed the city, thousands of Chicagoans fled through the tunnels. By 1884, however, few people used them. Traffic beneath the river increased after 1885, when electric lights and an underground cable car system were installed. The LaSalle Street tunnel was closed in 1939 to make way for the proposed Lake Street subway, but cable cars ran until the last tunnel closed in 1953. All the tunnels still exist beneath the Chicago River.

Notice some of Chicago's fine architecture as you head toward Wolf Point, near the the Merchandise Mart and slightly west of the Apparel Center at 350 N. Orleans Street. The Apparel Center has a landscaped walkway along its historic riverbank that provides lovely vistas of the city. In 1992, two beavers settled here and caused havoc when they toppled more than twenty trees in order to build their homes. The beavers were relocated. However, you can still enjoy the wildfowl and the fish that occasionally jump out of the water.

The area north of the Chicago River was settled by Irish laborers in the 1840s. After the 1871 fire, red brick factories and large homes were built and, years later, warehouses. Between World War I and World War II, homes became rooming houses. Through the 1970s, abandoned lofts became artists' studios, galleries, and restaurants—a rejuvenated area known as River North.

The river forks into a branch that flows around Goose Island—the only island within city limits. The island received its name because Irish and German immigrants who lived here raised geese in their yards.

From Madison Street to Jackson Boulevard the riverbanks are lined with tall buildings. In the 1830s, the area was woodland. Now it is a financial center and transportation hub.

## River Reversal

In the late 1830s, when Chicago was a very new town, its riverbanks were lined with cattails and marsh birds fished in the downtown area. The 450 citizens that lived here crossed the Chicago River by ferry because streets were so wet and muddy. As the town grew, log cabins and Fort Dearborn were joined by frame houses and factories along the main branch of the Chicago River. Unfortunately, river pollution accompanied the city's population explosion. The prairie stream became a sewer as people and factories polluted the water with their wastes. Because Lake Michigan supplied the city's drinking water, the contamination caused outbreaks of typhoid and cholera.

There were many unsuccessful attempts to keep industrial waste and sewage out of Lake Michigan before city leaders came upon a unique solution. They decided to stop the epidemics by reversing the flow of the polluted Chicago River. If the Main Branch of the Chicago River flowed backward, it would carry its pollution downstream to the Illinois River, which emptied into the Mississippi. Then Lake Michigan drinking water would remain pure.

In order to accomplish the engineering feat of reversing the flow of the Chicago River, the river bottom was lowered and the Illinois and Michigan Canal was deepened so it cut through the watershed at the present town of Summit. The canal's locks were removed and, on July 15, 1871, the Main and South branches of the Chicago River ran backward. Pollution flowed down the Illinois River, and Lake Michigan water remained clean—until a rainstorm in 1885 dropped more than five inches of rain and the Chicago River overflowed, pouring sewage into the lake. The contamination of the city's water supply again caused many Chicagoans to die of cholera and typhoid.

## The Sanitary and Ship Canal

Because the Illinois and Michigan Canal had not handled this flooding, engineers immediately went to their drawing boards and designed the much larger Sanitary and Ship Canal, with banks 201 feet apart and running parallel to the I & M, twenty-eight miles from Damen Avenue in Chicago to Lockport. Considered an engineering marvel, it became a model for the Panama Canal.

The Sanitary and Ship Canal was designed to send Chicago's sewage down the Mississippi River. That is why the city of St. Louis—which was downstream and would receive Chicago's pollution—announced it would petition the U.S. Supreme Court to prevent the canal from opening. On January 2, 1900, canal trustees circumvented the objections of St. Louis. They simply opened the canal and let the sewage flow downstream.

Today the Clean Water Act is aimed at preventing farms, industries, and cities from dumping wastes into lakes and rivers. That is why Chicago has waste and sewage treatment plants, and landfills lined with clay or plastic barriers that stop pollutants from leaching into underground water and surface streams and rivers. City workers and citizens work on many pollution prevention projects. They prevent soil erosion with plantings on riverbanks, and they preserve wetlands that clean urban streams. Nevertheless, during severe rains, floodgates still have to be opened and raw sewage still pours into Chicago's rivers and Lake Michigan.

The Tarp and Reservoir Project, or Deep Tunnel, is designed to store floodwaters in a series of large underground tunnels, in yet another attempt to control flooding in Chicago. When it is completed at the beginning of the twenty-first century, it will reduce urban flooding and perhaps end the pollution of Chicago's rivers and Lake Michigan during heavy rainstorms. Maybe the Deep Tunnel will make all of Chicago's waterways into great places for swimming and fishing.

## The Des Plaines River

Originating as a Wisconsin farm stream, the Des Plaines River flows south through northern Illlinois fields and prairies. It passes scenic Lake County Forest Preserve and the Des Plaines River Wetland Demonstration Project in Wadsworth (see Chapter 8) before it travels along the western edge of Chicago and the eastern edge of O'Hare Airport. Despite this urban route, a surprising number of birds, deer, and other wildlife make the river their home as it passes through Cook County forest preserves.

In Riverside, the Des Plaines is joined by Salt Creek. At Harlem Avenue and 47th Street south, it is part of the Chicago Portage National Heritage site, near the Laughton trading post and a ford across the river. The Des Plaines proceeds through an industrial area as it heads southwest in a man-made channel next to the Chicago Sanitary and Ship Canal. Once past Willow Springs, the river looks wild again as it twists around islands and wetlands filled with waterfowl. The river widens and passes by sandstone bluffs and forests in the I & M Canal National Heritage Corridor. At last, the Kankakee River joins the Des Plaines to form the Illinois River.

Along the length of the Des Plaines, you will find the historic Chicago Portage (above), Native American sites (Chapter 6), forest preserves and nature centers (Chapter 7), and wetlands (Chapter 8).

## The Calumet Flow

The Calumet river system includes the Little Calumet, the Grand Calumet, and the Calumet, as well as the man-made Calumet-Sag Channel.

The Little Calumet begins as a peaceful prairie stream with headwaters in LaPorte County, Indiana. "Calumet" is a Native American word meaning "pipe of peace." The river name may also be derived from a French word, "chalemel," meaning the wild irises or reeds that grew in the river. Or the Native American and French words may be linked in the name "Calumet," since some peace pipes seem to have been made of reeds.

The Little Calumet originally flowed west and north, branching around Blue Island, sand ridges, and lagoons until it joined with the Grand Calumet, a meandering stream that stretched across the extreme northwest corner of Indiana. The two rivers together form the Calumet River, which originally flowed through the south side of Chicago to empty into Lake Michigan. When coach drivers navigated the mouth of the Calumet, passengers held their breath because a hidden sandbar constantly shifted with Lake Michigan waves and currents, making the route treacherous.

Like the Chicago River, the flow of the Calumet was reversed because it carried pollution into the lake. To divert the wastes of industry in northwest Indiana and Chicago's south side, workers dug the Calumet-Sag Channel from where the Little Calumet turns east to the Des Plaines River. This diverted sewage and industrial pollution toward the Illinois River and kept it out of Lake Michigan. Today, the Thomas J. O'Brien Lock and Dam, near 134th Street, controls the direction of flow of the Little Calumet.

The Calumet-Sag Channel (Cal-Sag Channel) flows west from Ashland Avenue, east of Blue Island between 115th and 107th streets on the south side. Completed in 1922, it also keeps Lake Michigan clean by diverting wastes to the Chicago Sanitary and Ship Canal. The Cal-Sag has been an important route for barges that carried cargo to and from steel mills, refineries, and other industrial plants. Now it is being widened and deepened as a part of the Deep Tunnel system, to help prevent flooding and pollution.

Heavy cargo that used to be shipped on the Chicago River was transferred to the Calumet in the late nineteenth century. The Calumet also provides outlets for Lake Calumet and Wolf Lake.

Lake Calumet is being developed as a deep-water harbor. This will assist traffic in the Calumet industrial district and accommodate ocean-going vessels that come to Lake Michigan from Europe via the St. Lawrence Seaway.

## Calumet Division, Forest Preserve District of Cook County

Calumet Division Headquarters
Dan Ryan Woods
87th Street and Western Avenue
Chicago, IL
(773) 233-3766
(773) 233-3767

A surprising number of green places, including wetlands with flocks of migrating waterfowl and endangered birds, manage to survive in this industrial area encompassing the Little Calumet and Calumet rivers, Calumet-Sag Channel, Wolf Lake State Park and Conservation Area, Powderhorn Lake, Indian Boundary Line, Thornton–Blue Island Road (Hubbard's Trail), Beaubien Preserve and Calumet Woods, and Whistler Preserve. Obtain a map to guide you through this area.

## The Illinois and Michigan Canal

The War of 1812 made Congress realize the Chicago Portage had great military importance and heightened the need to populate the area as part of the water route from the Great Lakes to Louisiana Territory. That is why Congress gave Illinois a land grant for the Illinois and Michigan Canal right-of-way and additional land (alternate sections in a five-mile strip on either side of the planned canal) for Illinois to sell, thereby financing construction.

In 1829 the Canal Commission planned the towns of Chicago and Ottawa. Hundreds of construction workers, mostly Irish immigrants, died in malaria-like epidemics while excavating the canal and building towns between Chicago and LaSalle/Peru. Nevertheless, in 1848 the joining of the Mississippi River and the Great Lakes via the I & M Canal (or, as a reporter for Chicago's *Weekly Journal* put it, the "wedding of the Father of Rivers to our inland seas") at last took place. The first boat to pass through carried sugar from New Orleans, Louisiana and traveled the ninety-six-mile canal en route to the Great Lakes and Buffalo, New York.

Warehouses and towns such as Joliet and Lockport (the canal headquarters) sprouted up along the I & M Canal. Farmers could now bring their crops to the closest spot on the canal rather than going to Chicago. Natural resources headed east toward New York, Boston, and other markets. Canal boats carried wheat, corn, and oats from Illinois farms, lumber from the forests of Michigan and Wisconsin, and sugar from New Orleans. Manufactured goods were carried on the return trip to Chicago.

The I & M Canal also served as the major route for pioneers heading west. Horse-drawn packets carried passengers to Peru, where they transferred to steamboats or stagecoaches and continued their trips to the frontier.

In the late 1850s, railroads took passengers and trade from the canal. Nevertheless, even in the 1880s, the canal still profited in the cargo trade. In 1933, the Illinois Waterway—a federal project that is both natural and man-made—replaced the canal. Today, boats with names like Prairie Bird make infrequent journeys down the Illinois River. From Harlem Avenue to its terminus at the Chicago River, the I & M Canal is buried under Chicago's expressways. Yet barges on the Illinois waterway still carry bulk cargo such as wheat, corn, coal, petroleum, sand, salt, and gravel.

## 🍂🍂 Illinois and Michigan Canal National Heritage Corridor (3 hours to 1 week)

To obtain maps and information about Native American and other historic sites, sports facilities, land and river trails, state and local parks, and places with great natural beauty, contact:

National Park Service
U.S. Department of the Interior
(815) 740-2047

Illinois and Michigan Canal
Visitor Center
Gaylord Building
200 W. 8th Street
Lockport, IL 60441
(815) 838-4830

I & M Canal State Trail,
Gebhard Woods State Park, and
William G. Stratton State Park
P.O. Box 272
Morris, IL 60450
(815) 942-0796

Channahon State Park
P.O. Box 54
Channahon, IL 60410
(815) 467-4271

Kankakee River State Park
P.O. Box 37
Bourbonnais, IL 60914
(815) 933-1383

Buffalo Rock State Park
and Effigy Tumuli
P.O. Box 39
Ottawa, IL 61350
(815) 433-2220

Follow in the footsteps of Native Americans and the white settlers of the Old West as you take the land and water trail from Navy Pier in Chicago to LaSalle/Peru on the Illinois River. This National Heritage

Corridor (established in 1984) includes twenty Chicago neighborhoods, and goes along the Chicago River, the Sanitary and Ship Canal, the Des Plaines River, the Illinois and Michigan Canal, and the Illinois River. It encompasses state and local parks and forest preserves, forty towns, and sites that played a critical role in national history.

In summer, you can hike or bike on many trails or canoe between Channahon and Morris and between Utica and LaSalle. In winter, you can snowmobile on sixty miles of trail between Channahon and LaSalle/Peru.

🐚 Begin your journey in the I & M National Heritage Corridor at the Chicago River between Lake Michigan and LaSalle Street. Within the Chicago area, the trail contains the Chicago Portage National Historic Site, the Canal Bicycle Path, and Camp Sagawau.

🐚 At Romeoville (31 miles from Chicago), Centennial Trail parallels the Des Plaines River north of Romeo Road. The Isle à La Cache Museum relates tales of Native Americans and French voyageurs (see Chapter 6).

🐚 Lockport (33 miles from Chicago) has a variety of museums and visitor centers, a canal lock, and the old canal town national historic district with pre–Civil War buildings. Each June, the Old Canal Days celebration brings the history of the canal to life.

🐚 From Morris (60 miles from Chicago), the I & M Canal State Trail leads to the town of Ottawa, where a four-hundred-foot-long aqueduct crosses the Fox River. In the vicinity, you will find Goose Lake Prairie State Natural Area, with a visitor's center and trails through the largest remnant of prairie left in Illinois (see Chapter 5); and the Heidecke State Fish and Wildlife Area, which offers hunting (in season) and fishing. Other sights on the I & M Canal include the Aux Sable Aqueduct, locks, and a lockkeeper's house, as well as parks, campsites, and historic reenactments.

🐚 Channahon (48 miles from Chicago) has many ancient Native American sites. In the area, you will find McKinley Woods and the Aux Sable and Dresden accesses to the I & M Canal State Trail—great for hiking, biking, or snowmobiling along the sixty-one-mile path to LaSalle. The Seneca Grain Elevator, built in 1861, is slated for restoration soon. W. G. Stratton State Park has a boat launching area just below the bridge over the Illinois River.

🍂 Travel down Route 6 to the Channahon access to the I & M Canal State Trail, the site of a restored lock, a locktender's house, and the DuPage River Dam. Dresden, now a ghost town, was an important stop on the I & M Canal. It has an old barn where mules were quartered and a house that was a tavern and stagecoach stop. A short distance west is Lock 8 and an aqueduct over Aux Sable Creek.

🍂 Travel 33.5 miles west of Lock 8 along Route 6. You will come to Buffalo Rock State Park, where a sandstone bluff offers a panorama of the Illinois River and the countryside. Before the French established a military post there in 1673, the bluff was inhabited by Native Americans.

🍂 Still further west is Utica (88 miles from Chicago), another important canal port. It has a museum in a hundred-and-fifty-year-old warehouse that once stored grain, tile, and lumber.

🍂 End your trip at Locks 14 and 15 at LaSalle/Peru (94 miles from Chicago), where an aqueduct spans the Vermillion River and the steamboat basin once held 250 boats waiting for spring thaw.

Note: For more detailed information on Native American sites at Channahon, Starved Rock, Kaskaskia, Joliet, Buffalo Rock State Park, and Utica, see Chapter 6.

## Guided River Tours

To enhance your appreciation of the nature and history of Chicago waterways, take a guided tour.

Note: Admission fees are charged for all of the following.

### 🍂🍂 Friends of the Chicago River
(312) 939-0490

This nonprofit organization devoted to preservation and public use of the city's waterfront conducts two-hour summer walking tours at 10 A.M. daily. The group also offers canoe trips and cruises and sells maps for self-guided walking tours.

### The Chicago Architecture Foundation

(312) 922-3432

This organization presents an architectural tour of the river from Memorial Day to the end of September, middays for an hour and a half.

 ### Mercury Line

(312) 332-1353

Located at Michigan Avenue and Wacker Drive, this boat company has frequent cruises on the river and the lake. In spring and fall, it offers an Illinois and Michigan Canal National Heritage Corridor cruise.

### Navy Pier

600 E. Grand Avenue
Chicago, IL 60611
(312) 595-7437

Ask about cruises.

# 10

# Botanical Beauties

"Without the gift of flowers and the infinite diversity of their fruits, man and bird,
if they had continued to exist at all, would be today unrecognizable."
—Loren Eiseley (1907– ), anthropologist

## Recreation and Renewal

If you are like many people, you may not realize that to feel your best
you require the beauty, open space, and mystery of natural environments, or that parks and gardens are essential to ease the tensions of
urban stress and provide spiritual renewal. City people need to con-
nect with nature and, fortunately, Chicago abounds in green havens
for all to enjoy. You will find parks with meadows, groves of trees, lagoons, and flower beds in every sector of the city.

City planners made parks and gardens a priority here from the start.
They planned lakefront parks such as exquisite Grant Park, which was
built on the debris of the Chicago Fire, Lincoln Park, and Jackson
Park. These extraordinary tracts of public land contribute to Chicago's
great beauty.

Inland from the lake, world renowned landscape architects such as
Jens Jensen and Frederick Law Olmstead (who designed Central Park
in New York) also created lovely recreation areas with "prairie rivers"—that is, meandering streams through grasslands—wildflowers,
and lagoons, bringing a touch of wilderness and reminding urban dwellers of the city's natural history.

Chicago's motto, *Urbis in Horto* (City in a Garden), is aptly chosen. Plantings adorn public buildings, parks, and homes in every neighborhood. Schools and vacant lots, too, are sites where flowers bloom and vegetables and fruits are harvested. Exotic gardens with plantlife from all over the world grow in conservatories such as the ones at Garfield and Lincoln Park, and in the Chicago Botanic Garden and Morton Arboretum.

Like the plants themselves, Chicago's gardens show great diversity. Formal gardens have linear walkways and framed beds filled with colorful flowers. Some are devoted to a single species, such as peonies or roses. Others are herb or vegetable gardens. There are also rock gardens with alpine plants, and aquatic gardens with wetland plants and colorful *koi* (ornamental Japanese carp bred for color and pattern). Annual gardens, with orange marigolds, red geraniums, and purple petunias, die at the end of summer. Perennial gardens, with spring daffodils, tulips, and forsythia, summer lilies, and autumn chrysanthemums, bloom year after year. Naturalized gardens abound in wildflowers, for they recreate prairies, woodlands, and wetlands. All these living art forms make city life more pleasant.

## Immigrant Parks

The influx of foreigners into Chicago at the end of the nineteenth century led to the establishment of fourteen "immigrant parks." Fuller Park, and others in various sectors of Chicago, were designed to ease foreigners into American life. They provided immigrants with access to running water, so, on weekends, families lined up to receive towels and take showers; and they swam in the swimming pools. There were doctors and nurses and branch libraries on the premises, and immigrants took open-air gym classes, lessons in English, and vocational training. The open meadows and ball-playing fields, with a field house, gardens, and walkways lined with trees, made the immigrant park a model for parks across the United States.

## Designing Nature

Several of the major Chicago parks have gorgeous natural settings. Most of them began as ugly places that were reshaped by renowned landscape architects. Ossian C. Simonds brought wild plants into city parklands. Frederick Law Olmstead constructed natural oases with open meadows and quiet ponds. Jens Jensen created environments where city dwellers could reconnect with the rhythms of nature. He landscaped with sunlight, changing seasons, and native plants that attracted wildlife; and his work also had echoes of history in meandering prairie rivers and circular "council rings" built of stones.

## Lincoln Park (1 to 4 hours)
2400 N. Stockton Avenue
Chicago, IL 60614
(312) 747-2474

See ancient beach ridges, trees that survived the Chicago Fire, and gardens galore on twelve hundred acres of lakefront property. Relax at the beaches. Sail from the harbors. Play ball on the meadows or watch water birds and wild beasts in the zoo.

Lincoln Park originated on the site of a cemetery and grew through landfill projects. It was designed by landscape architects Swain Nelson, his partner Olaf Benson, and Ossian Simonds. Diversey Harbor, the beaches, and the South Lagoon may look like they were made by Mother Nature, but they were carefully designed engineering feats.

For an overview of this park that was named in memory of President Abraham Lincoln in 1865, follow Lake Shore Drive from Hollywood Avenue (5700 N.) to Oak Street (1000 N.). Detour east at Foster Avenue (5200 N.) and head south through the park to Montrose Harbor, then east for a great birding area and a city panorama. Reenter Lake Shore Drive at Montrose Avenue (4400 N.) and continue south. Exit and turn east at Belmont Avenue (3200 N.) to Belmont Harbor. Look for a bird sanctuary (a fenced area) near Recreation Drive, north of Belmont and southeast of the totem pole. Again, go south on Lake Shore Drive all the way to the Oak Street Beach (1000 N.). Or exit at Fullerton Avenue (2400 N.) and turn east to the Lincoln Park Conservatory and the Lincoln Park Zoo.

In some parts of the park, you will come upon bits of Chicago history. Ancient beach ridges are marked just southeast of Deming Place Bridge near Stockton Drive and near the sidewalk east of the middle of North Pond. Hundred-and-fifty-year-old bur oak trees may have been burned in the Chicago Fire of 1871. (Look for signs of fire damage—a rounded thickening on the trunk at eye level, or two trunks rising from a common base.) Find the oaks, and old cottonwoods and ash trees, on a sandbar near the South Field House at North Avenue (1600 N.).

Watch birds at North Pond Wildlife Preserve (2000–2600 N.), a resting and nesting habitat for waterfowl, shorebirds, and songbirds. Be on the alert for opossum, woodland squirrels, and turtles too. Rent a pedal boat at South Pond (2000 N.) to renew your energy before you head for Lincoln Park Zoo (see Chapter 11).

## 🍃🍃🍃 Lincoln Park Conservatory and Gardens (1 to 3 hours)

2400 N. Stockton Avenue
Chicago, IL 60614
(312) 294-4770
Hours: Daily, 9 A.M.–5 P.M. During flower shows, 9 A.M.–6 P.M.; Fridays, 9 A.M.–9 P.M.
Admission: Free.

Let flower shows herald the seasons and plants from distant places delight your eye. Escape bleak February by surrounding yourself with red and pink blossoms at the Azalea Show. Welcome March and April with fragrant hyacinths and bright-hued narcissus and tulips at the Spring Flower Show. Add warmth to November with many-colored mums at the Chrysanthemum Show. Proclaim December and January as time for poinsettias at the Holiday Show.

Any time of year, the greenhouses are gorgeous. The Palm House is a tropical world with tall palms, rare orchids, and plants that produce products—such as the breadfruit tree, the mahogany tree, and the vanilla vine. All parts of the coconut palm are valuable: the seed for food and oil, leaves for thatching roofs, and roots, bark, and flowers for medicine. The Fern House contains many plants with feathery fronds and the three-hundred-year-old giant dion, a living fossil that looks like a palm. The Cactus House is filled with desert plants that have leaves reduced to needles and stems bloated with water. The large century plant with sword-shaped leaves grows a central stalk that blooms only once before it dies.

The Main Garden, outside, is a summer rainbow with the "big five"— impatiens, geraniums, petunias, salvia, and marigolds. The Rock Garden contains alpine plants, and Grandmother's Garden, west of Stockton Drive, has perennials that grandma loved.

 **Grant Park (1 to 3 hours)**
Gateway: Michigan Avenue at Congress Street
Chicago, IL 60601
(312) 747-2474
Hours: Daylight hours and summer evenings.

Chicago's "great escape" extends along the lakefront from Randolph Street (150 N.) to Roosevelt Road (1200 S.) in the heart of city. Jog along the shoreline, skate at the sports plaza, meander through flower gardens and meadows, or walk on tree-lined paths to Buckingham Fountain and major museums. Come for marathons, summer concerts, July Fourth fireworks, Venetian Night, with decorated boats and fireworks, Taste of Chicago, and other events. This beautiful gathering place for Chicagoans is built on refuse that was dumped into Lake Michigan after the 1871 Chicago Fire.

The gateway—at Congress Plaza, on Michigan Avenue between Van Buren and Harrison streets—has two bronze statues, *The Spearman* and *The Bowman* (Ivan Mestrovic, 1928). In the Court of Presidents, *Seated Lincoln*, a statue of President Abraham Lincoln (Augustus Saint-Gaudens, 1926), overlooks a formal flower garden with brightly colored annuals. Nearby, one of the largest stands of American elms in the Midwest contains some hundred-foot-high trees.

Clarence Buckingham Fountain, dedicated in 1927, is patterned after the palace fountain in Versailles, France (Marcel Francois Loyou, sculptor, Bennett, Parsons and Frost, architects, Jacque H. Lambert, engineer). This tribute to Lake Michigan has jets of water that soar more than 130 feet high. Bronze sea horses represent the four bordering states: Wisconsin, Illinois, Indiana, and Michigan. On a summer night, come for the light show. You will be fanned by lake breezes as you delight in the fountain's rainbow of color.

The Daniel H. Flaherty Rose Garden (near the fountain) has new- and old-fashioned roses, including the deep-pink Chicago peace rose. A Cancer Survivor's Garden (at the northern end of the park, near Lake Shore Drive) is a lovely tribute.

## 🍃🍃🍃 Jackson Park (1 to 3 hours)

6401 Stony Island
Chicago, IL 60637
(312) 747-2474

This lovely lakefront park, between 53rd Street and 67th Street south and extending west to Stony Island Avenue, will please you with Lake Michigan panoramas and cityscapes. Swim at the beaches. Sail out of the harbor. Stroll along the shoreline, gardens, and nature sanctuary. Or look in on the Museum of Science and Industry.

Promontory Point, on the lakefront at 55th Street, is a favorite spot at sunset, for it offers splendid views of the city. A golden statue, *The Republic*, by Daniel Chester French (on East Hayes Drive), was made for the 1893 Columbian Exposition. At the Jackson Park Perennial Garden (59th Street and Stony Island Avenue) listen to warblers and feast your eyes on flowering crabapple trees in spring and multicolored annuals and perennials in summer.

The imposing Museum of Science and Industry, along with the reflecting pool and Wooded Island to the south, were also constructed for the 1893 Columbian Exposition. Cross the Clarence Darrow Bridge to Wooded Island. Also known as Paul H. Douglas Sanctuary, this sixteen-acre nature preserve is a birder's paradise. Pass through an oriental gate to Osaka Garden and meander along a path lined with red granite blocks taken from Chicago's streetcar tracks. Admire the floating lily pads, but tread carefully on stepping stones as you cross the water. Stop on the Moon Bridge and look north at the urban scene, then gaze at the small island constructed of rocks that symbolize mountains.

## 🍃🍃🍃 Garfield Park Conservatory and Gardens (1 to 3 hours)

300 N. Central Park Boulevard
Chicago, IL 60624
(312) 746-5100

Hours: Daily, 9 A.M.–5 P.M. During flower shows, 9 A.M.–6 P.M.; Fridays, 9 A.M.–9 P.M.
Admission: Free.

Roam through glass-domed rooms—the Palm House, the Fernery, the Cactus House, the Aroid House, and the Warm and Economic House—

The Palm House at Garfield Park Conservatory.

where waterfalls and sculptures by Loredo Taft are scattered amid unusual, beautiful, and economically important plants. Behind the scenes, cold frames and propagating houses grow three hundred thousand plants each year. Outside, you will find a lagoon and the Golden Dome Fieldhouse in the park.

Come for the seasonal flower shows. The February Azalea Show has azaleas in every shade of pink, plus camellias. The March/April Spring Flower Show delights the eye with red tulips, lavender hyacinths, and yellow daffodils. The November Chrysanthemum Show presents seventy-five hundred spidery, round, and daisylike flowers in a rainbow of white, yellow, lavender, and burgundy. The December/January Holiday Show is bright with ornamental pepper, Jerusalem cherry, and a poinsettia "tree" made of 250 single-stemmed poinsettia plants.

Be sure to wander through the conservatory. (Call to arrange a tour.) The Palm House has a coconut palm with six-foot-long leaves, a giant bird of paradise, and a large clump of bamboo that may grow six inches taller on a summer day. Children love the Fernery because they expect to find dinosaurs among these ancient land plants. See a variety of ferns with leaves divided into leaflets so they look like green lace, and stemless mosses and liverworts that spread over the soil and rocks near the waterfall. The tall sago palm is a missing link between ferns and flowering plants. It is related to the cycads, tropical trees with palmlike leaves, that lived 250 million years ago on the shore of Lake Michigan. The Aroid House is so humid that curtain vine and many other plants obtain water with their roots in the air. The Cactus House is dry, to accommodate desert plants with waxy or needle-like leaves that conserve water, such as the tiny living stone and the giant saguaro. The century plant received its name because it takes so many years to bloom. If you smell rotting meat, look for flowers on starfish cactus. It may seem odd, but the odor attracts flies that pollinate it. The barrel cactus almost died because of a movie with a hero that survived in the desert by quenching his thirst with cactus. During the run of the film, chunks of the cactus kept disappearing.

The Warm and Economic House displays plants that are valued for their fruit, wood, essential oils, perfumes, and spices. See mango, fig, and citrus fruit trees; the cacao tree, the source of chocolate; the annato tree that produces edible food coloring; and plants that produce chewing gum, tapioca, and spices such as cinnamon. Other plants are the source of fiber, such as hemp and cotton. Kapok, a tree with warty bark, provided the stuffing for life jackets during World War II.

Garfield Gardens consists of four and a half acres of parkland, a lagoon edged with cattails and inhabited by ducks and geese, and the Golden Dome Fieldhouse.

##  Douglas Park Formal Garden (½ to 1 hour)

1401 S. Sacramento Avenue
Chicago, IL 60626
(312) 747-7670

A natural lagoon and a pool with red, yellow, pink, and white water-lilies provide the backdrop for a formal garden with twenty thousand annuals.

## Gompers Park (½ to 1 hour)

4222 W. Foster Avenue
Chicago, IL 60630
(312) 742-7879

The northwest side of Gompers Park (named after Samuel Gompers, the labor leader) was originally a river floodplain wetland. It was filled with soil in the 1950s to make mowing easier. Plans for restoration of the wetland began when the Chicago Park District joined with the Urban Resources Partnership of the U.S. Department of Agriculture, Friends of the Chicago River, and community volunteers. In 1995 the fill soil was scraped away to allow river water to enter the wetland. Community volunteers and school groups planted four thousand plants on one and a quarter acres of wet meadow. As thousands of water-loving wildflowers and grasses are planted near the creek, the scenery grows ever more beautiful.

## Humboldt Park Flower Garden (½ to 1 hour)

1440 N. Sacramento Avenue
Chicago, IL 60622
(312) 746-5357

In a place that was once flat, treeless prairie, you can relax near a lagoon and view gorgeous formal plantings. Two large bronze bison flank the entryway to the sunken garden. In this three-hundred-foot circle, stroll on paved walkways past grassy areas and feast your eyes on flower beds filled with colorful blossoms and greenery.

## 🍃 Indian Boundary Park (½ to 1½ hours)

2500 W. Lunt Avenue
Chicago, IL 60645
(312) 742-7879

At this haven in the city you can visit a small zoo with alpaca, pygmy goats, and other animals, or feed waterbirds near a lagoon. You can also find a field house, tennis courts, and a delightful play area for children in this small park surrounded by apartment buildings.

## 🍃 Marquette Park (1 to 3 hours)

6734 S. Kedzie Avenue
Chicago, IL 60629
(312) 747-6136

This attractive park has a large lagoon, an oak savanna with twenty-four young trees, and some very old prairie. (See Ashburn Prairie, Chapter 5.) The rose garden, near the west end of the park, has four thousand hybrid teas, grandifloras, floribundas, and tree roses. Also visit the nearby trial garden with new annuals and perennials, a cactus and succulent garden, a poolside rock garden, and an herb garden. Boxwood, myrtle, and ivy topiaries and ornamental trees add to the beauty of the place.

## 🍃 Mary Berkemeier Quinn Park of Trees (½ to 1 hour)

Quinn Park
6239 N. McClellan Street
Chicago, IL 60646
(312) 742-7879

Some people wanted open space and others wanted woods on this lot that was donated to the community. They compromised with mowed grass at the center, edged by oak woods where Jack in the pulpit and wild geranium bloom each spring.

## 🍃 Hurley Playlot (½ to 1 hour)

Ridge Park
1901 W. 100ᵗʰ Street
Chicago, IL 60643
(312) 747-6639

Visit a remnant of ancient oak savanna with trees that may be descendants of those that lived at this site thousands of years ago. Restoration began when grass mowing was stopped, so oak seedlings and other savanna plants could develop. Further restoration will involve controlled burning to remove weeds, enrich the soil, and promote the growth of the fire-resistant grasses and wildflowers.

## 🍃 West Pullman Park (½ to 1 hour)

401 W. 123ʳᵈ Street
Chicago, IL 60628
(312) 747-7661

This park, on a south-facing slope of the Little Calumet River valley, has red, black, white, and bur oak, and hickory and cherry trees that are native to the Chicago area. Just north, at the Anker Site on the bank of the Calumet River, archeologists found shell masks dating back hundreds of years.

## 🍃 Grand Crossing Park (½ to 1 hour)

7655 S. Ingleside Avenue
Chicago, IL 60619
(312) 747-6136

This historic park is named in remembrance of an 1853 train wreck at 75ᵗʰ Street and South Chicago Avenue. Today the park is an urban refuge with an outdoor swimming pool and sports areas. Nearby Oak Woods Cemetery holds graves of Confederate soldiers.

Searching for a park in your neighborhood? Call the Chicago Park District:

Lakefront parks, (312) 747-2474
Near North parks, (312) 746-5357
North Side parks, (312) 742-7879
South Side parks, (312) 747-7661

Central area parks, (312) 747-7640
Southwest area parks, (312) 747-6136
Administration Office, (312) 747-2200, (312) 747-2001 TTD

# Suburban Parks

## 🍃 Skokie Northshore Sculpture Park (½ to 1 hour)

McCormick Boulevard between Main and Dempster streets
P.O. Box 692
Skokie, IL 60076
(847) 679-3010

Getting there: Located in Skokie, 16 miles north of Chicago. Take Sheridan Road north to Main Street in Evanston. Turn west on Main Street to McCormick Boulevard in Skokie. Turn north on McCormick Boulevard to Dempster Street.

Walk down paths adjacent to the north shore channel of the Chicago River to see fourteen sculptures in a naturalized setting. Look for abstracts inspired by nature, such as *Ripples*, by Fritz Olsen, *Bird of Fire*, by Ted Garner, and *Goat*, by Jerry Peart, as well as many other colorful and thought-provoking sculptures.

## 🍃🍃🍃 Chicago Botanic Garden (2 to 5 hours)

1000 Lake Cook Road
P.O. Box 400
Glencoe, IL 60022-0400
(847) 835-5440
Plant information, (847) 835-0972

Getting there: Located in Glencoe, 22 miles north of Chicago. Take I-94 (Edens Expressway) north and exit east at Lake Cook Road. Drive east on Lake Cook Road to the entrance on the south side of the street.
Hours: Daily, 8 A.M. to sunset. Closed December 25.
Admission: Fee.
Access: Wheelchairs are available at the information desk. The orientation center has assistive listening devices, closed captions, and raised letters.
Facilities: Greenhouses. Library. Indoor and outdoor restaurants. Gift shop.

The statue of Carl Linnaeus at the Chicago Botanic Garden.

Take pleasure in three hundred acres of gardens adorned with lagoons, fountains, statues, a waterfall, and fragrant and colorful plants. Enjoy formal and informal flower gardens, an aquatic garden, a vegetable garden, a sensory garden, and a Japanese garden on three islands. Stroll tree-lined paths past naturalized areas—places that resemble marshes, woodlands, and prairie. From mid-April through October, take a narrated tram ride. In winter, warm up in greenhouses alive with tropical and desert plants. Come for seminars and events such as the March Plant Society Fair with booths and talks; spring, autumn, and winter plant sales; a Halloween Walk; and a Christmas tree display.

Begin your visit at the Heritage Garden, a circular patio with ponds and plantings arranged by continent. A statue of Carl Linnaeus (who established our system of plant classification) hides among the greenery. Stop to smell the roses in the Rose Garden, where there is a dazzling array of yellow, orange, pink, and red blossoms. See the English Walled Garden with espaliered fruit trees, and the Dwarf Conifer Garden with low-growing evergreens. Listen to the water cascade down rocks planted with perennials and shrubs in the Waterfall Garden.

The large kasuga lantern and the arched bridge mark the entry to the Japanese Garden. Meander along paths lined with evergreens that represent the lasting quality of nature. The Island of the Auspicious Cloud has a seventeenth-century samurai's retreat house, boulders that represent islands, and a raked gravel garden that symbolizes the sea. The Island of Pure, Clear Breezes has an arbor, a dry garden, and a view of the Island of Everlasting Happiness.

The Naturalistic Garden has prairie, oak/hickory forest plants, and a plot that attracts butterflies and birds. Relax on the patio overlooking the lagoon. Then visit the nearby Landscape Garden with its herbs and ornamental grasses. At the Regenstein Fruit and Vegetable Garden, enjoy the colorful spectacle of chrysanthemums mingling with rhubarb and ornamental peppers.

Step onto wooden platforms to view water lilies blooming in the Aquatic Garden. Spring daffodils and summer lilies embellish the nearby Bulb Garden. Sniff the fragrant blossoms and touch the leaves of plants in the Sensory Garden.

In the Greenhouse, look for a prancing pony and other topiaries made with vines and moss growing on a wire skeleton. See pink azaleas, purple orchids, and insect-eating bog plants. Find the hundred-year-old jade tree in the Cactus House.

Continue your excursion at the Learning Garden for the Disabled, the Children's Vegetable Garden, the Plant Evaluation Garden, the Prairie, and the Turnbull Woods nature trail.

## Morton Arboretum (2 to 4 hours)

Route 53
Lisle, IL 60532
(630) 719-2465

Getting there: Located in Lisle, 25 miles west of Chicago. Take Route 88 (East-West Tollway) west. Exit north at Route 53 and go north to the entrance.

Hours: Daily, 7 A.M.–7 P.M. Daylight Saving Time; 7 A.M.–5 P.M. Central Standard Time.

Admission: Fee is $6 per car, half-price on Wednesday.

Facilities: Visitor's Center. Education Center. Library. Restaurant. Ginkgo Gift Shop.

Call the plant clinic at (630) 719-2424, 1–3 P.M., for woody plant advice.

If you are a tree-hugger, this museum of woody plants has more than seventeen hundred acres of trees from all over the world to love. Founded in 1922 (on land donated by the founder of the Morton Salt Company), the arboretum also has shrubs and vines, gardens, a reconstructed Illinois prairie, and lagoons with birding spots and wildlife refuges.

Attend adult and family classes in landscaping, horticulture, and nature appreciation. Join in family fun at overnighters, the April Arbor Day plant sale, and the September Family Fair. Bring preschoolers to junior high-schoolers to special activities including summer nature camps. Call for reservations on a guided tram tour or explore on your own. Drive along thirteen miles of road, or hike twenty-five miles of walking trails with lovely landscapes and exceptional trees.

The thirty-one hundred species that grow here are adapted to the climate and soil of northern Illinois. They are arranged in plant families such as oak, maple, or elm, each with twenty to forty tree species; habitat groups, such as northern Illinois forest; and geographic groups from China, Japan, Siberia, eastern Europe, western Europe, the Ozarks, and the Appalachian mountains.

Obtain a map and ask about tram tours and special attractions at the Visitor's Center. (Note that the arboretum is divided by Route 53 into east and west sides.) The map has driving loops, walking trails, and directions to plant collections, habitats, and birding spots.

Seasonal changes offer special treats. In early spring, visit the Daffodil Glade for a brilliant splash of yellow in the oak savanna. During May, woodland wildflowers blossom along Trees Trail Loops 1, 2, and 3 on the east side. In autumn, follow the Inner Loop Trail with its golden maples. In winter, hike through snow in the open forest and identify trees and shrubs by their silhouettes, buds, and branching style.

On the east side, the Groundcover Garden offers ideas for replacing lawn with variegated lily turf or lavender, and the Hedge Garden provides landscaping ideas.

If you are burning with curiosity about trees that lived here before European settlers, visit the northern Illinois collection. For evergreen trees, go to the pine and juniper collections. Also see the oak collection and the tree evaluation area, where trees that withstand city pollution are chosen for the streets of Chicago. Bur Reed Marsh is very noisy in late March when mating frogs call to one another and migrating birds sing out.

On the west side, see the evergreens on Spruce Hill, Hemlock Hill, and Pine Hill.

Sniff the pungent odors of wild nodding onion, skunk cabbage, and wild garlic around Lake Marmo. Visit the restored Schulenberg Prairie to enjoy more than 250 flowers and grasses. Near the Thornhill Education Center, walk through a new Forecourt Garden, a Fragrance Garden, and a Wild Garden.

## 🍃 Bergen Garden (½ hour; by appointment only)

Regents Park
5050 S. Lake Shore Drive
Chicago, IL 60615
(773) 288-5050

It is hard to imagine that this urban delight was once the roof of a parking garage. Tree-lined pathways take you through a landscape with lagoons, live ducks, fountains, a small waterfall, and thirty thousand plants.

# School Gardens

These cheery gardens are planned, planted, and cared for by teachers and children. Allow about half an hour each; by appointment only.

## 🍃 Jean Baptist Point Du Sable High School (south)

Contact:
Dr. Emil Hamberlin
(773) 535-1100

Stroll through an educational park in a courtyard where elm, honey locust, ginkgo, and sweet gum trees grow tall. Exotic birds—peacocks, pheasants, and guinea hens—will cross your path. You may also encounter pot-bellied pigs or "Miss Daisy," a goat.

In another courtyard, you will come upon a prairie, a flower garden, and a vegetable garden. Inside, Dr. Hamberlin's biology classroom is like a garden of Eden with tropical plants and animals such as pythons, ferrets, and jungle chickens. Don't be surprised if a macaw greets you. A memorial area—in remembrance of students who have lost their lives—will soon add another dimension to this remarkable urban sanctuary.

**Where to get gardening advice in the Chicago area**

Woody plants (trees, shrubs, and vines): plant clinic, Morton Arboretum. Call (708) 719-2424 between 1 and 3 P.M.

Vegetables, flowers, lawns, houseplants, soil: University of Illinois Cooperative Extension Service. Call (773) 292-4444.

## Von Steuben Metropolitan Science Center
(773) 534-5100

Honored as a national model, this lovely school site is being restored by horticulture science students as a landscape laboratory. Also look for new plantings on the North Branch of the Chicago River between Kimball and North Park College, where students work with community groups on cleanup and restoration.

## Avondale Elementary School
Contact:
Mrs. Christine Murphy
(773) 534-5244

A thousand students and forty teachers take plants grown in classrooms out to the schoolyard. Second- and third-graders till the soil and fourth- and fifth-graders plant the flowers.

Also visit Bontemps (773) 535-9176, James McCosh (773) 535-0570, Burbank (773) 534-3000, Hibbard (773) 534-5191, and other elementary schools; John Marshall (773) 534-6455, Lane Technical (773) 534-5400, Hubbard (773) 535-2200, and other high schools.

# Community Gardens (½ hour each)

Good neighbors in many areas of Chicago transform neglected ground into lovely urban gardens. Children as well as poor and homeless individuals work in harmony with residents to plant flowers and vegetables. Some of these community groups feed the hungry and assist service organizations. They all harvest enduring friendships.

### 🍃 Caryn Center

South 46ᵗʰ Street between Ellis (1000 E.) and Greenwood (1100 E.)
Chicago, IL 60643
(773) 324-7330

Homeless people work with neighborhood residents, and they are developing plans for a nature center, a children's garden, an orchard, and a food bank.

### 🍃 Ginkgo Organic Gardens

4057-4059 N. Kenmore (1040 W.)
Chicago, IL 60613
(773) 342-8430

Twenty-five raised beds overflow with flowers, vegetables, and fruit trees that are harvested for social service organizations.

### 🍃 St. Augustine (Su Casa) Neighborhood Community Garden

5043 S. Laflin (2 blocks east of Ashland at 52ⁿᵈ Street)
Chicago, IL 60609
(773) 376-9263

Vegetables, perennials, and bulbs are planted and cared for by families and the 4-H Club.

To locate other community gardens, contact:

Garden Clubs of Illinois, Inc.
(708) 778-8682

City of Chicago
Department of Environment
(312) 744-7468

University of Illinois Cooperative Extension Service
(773) 292-4444

Master Gardeners (trained by the University of Illinois Cooperative Extension Service) work with school and community groups.

# Suburban Gardens

##  Ladd Arboretum (1 to 2 hours)

Ecology Center
2024 McCormick Boulevard
Evanston, IL 60204
(847) 864-5181

Getting there: Located in Evanston, 13 miles north of Chicago. Take Sheridan Road north into Evanston. Turn west on Oakton Street to McCormick Boulevard. Follow McCormick Boulevard north to park near the Ecology Center at Bridge Street. The Arboretum extends between Green Bay Road on the north and Emerson Street on the south, along McCormick Boulevard and the east bank of the Sanitary District Canal.

Follow walking trails or go cross-country skiing along trails with lovely prairie plantings, meadows, tree groves, and a bird sanctuary on the banks of a flood-control channel. Attend programs at the Ecology Center, where commonly used landscape plants surround the building and native prairie plants cover the slope to the water channel.

Stroll south from the center through the International Friendship Garden, with 123 trees representing nations, Independence Knoll, with a flagpole and plantings, Washington Heritage Walk, with trees and shrubs President Washington knew, and Woman's Terrace, with plantings dedicated to outstanding Evanston women. Go north to see Aspegren Meadow, Pine Knoll, Oak Grove Knoll, Maple Knoll, and the bird sanctuary.

## Merrick Rose Garden (½ hour)

Oak and Lake streets
Evanston, IL 60201
Contact:
Assistant Superintendent of Parks
City of Evanston
(847) 866-2911

Getting there: Located in Evanston, 13 miles north of Chicago. Take Sheridan Road north into Evanston. Turn west on Lake Street and drive west past the railroad tracks to Oak Street.

Peace roses and All-America rose selections are some of the thousand plants contained in this fragrant and colorful garden.

## 🍃 The Shakespeare Garden (½ hour)

Northwestern University campus
220 Sheridan Road
Evanston, IL 60201
Contact:
Garden Club of Evanston
2703 Euclid Park Place
Evanston, IL 60201
(847) 491-0032

Getting there: Located in Evanston, 13 miles north of Chicago. Take Sheridan Road north into Evanston and park near Garrett Place. Walk on the Northwestern University campus to the east end of Garrett Place. The garden is just north of this spot.

Designed by renowned landscape architect Jens Jensen, this garden is enclosed by hedged walls and contains pansies, columbines, and many other flowers William Shakespeare mentions in his poems and plays.

## 🍃 Glencoe Gardens

Glencoe, IL 60022
Contact:
Superintendent of Parks
Glencoe Park District
(847) 835-4648
(847) 835-3030 to arrange a tour

Getting there: Located in Glencoe, 22 miles north of Chicago. Take I-94 north and exit east on Dundee Road.

See the Memorial Rose Garden and annual, perennial, and evergreen gardens. Tour greenhouses where volunteers work on the Plantlife Resources Project—raising flowers, trees, and shrubs that will be planted in Glencoe gardens and control erosion on Lake Michigan bluffs.

## 🍃 Wilmette Wildflower Garden (½ hour)

Gillson Park
Michigan Avenue south of Lake Avenue
Wilmette, IL 60091
Contact:
Wilmette Park District
(847) 256-6100

Getting there: Located in Wilmette, 16 miles north of Chicago. Take I-94 north and exit at Lake Avenue east. Go east on Lake Avenue to Michigan Avenue at the lakefront. Turn south on Michigan Avenue about one block to the garden entrance on the east side.

Walk a short winding trail through an everchanging wildflower garden on a park overlooking Lake Michigan.

## 🍃 Elmhurst College Arboretum and Wilder Conservatory (½ to 2 hours)

225 Prospect Street
Elmhurst, IL 60126
Wilder Park Conservatory, (630) 993-8909

Getting there: Located in Elmhurst, 17 miles west of Chicago. Take I-290 (Eisenhower Expressway) west and exit at St. Charles Road. Go west on St. Charles Road past York Street two short blocks to Cottage Hill Road. Turn north on Cottage Hill Road a short distance, and turn left into Wilder Park. Wilder Park has the conservatory and the Lizzadro Museum of Lapidary Art, and is across the street from Elmhurst College.

Hours: Conservatory, daily, 9 A.M.–5 P.M. Outside gardens open during daylight hours.

View tropical plants inside greenhouses, and herb, rose, and formal gardens outside the Wilder Conservatory. Across the street, magnolias, pears, dogwoods, and other flowering trees are some of the 270 varieties of plants that adorn the Elmhurst College campus.

## 🍃🍃 Lilacia Park (1 hour)

Between Maple and Parkside streets, west of Main Street
Lombard, IL 60148
Contact:
Lombard Park District or
Lombard Chamber of Commerce
(708) 627-5040

Getting there: Located in Lombard, 22 miles southwest of Chicago. Take I-290 (Eisenhower Expressway) west and continue southwest on Route 88. Exit Route 88 at Meyers Road (Route 25) north. Go north on Meyers Road, which becomes Westmore Avenue, to Maple Street. Turn west on Maple Street and go west past Main Street to the entrance.

Come for the spring lilac festival, when the air is filled with the scent of lilacs and you experience the visual pleasures of thirty-five thousand tulips and early-flowering trees. Jens Jenson designed this eight-and-a-half-acre park with its open lawns, splendid lilac collection, gardens with perennial flowers and prairie plants, and groves of conifers and hardwoods.

## 🍃🍃 The Oak Park Conservatory (1 hour)

617 Garfield Street
Oak Park, IL 60304
(708) 386-4700

Getting there: Located in Oak Park, 9 miles west of Chicago. Take I-290 west and exit at Austin Boulevard. The exit is on the left side of the expressway. Stay in the left lane on the ramp and turn left on Austin Boulevard, driving about 10 yards. Turn right (west) onto Garfield Street. Continue on Garfield to East Avenue. The conservatory is on the corner of East and Garfield. By CTA, take the Congress line to Oak Park Avenue and walk east on the platform to East Avenue.
Hours: Monday, 2–4 P.M. Tuesday, 10 A.M.–4 P.M. Wednesday–Sunday, 10 A.M.–6 P.M.

This conservatory for all seasons has desert, tropic, and fern houses, and outdoor perennial, prairie, and herb gardens. Pesticides are banned, so praying mantises and biological control methods protect the flora from insect damage. Birds thrive in cages scattered among the flora. Call about shows and special events. Come in October for daisy mums, in December for poinsettias and paper-white narcissus, in March for snapdragons, sweet peas, and other surprises, and in May for fuchsias. Children can join the Junior Naturalist Club and discover the tropical rainforest, prairies, and other ecological wonders.

## 🍃 Triton College Botanical Garden (1 hour)

2000 5th Avenue
River Grove, IL 60171
(708) 456-0300

Getting there: Located in River Grove, 15 miles west of Chicago. Take I-290 (Eisenhower Expressway) west and exit north on 1st Avenue. Go north on 1st Avenue (which becomes Thatcher Avenue) to North Avenue (1600 N.). Turn west on North Avenue to 5th Avenue and north to Triton College.

See medicinal plants, All-America selections, cut-flower plants, a nursery, experimental gardens, an educational greenhouse, and a Senior Center patio garden.

## 🍃 The Cuneo Museum and Gardens (1 to 2 hours)

1350 N. Milwaukee Avenue
Vernon Hills, IL 60061
(847) 362-2025

Getting there: Located in Vernon Hills, 31 miles north of Chicago. Take I-94 (Edens Expressway) north to Route 60. Go west on Route 60 to Route 21 (Milwaukee Avenue). Turn north on Route 21 and go ½ mile to the entrance.
Hours: Tuesday to Sunday, 10 A.M.–5 P.M.
Facilities: Restaurant.
Admission: Fee.

This seventy-five-acre estate has a Victorian mansion surrounded by formal gardens, antique statuary, fountains, a nine-hole golf course, and lakes. Visit the conservatory with exotic plants. Children will enjoy feeding white fallow deer in the deer park. Call to arrange a tour or a private party.

##  Cantigny Gardens (1 to 2 hours)

1 S. 151 Winfield Road
Wheaton, IL 60187
(630) 668-5161

Getting there: Located in Wheaton, 25 miles west of Chicago. Take I-290 west to Route 88 west. Exit Route 88 at Winfield Road. Drive north on Winfield 3 miles to the entrance, on the east (right).
Hours: Tuesday–Sunday, 10 A.M.–5 P.M. in summer; 10 A.M.–4 P.M. the rest of the year. Closed Mondays and the month of January.
Facilities: Visitors Center. Robert R. McCormick Museum. First Division (Military) Museum. Golf Course. Tack Room Cafe. Gift Shop. Shaded picnic grounds.
Admission: Fee.

On the estate once owned by Colonel McCormick, roam through ten acres of formal and semi-formal gardens to see a wide variety of midwestern plants and one of the area's largest displays of annuals. See a rose garden, a rock garden with conifers, and an idea garden, which demonstrates a variety of growing techniques for adults and fun gardening projects for children. Call for the schedule of garden lectures, outdoor concerts, greenhouse activities, and art shows and craft fairs.

##  Garfield Farm Museum

3 N016 Garfield Road
La Fox, IL 60147
(630) 584-8485

Getting there: Located 5 miles west of Geneva, about 40 miles northwest of Chicago off Illinois Route 38 on Garfield Road.

This working farm on an 1840s farmstead has horticultural seminars and heirloom plant events. (See Chapter 12.)

# 11

# Animal Encounters

"God is really only another artist. He invented the giraffe, the elephant, and the cat. He has no real style. He just keeps on trying other things."
Pablo Ruiz y Picasso (1881–1973)

If wildlife is your passion, go on a city safari. You will find all sorts of birds and other native animals wherever greenery exists amid concrete and asphalt. Colorful warblers and flocks of many other migrating birds feed on the Lake Michigan shore; bluegills, salmon, and trout swim in nearby waters. Stately herons rest in south side wetlands surrounded by junkyards and factories. Large mammals, including deer, foxes, coyotes, and elk, roam the forest preserves. Amphibians find shelter near ponds in parks. Reptiles such as the hognose snake slither through meadows, while katydids hop and butterflies wing their way across bits of prairie.

Until the 1800s, when Europeans settled here, millions of buffalo, birds, and other creatures thrived on the vast Illinois prairie. These native animals can be seen today in the forest preserves and remnants of wilderness that once covered the entire Chicago area. Native Americans fished in the Chicago and Des Plaines rivers and Skokie marsh, and they hunted in nearby wetlands. They hunted ducks, geese, and wild turkey for food, and beaver, otter, and raccoon for their furs. In the forests, they aimed their arrows at deer and fox.

If you prefer to hunt for exotic animals, Chicago has them, too. Pursue dolphins and whales from the deep oceans, and octopus, crabs, and fish from coastal waters at the Shedd Aquarium. Track gorillas, elephants, and leopards in the Lincoln Park Zoo; and crocodiles, anteaters, and giraffes in Brookfield Zoo.

# Flock to the Birds

Birds are especially plentiful in and around Chicago. On open meadows, robins gather worms from the ground. Hawks hunt for mice and other prey as they circle in the sky. About twenty-five thousand Canadian geese graze in the city and suburbs, and at least three hundred of them winter in Jackson Park. In backyard trees and woodlands, cardinals eat seeds and berries and nuthatches munch on insects. Ducks swim in ponds and herons and other migrating waterfowl rest in the Calumet wetlands, surrounded by industrial parks. Cliff-dwelling peregrine falcons nest on the ledges of downtown buildings and fledglings try their wings above traffic-clogged streets.

Spring and autumn are the best time for birding. Chicago is on the Mississippi Flyway, so in autumn, migrating birds from the midwestern provinces of Canada make stopovers in Chicago before continuing their long journeys south for the winter. The birds spread their wings and follow the Chicago and Des Plaines rivers to the Mississippi River Valley, then fly south to the Gulf of Mexico and Yucatan, or to Panama and Costa Rica. A few fly all the way to South America. The following spring, these long-distance travelers return to Chicago on their way to Canada. Therefore, in spring and fall you can see a tremendous variety of songbirds, waterfowl, and other migrating birds. Birding is also excellent in wetlands because they are so rich in vegetation. Many water birds such as ducks and herons rest and feed in south-side marshes and in suburban bogs and other wetlands.

To locate these feathered flyers, read *Chicago Area Birds*, by Steven Mlodinow. For suggestions about where to birdwatch, call:

Chicago Park District
(312) 747-2200
(312) 747-2001 TDD

Morton Arboretum
(630) 719-2465

Lincoln Park Zoo
(312) 742-2000

## Tips for Identifying Birds

In order to identify a bird in the wild, use binoculars to study its features. Then find its picture and description in a bird manual. Observe the bird's shape and outline (large or small, slender or round). Look at its color pattern. Notice the shape of its beak and its tail (square, forked, or curved). Look for a crest on the head and markings on the face. Note the wingspread (length from wingtip to wingtip) and the shape of the wings. Watch for markings on the wingtips and the shoulders. See if the bird's legs are long or short; how the toes are arranged; and whether the toes are webbed.

Brookfield Zoo
(708) 485-0263
(773) 242-2630

Forest Preserve District of Cook County
(312) 261-8400
(708) 366-9420
(708) 771-1190 TDD
(800) 870-3666

Chicago Audubon Society
(733) 539-6793

Chicago Ornithological Society
(708) 371-2124

Also call suburban park districts and forest preserve districts in other counties.

# Birding Spots

Forest preserves with nature centers often have bird walks. Doug Anderson, who has led bird walks in Chicago for many years, suggests the city birding places that follow.

###  Paul H. Douglas Nature Sanctuary

Jackson Park, on the south side of the lagoon behind the Museum of Science and Industry, near 57th Street and Lake Shore Drive, Chicago, IL 60637

This is one of the most accessible sanctuaries in the city and it abounds with birdlife. To find the sanctuary, also called Wooded Island, park near the reflecting pool south of the Museum of Science and Industry, then walk west across the Clarence Darrow Bridge. You will be rewarded with great biodiversity, for 243 species, including a great assortment of meadow birds, wading birds, and waterfowl, have been identified here.

###  North Park Village Nature Center (1 to 3 hours)

5801 N. Pulaski Road
Chicago, IL 60646
(773) 744-5472

Hours: Daily, 10 A.M.–4 P.M. Closed New Year's Day, Easter, Thanksgiving, and Christmas.

Come for bird walks in spring and fall. You will find excellent birding in the woodlands and restored prairie. Times vary, but they even have Owl Prowls at night.

###  Magic Hedge Bird Sanctuary

Lincoln Park
Montrose Avenue and Lake Michigan Shore

Exit Lake Shore Drive at Montrose (4400 N.) and drive north on the road that winds around the boat basin. Park at the "elbow" of the boat basin, where the road turns west again. Take the paved walkway east to the tip of Montrose Point. In mid-May and late September or early October, the hedge is a magnet for a variety of colorful warblers and many other species of migrating birds.

###  Lake Calumet Area

South side, from 116ᵗʰ Street and Torrence Avenue (2600 E.), about a mile west to Cottage Grove Avenue (500 E).

Tucked away between landfills and industrial sites, Dead Stick Marsh has a variety of shorebirds on mudflats. Amazingly, rare herons and many other birds return each year to two major rookeries. Many of the birds migrate from Central America to breed on unprotected private marshland. That is why environmentalists are trying to create a Calumet Ecological Park, with greenways for public recreation and refuges for bird nesting, between the I & M Canal National Heritage Corridor and the Indiana Dunes National Lakeshore.

### Peregrine Places

125 S. Wacker
Hyde Park (south side)
Lakeview (north side)

The Chicago Peregrine Release and Restoration Project and the Chicago Academy of Sciences brought endangered peregrine falcons, which ordinarily nest on cliffs, into the downtown area. In 1995, Harriet and Jingles were the first to nest on a ledge of the tall building at 125 S. Wacker, and four chicks made their fledgling flights.

## Suburban Birding

### Illinois Beach State Park

Wadsworth Road and the Lake Michigan shoreline
Zion, IL 60099
(847) 662-4811

Getting there: Located in Zion, 41 miles north of Chicago. Take Route 41 north to Wadsworth Road and go east 10 miles. The park extends from the railroad tracks to the shore and from Waukegan north to North Point Marina.

See many hawks during spring and late October migrations. Also look for shorebirds on the dunes and waterfowl in wetlands.

###  Palos area, including the Little Red School House Nature Center

9800 S. Willow Springs Road
Willow Springs, IL 60480
(708) 839-6897

Getting there: Located in Willow Springs, 19 miles southwest of Chicago. Take I-55 south and exit at Willow Springs Road. Go south to the schoolhouse.

Hours: March to October: weekdays, 8 A.M.–5 P.M., weekends, 8 A.M.–5:30 P.M. Winter: closes ½ hour earlier. Exhibit building opens at 9 A.M. and closes ½ hour earlier than the grounds; closed Fridays. Everything closed Thanksgiving, Christmas Day, and New Year's Day.

The many sloughs (shallow lakes) here offer good birding, with a bounty of ducks in fall.

###  MacArthur Woods Nature Preserve

Near Highway 60 and St. Mary's Road
Vernon Hills, IL 60061
Contact:
Lake County Forest Preserve District
(847) 367-6640

Getting there: Located in Vernon Hills, 31 miles northwest of Chicago. Take I-94 north to Highway 60. Go west on Highway 60 to St. Mary's Road. Turn north on St. Mary's Road and go north to the forest preserve.

This 446-acre preserve with upland and floodplain forest is a breeding habitat for forest interior birds.

###  Colored Sands Forest Preserve (by appointment only)

Haas Road
Shirland, IL 61079
Contact:
Tom Little
Sand Bluff Bird Banding Station
1509 Prairie Avenue
Rockford, IL 61102

Getting there: Located in Shirland, 97 miles northwest of Chicago. Hours: March to May and September to November: Saturday, dawn to dusk; Sunday, dawn to noon.

Migrating birds stop here to feed on rare plants in the sand prairie, river bottomland, and oak savanna. At Sand Bluff Banding Station, birds are caught in "mist nets" and banded to track their travels, changes in population, and life spans.

## Lake Renwick Heron Rookery Nature Preserve
Plainfield, IL 60544
Contact:
Forest Preserve District of Will County
(815) 727-8700

Getting there: Located in Plainfield, 37 miles southwest of Chicago. Take I-55 west and exit at Joliet Road (Route 30) north. Travel north to Renwick Road. Turn east on Renwick Road and drive ½ mile to the preserve on the north (left) side.

You cannot go onto the island. However, you can view nesting herons and cormorants from afar with binoculars. The heron rookery, located on an island in Lake Renwick, is the breeding ground of great egrets, great blue herons, black-crowned night herons, and double-crested cormorants.

# Illinois Animals

Illinois has 297 native species of birds, 196 of fish, and sixty-three of mammals. The white-tailed deer, the state mammal, is often seen in forest preserves, where it lives on twigs, shrubs, and grasses. Its coat is brown in summer and blue-gray in winter. When frightened, it can jump thirty feet as it runs away.

The bluegill, the state fish, has many names, including bream, sunfish, and prairie perch. Found in slow-moving streams, it has a distinctive black spot at the rear of its dorsal (back) fin, a small mouth, and, sometimes, vertical stripes.

The cardinal is the state bird. The female is yellow-brown, but the male, with a crest on its head, brings a touch of red and raucous whistles to woodlands and backyards.

# In Pursuit of Native Animals

A marvelous assortment of native aquatic and land animals live in the Chicago metropolitan area. Squirrels, chipmunks, and pigeons live in backyards and parks. Snails, slugs, and worms slide across the soil. Salamanders and field mice hide in leaf litter. Voles and woodchucks build underground burrows. Frogs croak at the edges of rivers and lakes. Clams live at the bottom of ponds and mosquitoes lay their eggs at the top. Crabs walk on jointed legs and fish swim in the shallow water along the Lake Michigan shoreline. Beavers build their homes and opossums and raccoons drink in cleaner sections of the Des Plaines and Chicago rivers. Bats, weasels, skunks, red fox, deer, and even elk and coyotes roam forest preserves. Occasionally, these mammals follow greenways along rivers and railroad tracks and find their way into the city.

To find the native animals that dwell in the Chicago metropolitan area, track them at the lakefront (Chapter 2), in the prairie (Chapter 5), at nature centers and in forests (Chapter 7), in wetlands (Chapter 8), in city parks (Chapter 10), in zoos (Chapter 11), and along rivers (Chapter 9).

Note the time, for each animal species operates on its own daily and seasonal schedule. At dawn, listen to bird choruses. At sundown, hear crickets buzz in the trees and frogs croak at the edge of ponds. In the darkness of night, your flashlight may shine on a bat flying quietly through the trees, using echolocation (sound that bounces off objects) to hunt insects. Because insects are so diverse and abundant, you can chase bees, beetles, and flies by day, and mosquitoes and moths by night.

In winter, when leaves lie beneath the snow and food is scarce, most animals disappear from view. However, you can find insect cocoons on brick buildings and tree branches. Search under leaf litter for salamanders and in hollow logs or a garage for sleeping mice. Groundhogs conserve energy by hibernating in burrows. But you can find footprints of active squirrels, foxes, and deer in the snow. In autumn, watch flocks of geese and other migrating birds fly along the Lake Michigan shoreline and head south. When spring comes, you will find caterpillars munching on new leaves and robins and other birds returning to city parks, prairies, and woodlands.

Because most wild animals are masters of camouflage that hide in the shadows of shrubs and shy away from people, they may be seem hard to spot in nature. However, if you are patient and remain silent and still, animals will approach you. Let your eyes adjust to the scene; you may be amazed to see a deer among the trees. Scan the treetops as well as the ground and listen for the rustle of a leaf or the snap of a twig. Search under leaf litter and rocks and dig in the soil. You will find larvae and eggs, ants, worms, and many other invertebrates there.

Be sure to pursue native species on the borders of woodlands and meadows, forests and prairies, and on riverbanks, the margins of ponds, and the shore of Lake Michigan. Along these edges, a great variety of food and shelter is available. That is why animals are more abundant and biodiversity is greatest at the meeting places of ecosystems. If you are looking for rare or endangered creatures, you are most likely to find them in bogs, fens, sedge meadows, sand prairies, or other unusual plant communities. If you want to spot wildlife in the city, find greenways—strips of vegetation along railroad tracks, rivers, roads, and the lakefront. Greenways provide food and cover within the urban environment, so these are the trails that birds and wildlife take into Chicago.

Where should you search for butterflies? In prairies, forests, and butterfly gardens at the Chicago Botanic Garden, the Sand Prairie Nature Preserve, and the Little Red Schoolhouse Nature Center.

Are you excited by snakes, lizards, and other reptiles? Or by frogs, salamanders, and other amphibians? Call the Chicago Herpetological Society at (773) 281-1800 or (773) 508-0034 TDD or TYY.

Do you admire snails, clams, and other molluscs? Call the Shell Club at the Field Museum at (312) 922-9410.

Do invertebrates and exotic (nonnative) animals intrigue you? See them at the Shedd Aquarium and at Lincoln Park and Brookfield zoos.

Do you prefer the antics of domesticated species? Attend cat shows, dog shows, and horse shows and visit farms and county fairs.

Aquatic life abounds where the water is relatively clean and contains enough oxygen, in Chicago's wetlands (see Chapter 8) and in Lake Michigan. Examine a drop of pond water and you will see many single-celled organisms, as well as insect larvae, tiny shrimp, and other microscopic beasts. Angle for bass, trout, and other native Illinois fish (see Chapter 13), in park lagoons, lakes, and less polluted sections of the Des Plaines and other rivers.

## 🍃 Willowbrook Forest Preserve and Wildlife Haven
Park Boulevard at 22nd Street
Glen Ellyn, IL 60138
(708) 790-4900, ext. 245

Getting there: Located in Glen Ellyn, 24 miles west of Chicago. Take I-290 (Eisenhower Expressway) west, and exit west on Roosevelt Road. Drive west on Roosevelt Road to Park Boulevard and turn south to 22nd Street.

This haven, where native birds and other wildlife are restored to health, has indoor exhibits and eagles, hawks, owls, red foxes, a coyote, and a badger on display outdoors. Learn how to bring wildlife into your backyard, and walk the interpretive nature trail (a half-mile outer loop and shorter inner loop) through shrubland and grassland. At the south end, permanently disabled water birds find refuge in the marsh.

# Aquatic Animals

The salty oceans, along with freshwater streams and lakes, cover most of the earth and contain a greater variety of animals than the continents. Some of these aquatic creatures attach themselves to the bottom while others swim thousands of miles across the oceans. Some filter bits of food from the water, others graze on seaweed or algae, and many are hunters. They range in size from tiny zooplankton (animals that drift on surface currents and graze on algae) to gigantic squid, fish, and whales that roam the deep seas.

Many water creatures are invertebrates (animals without backbones). They include arthropods (joint-footed animals with outside skeletons) such as shrimp and crabs; molluscs (soft-bodied muscular animals) such as clams, oysters, snails, squids, octopus, and the ancient nautilus; echinoderms (spiny creatures that slide along the bottom) such as sea stars and sea cucumbers; and cnidaria (almost transparent saclike animals with tentacles around their mouths) such as jellyfish, the sea anemone, and other coral animals that live in colonies and whose skeletons build coral reefs. Aquatic habitats also contain many vertebrates (animals with backbones). They include fish (swimmers with scales, gills, streamlined bodies, and fins) such as sharks, colorful reef fish, electric eels, bass and other native Illinois fish; and amphibia (animals with slimy skin that hatch from eggs in the water, then grow legs and move on land) such as frogs and salamanders. They also include reptiles (animals with lungs, scales, and claws) such as snakes, lizards, iguanas, and turtles (good swimmers but they must come up for air); and ocean mammals (streamlined swimmers with lungs and hair that produce milk for their young) such as dolphins, seals, sea lions, walruses, and whales.

## John G. Shedd Aquarium (2 to 6 hours)

1200 S. Lake Shore Drive
Chicago, Illinois 60605
(312) 939-2438

Hours: weekends, holidays, and daily in summer, 9 A.M.-6 P.M. September–May, 9 A.M.–5 P.M.
Closed Christmas and New Year's Day.
Admission: Fee. Thursdays, free admission to aquarium only. Half price for aquarium and oceanarium.
Access: wheelchairs and strollers available. Enter south of main entrance.
Facilities: Restaurants. Library. Gift shop.

Explore the underwater realm—an oceanarium, six galleries with fish from different parts of the world, and a coral reef exhibit—without scuba equipment. Marvel at acrobatic dolphins, graceful squids, colorful fish, and flowerlike coral creatures. Get close to dangerous sharks and electric eels; and watch sponges, snails, and sea stars that live on the bottom of the ocean.

Begin your undersea adventure at the Coral Reef—a circular ninety-thousand-gallon tank with examples of the colorful fish and coral that inhabit this tropical shallow ocean ecosystem. At feeding time (weekdays, 11 A.M. and 2 P.M.; weekends, 11 A.M., 2 P.M., 3 P.M.), watch agile turtles and a hungry six-foot-long shark gather around a diver.

Step inside the Oceanarium for a breathtaking view of Whale Harbor, the world's largest indoor saltwater pool, and Lake Michigan. Take a seat in the amphitheater to watch trainers in wetsuits encourage dolphins to demonstrate their physical and mental prowess. Go to the tidepool, where sea stars, pink chitons, and surf perch find refuge at low tide, and to the sea-otter pool. You can view dolphins, otters, and ghostlike beluga whales underwater, and find gentoo, Magellanic, and rockhopper penguins on a rocky shoreline. A variety of exhibits reveal the biodiversity and survival strategies of marine animals.

Stroll through six galleries representing different aquatic ecosystems. See a moray eel at Animals of the Caribbean; shark eggs, seahorses, a stingray, an ancient nautilus, and a "flashlight fish" at Animals of the Indo-Pacific. Look for Animals of Cold Oceans, where the John Woodworth Leslie Sea Anemone Exhibit contains a remarkable variety of coral reef residents. Don't miss the large rust-colored octopus slithering down a wall. At Animals of the Great Lakes, look for sportfishing favorites: salmon and trout, and the prehistoric sturgeon. At Freshwater Animals of the Americas, watch electric eels that produce a six-hundred-volt shock, and look at lungfish, stingrays, and river turtles. At Animals of Warm Fresh Water, see kissing gouramis, and piranhas that can devour a large animal in seconds. The Australian lungfish may be a 350-million-year-old link between land and water animals.

Solve mysteries of the deep on self-guided or group tours, at Youth and Family programs, night classes, the Adventures in Nature lecture series, and overnighters with classes and activities about sea animals and ecology. Come for programs during Water Quality Month and Wetland Month in autumn; and for Winterbreak and other seasonal festivals that offer crafts, experiments, and lakefront activities. Summer Worlds, a camp for six- to fourteen-year-olds, provides aquarium activities in conjunction with the Field Museum and Adler Planetarium.

### Lincoln Park Zoo (2 to 4 hours)
2200 N. Cannon Drive
Chicago, IL 60614
(312) 742-2000

Hours: Every day. Grounds, 8 A.M.–5 P.M. Buildings, 10 A.M.–5 P.M.
Admission: Free.
Access: Wheelchair accessible.
Facilities: Restaurants. Cafes. Shops.
Tours: Bird walks in Rookery: April, May, September, October, meet Sunday, Tuesday, and Thursday at 8:30 A.M. in front of the McCormick Bird House.

View a world-class collection of gorillas, chimpanzees, and other primates and see African lions, arctic bears, and antarctic penguins. Stroll through buildings and outdoor enclosures with large mammals, and lagoons with splashing waterfowl in this zoo near the heart of Chicago.

If you adore the antics of primates, enter the Lester E. Fisher Great Ape House. (The zoo has a breeding program for these endangered primates.) Orangutans often hunker down, but agile chimpanzees climb poles and gorillas climb rope nets and balance like tightrope walkers. At the Helen Brach Primate House you will see acrobatic gibbons and hear howler monkeys. At Kovler Lion House, watch leopards and other big cats in cages adorned with vegetation and paintings that re-create their natural habitats.

The Joseph Regenstein Large Mammal Area has an elephant training session. You will also see the tall giraffe, the nearsighted rhinoceros, the red-toed capybara (the largest rodent), and the pigmy hippopotamus.

If you are a bird lover, watch waterfowl in the lagoons and see birds of the savanna, seashore, and wetland in the McCormick Bird House. Take a bird walk in the Rookery (see times above).

Other zoo attractions include outdoor enclosures with camels, zebras, and alpacas; the Robert R. McCormick Bear and Wolf Habitat; Koala Plaza; Penguins and seabirds; and Farm-in-the-Zoo. The Pritzker Children's Zoo has mammals, birds, and reptiles and hands-on fun at Conservation Station.

Watch Animals in Action—feedings of great apes, seals, and sea lions. Or attend an elephant workout and Wildlife Encounters with reptiles, mammals, and birds of prey. Look out for Curiosity Carts, activity stations on conservation, and farm events. Come for the ZooLights Festival and enjoy ice sculptures, wildlife outlined in lights, holiday scenes, music, and children's activities (November 29 to December 31, nights, except Christmas). (The zoo is open Christmas Day.)

##  Brookfield Zoo (2 to 4 hours)

1st Avenue and 31st Street
Brookfield, IL 60513
(708) 485-0263
(773) 242-2630

Getting there: Located in Brookfield, 13 miles west of downtown Chicago. Take I-290 (Eisenhower Expressway) west and exit at 1st Avenue south. Go south on First to the entrance at 31st Street. Or take the Burlington Northern commuter line or PACE bus.

Hours: Animal exhibits: daily, 10 A.M.–4:30 P.M. Dolphin shows: weekdays, 11:30 A.M., 2:30 P.M.; weekends and holidays, 1 P.M., 3 P.M.
Admission: Entrance fee. Parking fee.Dolphin Show fee. From October to March, Tuesdays and Thursdays are free.
Access: Wheelchair and stroller rentals.

Take safaris to Habitat Africa!, Seven Seas Panorama, Tropic World: A Primate's Journey, The Fragile Kingdom, The Swamp: Wonders of Our Wetlands, and twenty other major exhibits. You will have close encounters with almost four hundred species of birds and beasts in naturalized outdoor enclosures and superb indoor habitats.

Habitat Africa! has a waterhole and a kopje (rocky outcrop) where you can view zebras, giraffes, ostriches, African wild dogs, and other animals of the savanna. Seven Seas Panorama offers sea lions and harbor seals swimming in outdoor pools, and indoor dolphin presentations. At Tropic World: A Primate's Journey, scan the rainforest scenery for a giant anteater, a golden lion tamarin, and a two-toed sloth climbing head down. In the Asian section, look for gibbons, tree shrews, small-clawed otters, and an orangutan. Pass through the doors to African Habitat, where gorillas reside.

At The Fragile Kingdom, wander through an Asian rainforest for a glimpse of a python, a snake that swallows rats whole. Go on to the African desert for a look at a naked mole-rat and a rock hyrax—the elephant's closest relative. At The Swamp: Wonders of Our Wetlands, enjoy alligators, turtles, and frogs; and see otters and game fish in an Illinois Wetland.

Outdoors, you will find big cats, giraffes, endangered animals, Ibex Mountain, Bear Grotto, and a children's zoo.

The Small Mammal House has a harvest mouse so small it can build its nest on a blade of grass. The Australia House contains hairy-nosed wombats. The Pachyderm House has elephants, rhinoceros, and hippopotamus. The Reptile House offers a grand collection of venomous snakes, lizards, alligators, and turtles. Also look for a giant cockroach, tarantula, and scorpion. Find flamingos, penguins, pelicans, and other birds in birdhouses and outdoor lagoons.

Come for year-round fun with the animals. Programs (for preschoolers, children over twelve, teens, and adults) vary throughout the year and cover subjects such as conservation, the swamp, and many animal topics. Families are welcome at Windows into the Zoo—hour-long tours of different animal areas. Celebrate wild beasts at Ground-hog Day in February, National Pig Day in March, and Affie Elephant's Birthday Party in June. During the May Memorial Day Weekend Festival, see animal action at the children's zoo and elephant demonstrations. At the July Fourth Celebration, enjoy the Animals in Action show and Native North American animals. In August, come for the Teddy Bear Picnic, with a teddy bear contest and "bearious" other activities. In September, look at the photo contest display. In October come for the Zoo Run Run. Join in a three-kilometer walk, a five-kilometer run, or a half-mile Fun Run (open to children age ten and under and to young adults with physical disabilities) that supports animals at the zoo and in the wild. (Registration required: Call (708) 485-0263.) At the November Thanksgiving Day Feast, assist Children's Zookeepers. At the December Holiday Magic Festival, spend a joyful night with storytellers and musical groups. In spring, enter the Brookfield Zoo Photo Contest, (708) 485-0263, ext. 352.

*12*

# Museums on the Wild Side

"All my life through, the new sights of Nature made me rejoice like a child."
—Marie Curie (1867–1934), physicist

Escape Chicago's spring rains, summer heat, and winter snows with an indoor array of nature's wonders. Peer at the heavens. Dive under the sea. Meet the entire animal kingdom. Immerse yourself in habitats, from arctic to tropical. Or go back in time with rocks and fossils, Native Americans and pioneers. See the environment as it is and as it used to be. Take a walk on the wild side at Chicago's many museums.

### 🌿🌿🌿 Adler Planetarium and Astronomy Museum (2 to 5 hours)
1300 S. Lake Shore Drive
Chicago, IL 60605
(312) 322-0325

Tour the sky and discover how stars and other heavenly bodies influence nature on Earth. (See Chapter 4.)

## 🍃🍃🍃 The Art Institute of Chicago (1 to 4 hours)

111 S. Michigan Avenue
Chicago, IL 60603-6110
(312) 443-3600

Hours: Monday, Wednesday, Thursday, Friday, 10:30 A.M.–4:30 P.M. Tuesday, 10:30 A.M.–8 P.M. Saturday, 10 A.M.–5 P.M. Sunday and holidays, noon–5 P.M.
Admission: Fee. Suggested fee for adults, $7.00; for children, students, and seniors, $3.50. Tuesdays are free.
Access: Wheelchairs and strollers available.
Facilities: Library. Restaurants. Checkroom. Shop.

Masterpieces of sculpture and painting reveal the awe-inspiring, lovely, threatening, and strange aspects of nature. See how artists often employ animals—such as a lion for strength or a dove for peace—to express human qualities or abstract ideas. You will be fascinated by the colors and lines in landscapes and by the grandeur of mountains, the mystery of forests, and the fury of the sea.

Come for daily lectures or gallery walks, or for special events. Group tours can be arranged. Let the animals and plants represented in ancient Egyptian, Greek, Etruscan, and Roman art transport you into the world of the supernatural; the African and Native American art bring you new perspectives on human qualities. Allow fruits, flowers, trees, and beasts in still lifes by Henry Matisse and Pablo Picasso, scenes by Vincent van Gogh and Paul Gauguin, and abstract sculpture by Alexander Calder give you an appreciation of nature's influence in everyday life.

Sense the mystery and power of the natural world in landscapes by Jean Baptiste Camille Corot, Gustave Courbet, Joseph Mallord William Turner, Jules Breton, Peter Blume, and Henry Rousseau. Delight in the colors of sunlight in the artistry of Claude Monet.

All these masterworks of art offer you new insights into wilderness and the dynamic forces of the natural world in which you live.

## 🍃🍃 Chicago Academy of Sciences (1 to 2 hours)

North Pier
435 E. Illinois Street, 3rd Floor
Chicago, IL 60614
(773) 549-0606

Hours: Monday to Friday, 9:30 A.M.–4:30 P.M. Saturday, 10 A.M.–6 P.M. Sunday, noon–6 P.M. Closed Thanksgiving, Christmas, and New Year's Day.
Admission: Fee.
Note: By mid-1998, the museum will be in a new building at Fullerton and Cannon Drive in Lincoln Park.

Greet live animals, take part in science demonstrations, and listen to stories that reveal the wonders of nature and science. Adventurous children and adults can enjoy hands-on exhibits such as the Water Works Lab, where a replica of the Chicago River and lock system demonstrates the complex control of nature; and the Children's Gallery, where games, storytelling, and other activities introduce basic concepts of natural history.

Many special events correspond to the changing seasons. Celebrate Earth Day in April, and meet iguanas, snakes, turtles, and frogs at the September HerPETological Weekend. Knee-High Naturalists (four- to five-year-olds) can attend monthly programs; four- to twelve-year-olds can come for week-long summer day camps; and teens may participate in December activities. Families are welcome at Weekend Adventures related to nature and science. Teachers are invited for professional development classes on environmental and other sciences.

## Chicago Historical Society (1 to 3 hours)
Clark Street at North Avenue
Chicago, IL 60614-6099
(312) 642-4600
Hours: Monday–Saturday, 9:30 A.M.–4:30 P.M. Sunday, noon–5 P.M.
Admission: Fee. Mondays are free.
Access: Wheelchairs available, adjacent parking.
Facilities: Library. Cafe. Gift shop.

Chicago's natural and human history comes alive as you view the tools of pioneer life and the products, photographs, and paintings of the city. Original documents and captivating exhibits take you back to the events that shaped this great midwestern city.

In the Chicago History Galleries, learn about the symbolism of the Chicago flag, with blue stripes representing the North and South branches of the Chicago River and four stars standing for the Fort

Dearborn Massacre of 1812, the Chicago Fire of 1871, the World's Fair of 1893, and the Century of Progress, 1833 to 1933. Investigate how Chicago changed from a wilderness outpost to a growing town. Look at a pioneer home, farm equipment, a covered wagon, printing machines, and demonstrations of frontier life.

Become acquainted with the Union Stockyards, where cattle, sheep, and pigs that grazed western rangeland were slaughtered. Discover how nature's raw materials and a strategic lakeshore location made Chicago a manufacturing and merchandising center. Find out how speculators at the Chicago Board of Trade and the Chicago Mercantile Exchange made fortunes on wheat, corn, and soybeans grown on farms. Don't miss the Bootlegging display, which shows how fermented grain in alcoholic beverages gave rise to gang warfare during Prohibition (from 1919 to 1933, when alcohol was illegal); and to Chicago's reputation as a gangster city.

Take advantage of gallery walks and group tours by reservation. Attend demonstrations of pioneer life and lectures on Chicago's natural and human history, famous citizens, and city planners. Children's Summer Camp, in conjunction with Lincoln Park Zoo, links Chicago history with nature. February Winterbreak presents winter on the prairie, with Illinois folk songs and traditional life activities.

## 🍃 Chicago Children's Museum (½ to 2 hours)
Navy Pier
700 E. Grand Avenue, Suite 127
Chicago , IL 60611-3428
(312) 527-1000
Hours: Tuesday–Sunday, 10 A.M.–5 P.M. Thursday, 10 A.M.–8 P.M. Memorial Day–Labor Day, open every day.
Admission: Fee. Thursdays are free.
Access: Friendly and encouraging for children with physical disabilities.

Child's play is great fun here, where hands-on exhibits foster understanding and respect for nature. Six- to ten-year-olds can uncover the secrets of the Stinking Truth about Garbage; preschoolers can follow Treehouse Trails; and all children can do experiments at Waterways. Climbing Schooner, a fantasy version of a lake-faring vessel, sets the stage for programs about the Great Lakes and the Chicago River. PlayMaze offers adventures in an urban environment. Lies about Animals—with photographs, specimens, and a game—reveals the truth about misunderstood insects, snakes, and other creatures. Changing displays and programs may offer Native American stories, family nights, youth concerts, art, or a variety of experiences with nature.

### 🌲🌲🌲 The Field Museum (2 to 6 hours)

Lake Shore Drive at Roosevelt Road
Chicago, IL 60605-2496
(312) 922-9410
(312) 341-9299 TDD

Hours: Daily, 9 A.M.–5 P.M. Closed Thanksgiving, Christmas, and New Year's Day.
Admission: Fee. Wednesdays are free.
Access: Wheelchairs at Coat Check, first floor, and west door.
Facilities: Shops. Library. Cafeteria.

Explore the earth and its people in this magnificent museum. Venture across America to Africa, Asia, and other parts of the world. Look at artwork from many cultures, Portraits of Man, and a mind-boggling collection of plants, animals, fossils, and precious stones from all over the world. Follow "nature trails" through various continents and artistically rendered habitats.

Begin your visit by walking under a dinosaur. Then see two fighting African elephants in Stanley Field Hall (Main Floor Lobby).

At Life Over Time (one to two hours), take a journey that begins with the origins of life nearly four billion years ago. Take a Dive to Old Chicago, four hundred and ten million years ago, and see fossils found at Mazon Creek near Chicago. Then enter Jurassic time, three hundred and fifty million years ago, to view dinosaur dioramas, skeletons, and paintings. Don't miss the Great Plains, forty million years ago; Darwin's Origin of Species; Ice Station Chicago; and Teeth, Tusks, and Tar Pits.

At east-side exhibits, compare your size with other creatures and marvel at the diversity of the insect world. See the American bison, buckskin clothing, food-gathering gear, the paraphernalia of medicine men, and trade items in Indian galleries.

On the west side, find a world of birds and headless, spineless, and legless beasts in What Is an Animal? Take a Nature Walk through wetlands, cliffs, prairie, ocean shores, woodlands, and local lakes and see animals adapted to these environments. Find Messages from the Wilderness, eighteen artistically rendered habitats with native animals. Experience the World of Mammals by listening to whale songs and learning how moving continents influence animal evolution. At the African exhibits, see a splendid savanna scene with cheetah, giraffe, and elephants. See if you can recognize gorilla sounds or track animals by identifying their spoor (footprints) and dung (droppings).

Stroll around the balcony and enjoy Malvina Hoffman's Portraits of Man—an extraordinary series of sculptures that illustrates the diversity of the human species.

The Grainger Hall of Gems displays dazzling jewels, including pearls and coral made by animals. At Plants of the World, find out what plant parts you eat and drink, and what plants are deadly. See spices that influenced history; grasses that feed the world; legumes that fertilize the soil; and plants that produce fiber, wood, and medicine.

Tours of museum highlights take place Monday through Thursday at 11 A.M. and 2 P.M. A calendar lists the schedule of lectures, courses for adults and children, and events such as overnights, Earth Day, music fests, workshops, Chicago wilderness field trips, and holiday programming in celebration of Chicago's cultural diversity.

## 🌿🌿🌿 Museum of Science and Industry (2 to 6 hours)

57th Street and Lake Shore Drive
Chicago, IL 60637-2093
(773) 684-1414
(773) 684-DEAF TDD

Hours: Between Labor Day and Memorial Day: Monday–Friday, 9:30 A.M.–4 P.M., Saturday, Sunday, and holidays, 9:30 A.M.–5:30 P.M. Extended hours in summer.

Admission: Fee. Thursdays are free. Purchase combined ticket for Omnimax Theater.

Access: Wheelchair accessible from the Henry Crown Space Center, east side.

Facilities: Restaurants. Shops. Theaters.

Discover how science solves the mysteries of the natural world and how technology taps natural resources for human benefit. Perform experiments, push buttons, use computers, and see live demonstrations at exhibits organized in seven zones: Communication, Energy and Environment (look for a major environment exhibit in the near future), Human Body, Manufacturing, Space and Defense, Transportation, and Imagination Station (a children's area).

See if you can figure out how the Foucault pendulum demonstrates the earth's rotation. Watch baby chicks hatch out of eggs. Travel through a coal mine and explore for oil. Explore the birth of the universe and the evolution of stars and black holes. Investigate earthquakes, volcanic eruptions, and mountain-building. Find out about evolution and "primordial soup," where life may have begun with a flash of lightning. See the History Wall: Landmarks in Science, for breakthroughs in understanding nature. At Energy Lab, What's Watt reveals how much electricity Americans consume each day, and a computer allows you to calculate your radiation exposure. The Henry Crown Space Center and the Omnimax Theater offer outer space and Earth wilderness adventures.

## Suburban Museums

###  Cernan Earth and Space Center (2 hours)

Triton College
2000 5th Avenue
River Grove, IL 60171
(708) 583-3100
(708) 456-0300 ext. 3372 for field trips and special events

Attend monthly skywatches and come for films on astronomy. See Chapter 4.

###  Isle à La Cache Museum (1 to 2 hours)

501 E. Romeo Road
Romeoville, IL 60441
(815) 886-1467

Enter the past, when French voyageurs and Native Americans roamed the prairie and rivers of Illinois. See Chapter 6.

## 🦋🦋 Lizzadro Museum of Lapidary Art (1 to 2 hours)

Wilder Park
220 Cottage Hill Avenue
Elmhurst, IL 60126
(630) 833-1616

Getting there: Located in Elmhurst, 17 miles west of Chicago. Take I-290 (the Eisenhower Expressway) west. Exit at St. Charles Road west and drive west along St. Charles Road past York Road to Cottage Hill Avenue. Turn north on Cottage Hill to the museum in Wilder Park.
Hours: Tuesday to Saturday, 10 A.M.–5 P.M., Sunday, 1 P.M.–5 P.M.
Admission: Fee. Children under 13, active members of the Armed Forces, and teachers with school groups are free. Fridays are free.
Access: Accessible for physically disabled visitors.

See a multitude of minerals—the source of diamonds, gold, and silver; the substances from which nuclear and fossil fuels are extracted; and the raw materials from which glass, steel, and many manufactured products are made. Admire a variety of gems and enjoy exhibits featuring lapidary art and artists that change every six months.

Roam the art gallery with delightful dioramas of forest, wetland, coral reef, and desert environments. Look closely and you will find obsidian stag beetles, tiger's-eye turtles, serpentine cacti, and agate fishes. Be sure to examine the cases beneath the dioramas, for they contain large mineral specimens, including petrified oak and quartz. Notice the splendid stone carvings, the blue jade Imperial Pagoda, and the stone mosaic picture. Amid the jewelry, you will come upon a sixty-seven–carat aquamarine.

Downstairs, the Rocks and Minerals of Illinois exhibit contains fluorite, the official state mineral. Don't miss Castle Lizzadro, a miniature castle of eighteen-carat gold with diamonds that rests on amethyst, malachite, and azurite "mountains" surrounded by a Brazilian agate "lake."

Come on Sunday afternoon for the video Collecting Earth's Natural Treasures if you want advice about starting a mineral and fossil collection. On select Saturdays, seven-year-olds to adults are welcomed at programs on topics that range from lapidary (such as faceting stones and stone carving) and Native American burial grounds to paleontology, earth science, anthropology, and archaeology. Group tours should be arranged in advance.

## 🍃 Garfield Farm Museum (1 to 3 hours)

3 N016 Garfield Road
La Fox, IL 60147
(630) 584-8485

Getting there: Located 5 miles west of Geneva, about 40 miles northwest of Chicago, off Illinois Route 38 on Garfield Road.
Hours: June to September: Wednesday, and Sunday, 1-4 P.M., or by appointment any time during the year.
Admission: Donations.

Experience a working farm on the 280 acres of an 1840s farmstead. Tour the original buildings and see a demonstration prairie plot. Meet the animals that prairie farmers raised, such as Devon oxen, merino rams, and black java chickens.

Come for one of the monthly prairie walks. Hike through a ten-thousand-year-old unplowed prairie, wetlands, and oak savanna. Or attend a Fruit Tree Grafting Seminar (which emphasizes antique apple grafting) in March; the Rare Breeds Livestock Show in May; and the Heirloom Garden Show in August. Attend programs on prairie restoration, antique roses, bluebird and bat boxes, and more. Group tours can be arranged.

## 🍃 Jurica Nature Museum (1 to 2 hours)

School Science Center
Illinois Benedictine College
Maple Avenue and College Road
Lisle, IL 60532
(630) 829-6545

Getting there: Located in Lisle, 25 miles southwest of Chicago. Take I-290 (Eisenhower Expressway) west and continue on Route 88 west. Exit Route 88 at Route 53 south. Go south on Route 53 to Maple Avenue. Turn west on Maple to College Road (Yackley Road). The museum is on the Illinois Benedictine College campus.
Hours: Tuesday–Friday, 1–5 P.M. Sunday, 2–4 P.M. Closed when college is not in session.
Admission: Free.

See strange and wonderful beasts such as marine animals, insects, birds, anteaters, and bears that were collected by two Benedictine monks.

Enjoy a large diorama of the African savanna with antelope, giraffe, zebra, and other animals; and a northern Illinois diorama with wetlands, woodlands, and prairie as it was two hundred years ago. You can also view small habitat displays of the North American desert, tropical rainforest, salt marsh, and mangrove swamp. Don't miss the whale and gorilla skeletons or the Extinct and Endangered exhibit. Ask about tours and workshops for elementary science teachers.

*13*

# Outdoor Action

"Nature bats last."
—Bumper sticker, 1989

If you are sports-minded, Chicago offers many wild spots for outdoor recreation. In spring, hike on riverbanks and in forests filled with wildflowers. In summer, roller-blade through gardens, fish in lagoons, and sail or swim in the refreshingly cool water of Lake Michigan. In autumn, bike through colorful forests and play golf in scenic parkland. In winter, ski on the beach, ice-skate on frozen ponds, and toboggan near nature centers. Whether you seek team sports, therapeutic programs, or instruction, you will find that Chicago has many leisure activities linked with nature.

## Basketball
Three on Three Basketball Tournament
(312) 744-3315
Taps Gallagher: (708) 690-2078

Compete in a half-court basketball tournament with three players on each team. It attracts five hundred teams in three divisions. The basketball competition is part of the July Inner City Games, with swimming, baseball, soccer, and track and field in an Olympics-type competition. Cosponsored by the Mayor's Office of Special Events, the Chicago Bulls, and the Chicago Park District, it benefits many Chicago charities.

# Biking

Obtain bike trail maps from any of the following organizations:

Chicagoland Bicycle Federation
343 S. Dearborn Street
Chicago, IL 60604
(312) 42-PEDAL

Attend meetings on the third Tuesday of each month for technical advice and safety tips. Join scheduled rides that range from leisurely to fast.

Chicago Park District
(312) 747-2200
(312) 747-2001 TDD

Ride eighteen miles of bike paths through city parks. New paths are being added.

Chicagoland Trails Northeastern Illinois Planning Commission
400 W. Madison Street
Chicago, IL 60606
(312) 454-0400

Forest Preserve District of Cook County
536 N. Harlem Avenue
River Forest, IL 60305
(312) 261-8400
(708) 366-9420
(800) 870-3666
(708) 771-1190 TDD

Ride eighty miles of bike trails along rivers and through meadows and forests in the Cook County forest preserves. A sampling:

## 🍂 Busse Woods Trail

Follow an eight-mile loop through wooded areas, around lakes, and near an elk pasture.

Many sports teams have animal names that symbolize how tough they are. For example:

**Chicago Blackhawks (hockey), Chicago Cubs (baseball), Chicago Bears (football), and Chicago Bulls (basketball).**

## North Branch of the Chicago River

Pass through woodlands and the Skokie Lagoons on the way to the Chicago Botanic Garden.

## Salt Creek Trail

Follow a six-and-one-half-mile path along Salt Creek that enters woods, passes Brookfield Zoo, and goes to the Wolf Road Prairie.

## Tinley Creek Bike Trail

Ride an eighteen-mile-long path through woods near Arrowhead and Turtlehead lakes and Midlothian Reservoir.

## Lakefront Ramble

Pedal twenty-four miles through parks with splendid views of the Chicago skyline and major museums and other attractions on the Lake Michigan shoreline.

Start at Foster Avenue near the Lake Michigan shore. Travel south along the lakefront through Lincoln Park past the Lincoln Park Zoo and Chicago Historical Society. Bike through Grant Park, near the Art Institute and Buckingham Fountain. Detour east along Solidarity Drive past Shedd Aquarium and the Adler Planetarium for splendid views of the city skyline. Return to Lake Shore Drive and the Field Museum. Continue south past Soldier Field and McCormick Place to Jackson Park, with the Museum of Science and Industry and Paul H. Douglas Nature Sanctuary. For details on the Lake Michigan shoreline see Chapter 2, for museums see Chapter 12, for lakefront parks see Chapter 10, and for animals along the way see Chapter 11.

**Sheridan Road Trail**

Start at South Boulevard and Sheridan Road in Evanston. Head north along Sheridan Road to the Chicago Botanic Garden at Lake-Cook Road. You will have glimpses of Lake Michigan as you ride past Northwestern University, residential areas, and suburban parks with wooded areas.

Jim Hochgesang, author of *Hiking and Biking in Cook County, Illinois,* suggests the following bike paths north of Chicago:

 **Des Plaines River Trail in Lake County**

Start at Russell Road (near Highway 41 and the Wisconsin state line) and go south along the Des Plaines River to the Half Day Forest Preserve in Lincolnshire. You will travel twenty-two miles on mostly flat paths through woods, savanna, and the Des Plaines River Wetland Demonstration Project in Wadsworth. Farther south, you will pass through MacArthur Woods in Libertyville and end at Half Day Forest Preserve in Lincolnshire.

 **Deer Grove Forest Preserve Trail**

Follow this eight-mile trail in Palatine. Begin at Dundee and Quentin roads and wind through meadows, woodlands, a creek, and ravines.

 **Illinois and Michigan National Heritage Corridor**

I & M Canal State Trail
P.O. Box 272
Morris, IL 60450
(815) 942-0796

Bike along sections of a ninety-six-mile-long canal that echoes with the history of Native Americans and the settlement of the American West. The trail goes from Chicago to La Salle/Peru, past the Chicago Portage National Historic Site, river locks, early farm towns, state parks, and other nature preserves (see Chapter 9).

Suggested books on bike excursions:
  *Chicago Bicycle Guidebook*, by Michael Palucki
  *Hiking and Biking in Cook County, Illinois*, by Jim Hochgesang

For more suburban bike trails:

DuPage County Bikeways
DuPage County Regional Planning Commission
(708) 682-7230

Illinois Bikeways
Illinois Department of Conservation
524 S. 2nd Street, Room 500
Springfield, IL 62701-1787
(217) 782-7454

Illinois Prairie Path Trail
P.O. Box 1086
Wheaton, IL 60189
(708) 752-0120

Kane County, Fox River,
Great Western, and
Virgil L. Gilman Bike Trails
Kane County Forest Preserve District
719 Batavia Avenue, Building G
Geneva, IL 60134
(708) 232-1242

# Boating

Cool breezes and calm water make sailing, canoeing, kayaking, and motorboating a pleasure on Chicago's lakes, rivers, and canals.

## 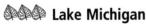 Lake Michigan

Enjoy twenty-eight miles of shoreline with spectacular views of Chicago.The boating season begins in mid-May and finishes in mid-October. During that time, you can take lessons, rent a fishing charter, take harbor cruises or party boats, enter regattas, and watch the annual parade of boats on Venetian Night.

## Chicago Park District Harbors

About five thousand boats are docked at the nine city harbors, where boating activities include lessons and regattas as well as rentals and docking and launching facilities.

Belmont Harbor
3200 N. on Lake Shore Drive
Chicago, IL 60657
(773) 742-7673

Burnham Harbor
1200 S. on Lake Shore Drive
Chicago, IL 60605
(773) 747-7009

Diversey Harbor
2800 N. on Lake Shore Drive
Chicago, IL 60657
(773) 742-7762

59th Street Harbor
5900 S. on Lake Shore Drive
Chicago, IL 60607
(773) 747-7019

Jackson Inner and Outer Harbors
6400 S. on Lake Shore Drive
Chicago, IL 60607
(773) 747-6189

Monroe Harbor
100 S. on Lake Shore Drive
Chicago, IL 60603
(773) 742-7643

Montrose Harbor
4400 N. on Lake Shore Drive
Chicago, IL 60640
(773) 742-7527

Calumet Harbor
9500 S. on Lake Shore Drive
(launch ramps only)
Chicago, IL 60619

Note: When it is not boating season, call the Marine Department, (312) 747-0737.

Yacht clubs at harbors sponsor regattas (sailing races) and other special events.

## Sailing

Chicago Park District and Westrec Corporation
Contact:
Ted Sutherland
Coordinator for sailing programs
(312) 747-0739

Learn the basics between mid-June and Labor Day.

The Rainbow Fleet Program is for anyone over ten years old. Choose group classes (four three-hour sessions), or individual lessons (five one-hour sessions) that meet during a one-week period. You will learn sailing terminology, right-of-way rules, calculating speed in knots, and how to read the wind. Practice how to launch, dock, and capsize the boat and right it again. Then take written and "on the water" tests that cover sailing fundamentals so you can sail a small boat in good weather.

The Judd Goldman Adaptive Program is for people with disabilities (see below).

Special sailing events include a formal regatta on Labor Day weekend, when sailboats leave Burnham Harbor to compete on racing courses a distance from the Lake Michigan shore.

## Suburban Boating

Forest Preserve District of Cook County
536 N. Harlem Avenue
River Forest, IL 60305
(312) 261-8400
(708) 366-9420
(800) 870-3666
(708) 771-1190 TDD

From the Skokie Lagoons in the north to Saganashkee Slough in the south, you will find boat ramps and boating waters. Obtain a Forest Preserves Facilities map and boating waters guide. Some scenic waterways:

###  Des Plaines River
In the northwestern suburbs from Wheeling to Lemont

### Skokie Lagoons
In the northern suburbs from Glencoe to Winnetka

### Little Calumet River
On the south side of Chicago and in Riverdale

### Illinois and Michigan National Heritage Corridor
Along the Chicago, Des Plaines, and Illinois rivers, and the Illinois and Michigan Canal from Chicago ninety-six miles to Peru/LaSalle. (See Chapter 9.)

## Canoeing
Chicagoland Canoe Base
4019 N. Naragansett Street
Chicago, IL 60634
(773) 777-1489

"The canoe was responsible for the early discovery, settlement, and trade and commerce in our area," says Ralph Frese, who started the Annual Des Plaines River Canoe Marathon. Many canoeists join him on Chicago's rivers to celebrate the New Year, on nights of the full moon, and at more traditional times. He also builds canoes, sells gear, and knows the river trails in the Chicago region.

Many Chicago-area streams have been dammed or straightened. Yet they appeal to canoeists for their scenery, history, fishing, and wildlife. Frese recommends the following one-day excursions:

### Skokie Lagoons
Launch: Below main control dam on Willow Road, east of I-94 in Winnetka, 18 miles north of Chicago

Paddle through seven miles of wooded scenery in Winnetka and Glencoe. You will be surrounded by birdsongs and see deer and other wildlife. From the main control dam at Willow Road, go northward taking the right-hand channels. Portage over small control dams and one causeway until you arrive at Dundee Road. Turn south and again take the right-hand channels.

## 🍃🍃 Winter Canoe Ride, Skokie Lagoons

Launch: Main control dam on Willow Road, east of I-94 in Winnetka, 18 miles north of Chicago.

From the Willow Road dam, paddle south down the Skokie Branch (East Fork) of the North Branch of the Chicago River six miles to Dempster Street in Morton Grove. The Harms Woods section in Glenview is particularly scenic and has wildlife.

In summer, extend your trip to Whealan Pool at Devon Avenue (6400 N.) or to the junction with the North Shore Channel at Foster Avenue (5200 N.) and Albany Avenue in Chicago.

## 🍃🍃 Bahai Temple to Baja Beach Club

Launch: North side of the North Shore Channel, opposite the Bahai Temple at the junction of Sheridan Road at Linden Avenue, Wilmette, 16 miles north of Chicago.

Take an unusual canoe trip from the Bahai Temple in Wilmette, a northern suburb, to the Baja Beach Club at North Pier, in downtown Chicago. You pass through woodlands, the Ladd Arboretum, residential neighborhoods, boatyards, and industrial areas. At Wolf Point, where the North Branch and Main Branch of the Chicago River meet, paddle east on the Main Branch past skyscrapers, excursion boats, and the jet of water that periodically shoots across the river in commemoration of river cleanup. Enter the inner harbor of the Port of Chicago where a lock separates the river from the higher waters of Lake Michigan. To the left is Ogden Slip, a channel dug as part of the Illinois and Michigan Canal. Dock at North Pier, where cargo from Great Lakes freighters was transferred to river barges in the past, and disembark for refreshment at the Baja Beach Club.

##  The Annual Des Plaines River Canoe Marathon

Sunday before Memorial Day weekend

Launch: Canoe landing at Oak Spring Road and the Des Plaines River, Libertyville, 35 miles north of Chicago.

Canoe through picturesque woodlands with deer and beaver cuttings. Along the Des Plaines River you will pass Ryerson Nature Preserve near Half Day Road and River Trail Nature Center at Milwaukee Avenue south of Wheeling. The finish line is at Dam 2 in the Cook County Forest Preserve south of Wheeling.

##  Chicago Portage Canoe Trail

Launch: Stony Ford on the Des Plaines River west of Joliet Road, Lyons, 12 miles west of Chicago. Obtain maps from:

Forest Preserve District of Cook County
536 N. Harlem Avenue
River Forest, IL 60305
(312) 261-8400
(708) 366-9420
(800) 870-3666
(708) 771-1190 TDD

Follow the historic water route of Louis Joliet and Father Jacques Marquette on the Des Plaines River. (See Chapter 9.) The trail from Stony Ford to Columbia Woods is 7.5 miles; from Columbia Woods to the Lemont Landing, 6.9 miles; and all the way from Stony Ford to Lemont Landing, 14.4 miles. As you journey south and west on the Des Plaines River, you will parallel the Chicago Sanitary and Ship Canal and the Illinois and Michigan Canal. You will pass Laughton Ford, the site of a trading post, where the Ottawa Trail crosses the river. Just east of Laughton Ford, south of 47th Street, stop to see the monument at the Chicago Portage that commemorates where Father Jacques Marquette and Louis Joliet crossed in 1673. South of Willow Springs Road, the river looks wild again as you paddle through Columbia Woods. Pass under bridges at Lemont Road and Stephen Street to disembark on the north side of the river at Lemont Landing.

From Lemont downstream, you may see great numbers of herons and egrets, or spot deer and beaver in the wetlands. You will come upon the largest island in the Des Plaines River—Isle à La Cache, with a museum (see Chapter 6). Just above Lockport is a dam owned by Material Service Corporation (caution: it is under the bridge). After an easy portage under the right side of the bridge, the river widens and flows over bedrock and braids its way through many islands, creating "fishnet rapids." Disembark at Division Street Bridge (reached only from the north from Joliet Road, Route 53), or travel on.

If you continue south along the Des Plaines River, it joins the Sanitary and Ship Canal, a commercial waterway that goes through Joliet to the Brandon Road Lock and Dam. Below the Brandon Road Dam, Hickory Creek and then the Du Page River enter the Des Plaines River. The Illinois and Michigan Canal soon flows alongside. Pass McKinley Woods Forest Preserve, with a massive bluff on the north bank of the Des Plaines. Near this point, the Des Plaines River is joined by the Kankakee River, giving birth to the Illinois River. At this junction, a large backwater fills with huge American lotus that bear yellow flowers in August.

## 🍃 Salt Creek Canoe Trail

Launch: Busse Woods, at Salt Creek and Arlington Heights Road, Elk Grove Village, 26 miles northwest of Chicago.

As you paddle southeast on Salt Creek from Busse Woods to the Des Plaines River at Brookfield, you pass through residential areas, forests and meadows, and marshlands where ducks and geese gather and there are signs of beaver. Lush foliage adorns Salt Creek in late spring and you may spot a yellow-headed blackbird. Beyond Oakbrook, enter Fullersburg Forest Preserve and the millpond of the Old Graue Mill. Portage the dam on the left side and continue on Salt Creek through the forest preserve and around Brookfield Zoo to the Des Plaines River.

## 🍃 The Lower Fox River

Lower Fox River Coalition
Chicagoland Canoe Base
4019 N. Narragansett Street
Chicago, IL 60634
(773) 777-1489

This waterway, rich in the geology of glaciers and the history of Native Americans, also has lovely sandstone bluffs and the nesting places of hawks and herons. It is the only place in Illinois where you can find stands with five species of native evergreen trees.

## Camping

Illinois Department of Conservation
524 S. 2nd Street, Room 500
Springfield, IL 62701-1787
(217) 782-7454

I & M Canal State Trail
Box 272
Morris, IL 60450
(815) 942-0796

Illinois Beach State Park
Wadsworth Road and the Lake Michigan shoreline
Zion, IL 60099
(847) 662-4811

Indiana Dunes National Lakeshore
1100 N. Mineral Springs Road
Porter, IN 46304-1299
(219) 926-7561

## Fishing

Chicago Park Lagoons
Urban Fisheries Program
Illinois Department of Natural Resources
Division of Fisheries
9511 Harrison Street
Des Plaines, IL 60016
Contact:
Brenda Harris
Chicago Urban Program Coordinator
(847) 294-4134

Fishing is a pleasure in Chicago park lagoons, for they are stocked with many of the favorites of anglers. There are bullheads in spring, easy for novices to catch; channel catfish, active during hot summer months; and bluegill, which are large and aggressive. Carp, largemouth bass, white crappie, pumpkinseed, and northern pike are also ready to be hooked. To maintain these lagoons, aquatic "weeds" are removed; fish populations are examined; water quality is tested; and anglers are interviewed to determine the harvest of stocked fish and sport fish.

In June and July, the Chicago Park District and the Urban Fisheries Program run fishing clinics at thirteen Chicago lagoons. The clinics cover ecology, fish identification, fishing equipment, safety, and fishing regulations. Rods and reels are provided but bring your own bait. The Access to Fishing program allows you to borrow fishing rods and reels from several libraries. Adult and youth groups—including organizations for the physically challenged—may arrange clinics and events through the Urban Fisheries Program.

Adults and children may participate in a Fishing Derby with catch competitions and instructors. In June and July, join Hooked on Fishing. In September, meet the challenge of Mayor Daley's Fishing Derby.

If you want to brave the cold, come to a Winter Fishing Clinic. Caution: Ice fishing is illegal at Chicago lagoons but can be done on Lake Michigan and in the forest preserves.

Forest Preserve District of Cook County
536 N. Harlem Avenue
River Forest, IL 60305

For a fishing guide and locations of boating waters, call (708) 771-1330.

In the Cook County Forest Preserves, you can fish at forty lakes stocked with game fish including rainbow trout, walleye, largemouth bass, smallmouth bass, and catfish.

For more fishing information, contact:

Chicago Sportfishing Association
Burnham Harbor
(312) 922-1100

Illinois Urban Fishing Program
Illinois Department of Conservation
Division of Fisheries
Springfield, IL 62706

## Golfing

For tee times and reservations at the following Chicago Park District golf courses, call (312) 245-0909.

Hours: Golf courses: Dawn to dusk. Driving ranges and mini-golf course: Daily, 7 A.M.–10 P.M.

Diversey Driving Range and Miniature Golf
141 W. Diversey
Chicago, IL 60657
(773) 281-5722

Jackson Park Driving Range
63rd Street and Lake Shore Drive
Chicago, IL 60621
(773) 288-6104

Sydney R. Marovitz Golf Course
3600 Recreation Drive (Lake Shore Drive)
Chicago, IL 60611

Located downtown, it has a 3,290-yard, par-36 course with tight greens, numerous bunkers, and above-average length.

Robert A. Black Golf Course
2045 W. Pratt Boulevard
Chicago, IL 60645

This north-side facility has a 2,450 yard, par-33 course for all skill levels.

Columbus Golf Course
500 S. Central Avenue
Chicago, IL 60644

This west-side course has wide-open fairways with a 2,753-yard, par-34 layout suited for all skill levels.

Marquette Golf Course
6700 S. Kedzie Avenue
Chicago, IL 60629

This west-side course has a 3,300-yard, par-36 layout. With water surrounding seven of its nine holes, it is very challenging.

Jackson Park Golf Course
63rd Street and Lake Shore Drive
Chicago, IL 60621

Located on the south side, this course has eighteen holes with trees protecting fairways; par 5s reaching 560 yards, and par 3s extending to 215 yards.

South Shore Golf Course
71st Street and South Shore Drive
Chicago, IL 60619

This south-side facility is a 2,900-yard, par-33 course with tree-lined fairways and views of Lake Michigan.

To locate other golf courses, contact forest preserves of Cook County and other counties; and suburban park districts.

## Hiking

Choose your favorite environment, any time of year, and you will find a trail with natural beauty. There are trails along the lakefront (Chapter 2), in the prairie (Chapter 5), along Native American pathways (Chapter 6), through forests and near nature centers (Chapter 7), in wetlands (Chapter 8), and along rivers (Chapter 9).

Take hiking paths with spectacular views of the city skyline that go through city parks with gorgeous gardens, ancient beach ridges, and trees that survived the Chicago Fire (see Chapter 10). Walk through downtown Chicago, where you will view historic sites, famous architecture, and outdoor art (see Chapter 1).

For eighty miles of hiking trails in the forest preserves, call:

Forest Preserve District of Cook County
(312) 261-8400
(708) 366-9420
(800) 870-3666
(708) 771-1190 TDD

# Horseback Riding

For trails, lessons, and rentals, contact:

Forest Preserve District of Cook County
(708) 771-1330

Forest View Farms
5300 W. 167th Street
Tinley Park, IL 60477
(708) 560-0306

This stable offers English and Western lessons, and trail, hay, and sleigh rides.

# Running and Jogging

For paths with exercise stations and noncompetitive events, call:

Chicago Park District
(312) 294-2200

For running and marathons, call:

Chicago Park District
(312) 294-2200

Chicago Area Runners Association
(312) 666-9836

LaSalle Bank's Chicago Marathon
(312) 243-3274

New Year's Day 5 K Run and Walk
Lincoln Park
(773) 868-3010

Zoo Run Run
Brookfield Zoo
(708) 485-0263
(773) 242-2630
(See listing in Chapter 14.)

# Skating
Chicago Park District
(312) 294-2200

Ice skate in winter or do in-line skating at sixty-five indoor and outdoor skating rinks in various Chicago parks. In downtown Chicago you can in-line skate on park paths or practice your skills on the rink at the Sports Plaza at the north end of Grant Park. In winter, skaters congregate at the Daley Bicentennial Plaza Ice Rink (on the roof of the Monroe Drive Parking Garage at Lake Shore Drive, between Monroe and Randolph). Join the Green Team of the Chicago Park District (312) 747-2121 and skate along lakefront parks, reporting problems and promoting safe and sound use of the parks.

Sears "Skate on State"
State Street between Randolph and Washington streets
(312) 744-3370
(312) 744-2964 TTY
(See listing in Chapter 14.)

# Skiing
Nordic Ski Program
Camp Sagawau
1255 W. 111th Street
Lemont, IL 60439
(630) 257-2045

Adults and children from fourth grade up can participate in the Nordic Ski Program. Take cross-country skiing lessons that improve your technique and assist you in selecting equipment. There is a waxing clinic and ski equipment rental. Come for lessons in January and February on weekends (fee required). The camp also offers school and group lessons and ski-skating lessons. Kids Ski Too, a program with games and other activities, is designed to improve skiing skills for younger children. (Parent or guardian must sign a waiver.) Nature Ski, held on Sundays at 1:30 P.M. from January to March, provides a slow-paced ski tour with a naturalist for adults and children over twelve (free). The January Ski Fest has games, free lessons, and two-for-one ski rentals. The camp also offers moonlight skiing and a Cross-Country Slide and Glide Party.

###  Lake Michigan Shoreline ski trails
Grant Park on the lakefront
Chicago, IL 60601

Chicago terrain is very flat, so cross-country skiing is a common winter pastime in Chicago parks. One trail runs through Grant Park, at the north end. Also ski on the Lake Michigan beaches.

###  Cook County Forest Preserve Trails
Forest Preserve District of Cook County
536 N. Harlem Avenue
River Forest, IL 60305
(312) 261-8400
(708) 366-9420
(800) 870-3666
(708) 771-1190 TDD

Ski trails follow rivers and pass through woodlands and meadows in many parts of the forest preserves. For additional ski trails, call suburban park and forest preserves.

## Swimming
Chicago Park District
Beaches and Pools
(312) 747-2200
(312) 747-2001 TDD

Caution: Lake Michigan is lovely but it can be treacherous. For safety, swim only in guarded areas. Beware of rip currents and strong waves. Keep off rocks near the edge.

## North Suburban Beaches
Many of these require that you purchase day or season passes during months when lifeguards are present. Call the recreation department in individual north shore towns or suburbs for resident and nonresident information.

# Tennis

Court locations and lessons:
Chicago Park District
(312) 747-2200
(312) 747-2001 TDD

# Tobogganing

Experience the delight of sledding down snowy hills in parks and forest preserves.

Forest Preserve District of Cook County
536 N. Harlem Avenue
River Forest, IL 60305
(312) 261-8400
(708) 366-9420
(800) 870-3666
(708) 771-1190 TDD

Little Red Schoolhouse Nature Center
9800 Willow Springs Road
Willow Springs, IL 60480
(708) 839-6897

Swallow Cliff Sports Area
Route 83 and Route 45
Palos Park, IL 60464

# Volleyball

Play volleyball in parks and on the beaches. For scheduled activities, contact:

Midwest Volleyball Professionals
1229 N. North Branch Street, #122
Chicago, IL 60622
(312) 266-8580

June Sand Volleyball Tournament
Summerfest
Prospect Heights Park District
110 W. Camp McDonald Road
Prospect Heights, IL 60070
(847) 394-2848

## Sports for the Physically Challenged

Special Olympics
(312) 747-0827

Special Olympics, with basketball, powerlifting, track and field, and other competitions, takes place each summer. The first Special Olympics games, in 1968, took place at Soldier Field. Created by the Joseph P. Kennedy, Jr. Foundation and sponsored by the Chicago Park District, Special Children's Charities, and Illinois Special Olympics, the tradition continues. In every sector of Chicago, there are training sites with classes Tuesday through Saturday. Winter training programs include basketball, wheelchair skills, unified bowling, and soccer. Spring training encompasses aquatics, powerlifting, gymnastics, track and field, and motor activities. Summer training is offered in bowling, tennis, and softball. Autumn training covers golf, volleyball, hockey, and ice skating.

## Therapeutic Recreational Programs and Sites

Chicago Park District
(312) 294-4768
(312) 986-0726 TDD

Programs are located at field houses and pools equipped with lifts or ramps, beaches with surf chairs (beach wheelchairs), and accessible comfort stations. You will find programs such as Cubs Care Baseball Leagues and Sledge Hockey for children or adults with developmental and/or physical disabilities.

# Fishing

Urban Fisheries Program
Illinois Department of Natural Resources
Division of Fisheries
9511 Harrison Street
Des Plaines, IL 60016
Contact:
Brenda Harris
Chicago Urban Program Coordinator
(847) 294-4134

Fish in Chicago park lagoons. Attend fishing clinics and fishing derbies.

# Sailing

The Judd Goldman Adaptive Program
Chicago Park District and Westrec Corporation
Burnham Harbor
Chicago, IL 60605
Contact:
Ted Sutherland
Coordinator for sailing programs
(312) 747-0739

Lessons and boat rentals are offered to amputees, quadriplegics, paraplegics, and visually and hearing-impaired individuals. Sessions take place at Burnham Harbor, where special equipment transfers individuals to special chairs on boats. Lessons cover the fundamentals of sailing. Assisted by instructors, individuals with visual or other disabilities avoid obstacles and steer the boat. "It is amazing what they can do," says the instructor. "Sailing is very therapeutic and brings out the best of their abilities." Experienced sailors can participate in weekly races or a regatta in August in which eighteen teams compete for the North American Championship.

## Nature Trails, Nature Centers, and Sensory Gardens

Forest Preserve District of Cook County
(312) 261-8400
(708) 366-9420
(708) 771-1190 TDD
(800) 870-3666

Chicago Botanic Garden
(847) 835-5440

Also contact suburban park districts and forest preserve districts.

*14*

# Celebrate Nature

"Those who dwell . . . among the beauties and mysteries of the earth are never alone or weary of life. . . . Those who contemplate the beauty of the earth find reserves of strength that will endure as long as life lasts."
—Rachel Carson (1907–1964) science writer

For everyone who adores glorious flowers, superb trees, and wondrous beasts, Chicago is the place. Celebrate these natural treasures at lakefront happenings and in festivities at museums, parks, and forest preserves in every season of the year. Remember to check Chapter 13 for specific outdoor sporting events and Chapter 15 for animal clubs, garden groups, and environmental action organizations.

## Calendar of Nature Festivities

### January

New Year's Day 5 K Run and Walk
Starts in Lincoln Park
Chicago, IL
(312) 868-3010

Warm up with a run through one of Chicago's lakefront parks.

Sears "Skate on State"
State Street between Randolph and Washington streets
Chicago, IL 60601
(312) 744-3370
(312) 744-2964 TTY

Glide and slide on an outdoor rink at State Street, a prairie path that has become one of Chicago's main shopping areas.

Arctic Blast
Lincoln Park Zoo (see Chapter 11)
2200 N. Cannon Drive
Chicago, IL 60614
(312) 742-2000

Owl Prowl
North Park Village Nature Center (see Chapter 7)
5801 N. Pulaski Road
Chicago, IL 60646
(773) 744-5472

Whoooo will come to prowl for owls? You will see slides, then do owl calls as you search the forest for these big-eyed birds that hunt at night.

## February

Groundhog Day
Brookfield Zoo (see Chapter 11)
1st Avenue and 31st Street
Brookfield, IL 60513
(708) 485-0263
(773) 242-2630

Will the groundhogs Sunshine and Shadow see their shadows? Watch these furry animals come out of hibernation to solve the mystery of whether spring will arrive early or if there will be six more weeks of wintry weather.

Winterbreak Chicago
Various locations near downtown Chicago
(312) 744-3370
(312) 744-2964 TTY

Get rid of winter blues with a variety of activities.

Ski-Fest
Camp Sagawau (see Chapters 3 and 13)
1255 W. 111th Street
Lemont, IL 60439
(630) 257-2045

Enjoy aerobic exercise at this snow-covered nature reserve. Come to the Ski-Fest, featuring fun and games and cross-country rentals, and take the chill out of winter during romantic moonlight tours and the Cross-Country Glide and Slide Party.

Totally Trees
Sand Ridge Nature Center (see Chapter 7)
15890 Paxton Avenue
South Holland, IL 60473
(708) 868-0606

Hike through the open forest to identify trees by branching, bark, and bud.

A Winter Weekend of Trees
Morton Arboretum (see Chapter 10)
Route 53
Lisle, IL 60532
(630) 719-2465

Winter is a wonderful time to learn how to identify trees by their out-lines, branching patterns, bark, and bud scars.

Animal Tracking
The Hal Tyrrell Trailside Museum (see Chapter 7)
238 Thatcher Avenue
River Forest, IL 60305
(708) 366-6530

Trek through the snow and identify the footprints of mice, opossum, deer, raccoon, and other native animals of Illinois.

Azalea Flower Show
Lincoln Park Conservatory (see Chapter 10)
2400 N. Stockton Avenue
Chicago, IL 60614
(312) 294-4770

Azalea Flower Show
Garfield Park Conservatory and Gardens (see Chapter 10)
300 N. Central Park Boulevard
Chicago, IL 60624
(312) 746-5092

## March

Sun Fest
Adler Planetarium and Astronomy Museum (see Chapter 4)
1300 S. Lake Shore Drive
Chicago, IL 60605
(312) 322-0304

Bring the family for this celebration of the spring (vernal) equinox: the time when day and night are equal in length.

National Pig Day
Brookfield Zoo (see Chapter 11)
1st Avenue and 31st Street
Brookfield, IL 60513
(708) 485-0263
(773) 242-2630

This is your big chance to watch an Ossabaw Island pig and a Yucatan miniature pig demonstrate their skills.

Owl Census
The Chicago Ornithological Society (see Chapter 15)
559 Clinton Place
River Forest, IL 60305
(708) 366-2409

Meet at 3 A.M. in the forest preserve to count owls.

Annual Cook County Owl Count
Chicago Audubon Society (see Chapter 15)
5801 N. Pulaski Road
Chicago, IL 60646
(773) 539-6793

Spring Flower Show
Lincoln Park Conservatory (see Chapter 10)
2400 N. Stockton Avenue
Chicago, IL 60614
(312) 294-4770

Tiptoe through red and yellow tulips and other harbingers of spring.

Spring Flower Show
Garfield Park Conservatory and Gardens (see Chapter 10)
300 N. Central Park Boulevard
Chicago, IL 60624
(312) 746-5092

Smile at the daffodils and don't let the hyacinth make you blue. Delight in the flowers that bloom in the spring.

Plant Society Fair
Chicago Botanic Garden (see Chapter 10)
1000 Lake Cook Road
P.O. Box 400
Glencoe, IL 60022-0400
(847) 835-5440

Chat about irises, lilies, African violets, and other species. Or talk about gardening, flower arranging, and the techniques of bonsai as you tour the booths and meet members of more than twenty plant societies.

Fruit Tree Grafting Seminar
Garfield Farm Museum (see Chapter 12)
3 N016 Garfield Road
La Fox, IL 60147
(630) 584-8485

Prepare for a harvest of antique apples and modern nectarines. This is your opportunity to learn the techniques of fruit tree grafting.

Maple Syrup Festival
North Park Village Nature Center (see Chapter 7)
5801 N. Pulaski Road
Chicago, IL 60646
(773) 744-5472

Learn how to tap trees and make maple syrup.

Chicago Flower and Garden Show
Navy Pier (see Chapter 2)
600 E. Grand Avenue
Chicago, IL 60611
(312) 595-7437

Oh so many flowers are on display at this large exhibition. Walk through gardens and enjoy flower arrangements. Talk with flower sellers and garden suppliers.

Sugar Maple Festival
River Trail Nature Center (see Chapter 7)
3120 N. Milwaukee Avenue
Northbrook, IL 60062
(847) 824-8360

See how Native Americans and European pioneers collected tree sap and made pure maple syrup. Then sample the results.

Adventures in Nature Lecture Series
John G. Shedd Aquarium (see Chapter 11)
1200 S. Lake Shore Drive
Chicago, Illinois 60605
(312) 939-2438

Hear odd facts about fish and other animals of the deep and uncover the secrets of the underwater realm.

International Cluster of Dog Shows
Location: McCormick Place East
2301 S. Lake Shore Drive
Chicago, IL 60616
Sponsor:
International Kennel Club of Chicago
6224 W. North Avenue
Chicago, IL 60639
(773) 237-5100

Revel in the biodiversity of canines. Watch obedience, herding, and agility demonstrations. See demonstrations by service dogs that are trained to assist the physically challenged, such as small dogs that "tell" a hearing-impaired individual the telephone is ringing; and larger dogs that guide blind individuals or open refrigerators and turn off lights for people who cannot move easily.

# April

Earth Day
Sand Ridge Nature Center (see Chapter 7)
15890 Paxton Avenue
South Holland, IL 60473
(708) 868-0606

Take nature hikes, participate in a walk-a-thon, and tour booths set up by conservation organizations to celebrate Earth Day.

Earth Day
The Grove National Historic Landmark (see Chapter 7)
1421 Milwaukee Avenue
Glenview, IL 60025
(847) 299-6096

Midwest's Largest Environmental Cleanup
of Parks and Beaches
Friends of the Parks
407 S. Dearborn Street
Chicago, IL 60603
(312) 922-3307

Call this and other environmental organizations to participate in Earth Day cleanups, plantings, and other conservation action. Major museums, nature centers, forest preserves, and city parks also have celebrations of our earthly ecosystem.

Arbor Day
Brookfield Zoo (see Chapter 11)
1st Avenue and 31st Street
Brookfield, IL 60513
(708) 485-0263
(773) 242-2630

Participate in a tree planting ceremony and obtain free saplings to plant on your lawn (as long as the supply lasts).

Arbor Day Plant Sale
Morton Arboretum (see Chapter 10)
Route 53
Lisle, IL 60532
(630) 719-2465

Green and Growing Fair
University of Illinois Cooperative Extension Service (see Chapters 10 and 15)
Cook/Chicago North Office
1000 N. Milwaukee Avenue, 4th Floor
Chicago, IL 60622
Contact:
Chris Eiler
(773) 292-4444
Buy flowers, vegetables, and other fine plants for your garden.

## May

Bark in the Park
Montrose Harbor
Lincoln Park
Chicago, IL 60640
Sponsor:
Anti-Cruelty Society (see Chapter 15)
157 W. Grand Avenue
Chicago, IL 60610
(312) 644-8338
Start at Montrose Harbor and get ready to go on a five-kilometer run with an obstacle course for you and your dog. Watch demonstrations on dog obedience and performances by groups such as the Chicago Canine and Equine Police Unit.

Be Kind to Animals Week
Animal Welfare League (see Chapter 15)
6224 S. Wabash Street
Chicago, IL 60637
(773) 667-0088
10305 Southwest Highway
Chicago Ridge, IL 60415
(708) 636-8586
Attend programs on responsibility and humane care for animals.

Spring Bird Count and Bird Migration Field Trips
The Chicago Ornithological Society (see chapter 15)
3417 W. 123rd Street
Alsip, IL 60658
Contact:
Mike Kutska
(708) 366-2409

Migratory Bird Day
Crabtree Nature Center (see Chapter 7)
Palatine Road, 1 mile west of Barrington Road
Barrington, IL 60010
(847) 381-6592

Annual Spring Plant Sale
Chicago Botanic Garden (see Chapter 10)
1000 Lake Cook Road
P.O. Box 400
Glencoe, IL 60022-0400
(847) 835-5440

Live Reptile and Amphibian Show
Contact: Chicago Herpetological Society (see Chapter 15)
2060 N. Clark Street
Chicago, IL 60614
(773) 281-1800
(773) 508-0034 TDD or TTY

See reptiles and amphibians on display and for sale.

Memorial Day Weekend Festival
Brookfield Zoo (see Chapter 11)
1st Avenue and 31st Street
Brookfield, IL 60513
(708) 485-0263
(773) 242-2630

See Children's Zoo animal action and elephant demonstrations.

Spring Garden Walks
The Garden Clubs of Illinois, Inc. (see Chapter 15)
1717 West 31st Street, Suite A
Oakbrook, IL 60521
(630) 794-9625

Their publication, *Garden Glories*, lists garden walks and other events throughout the state.

Herb and Scented Plant Sale
Oak Park Conservatory (see Chapter 10)
615 Garfield Street
Oak Park, IL 60304
(708) 386-4700

Rare Breeds Livestock Show
Garfield Farm Museum (see Chapter 12)
3 N016 Garfield Road
La Fox, IL 60147
(630) 584-8485

Meet Devon oxen, merino rams, black java chickens, and other animals that prairie farmers raised in the early 1800s.

Annual Des Plaines River Canoe Marathon (see Chapter 13)
Launch: Canoe landing at Oak Spring Road and the Des Plaines River
Libertyville, IL
Contact:
Chicagoland Canoe Base
4019 N. Naragansett Avenue
Chicago, IL 60634
(773) 777-1489

Canoe 19 miles from Libertyville through wildlife-filled woodlands to Dam 2 in the Forest Preserves, just north of Wheeling.

Spring Bird Count
The Chicago Ornithological Society (see Chapter 15)
559 Clinton Place
River Forest, IL 60305
(708) 366-2409

Count every bird that you see. If you are lucky, you may spot some of the thirty species of colorful warblers that come to the Chicago area.

The information will be compiled with bird counts from all over the country to establish patterns and identify problems with bird populations.

## June

Sun Fest
Adler Planetarium and Astronomy Museum (see Chapter 4)
1300 S. Lake Shore Drive
Chicago, IL 60605
(312) 322-0304

Bring the family for this celebration of the summer solstice: the time the sun appears at its peak in the sky.

Breeding Bird Census throughout Cook County
Chicago Audubon Society
5801 N. Pulaski Road
Chicago, IL 60646
(773) 539-6793

Watch woodpeckers enter holes in tree trunks. Listen to yellow warblers sing. Look for young geese. Do all this as you do a bird census and confirm nesting.

Rendezvous: A French and Indian Trade Fair
Isle à La Cache Museum (see Chapter 6)
501 E. Romeo Road
Romeoville, IL 60441
(815) 886-1467

Go back in time to the 1750s as you enjoy canoe races, tomahawk throws, and musket shoots.

Nature Artist Guild Exhibition
Morton Arboretum (see Chapter 10)
Route 53
Lisle, IL 60532
(630) 719-2465

National Garden Week
Contact local garden clubs for flower shows, garden walks, and talks.

Mid-America Canoe Race (see Chapter 13)
On the Fox River from South Elgin to North Aurora
Contact:
Chicagoland Canoe Base
4019 N. Naragansett Avenue
Chicago, IL 60634
(773) 777-1489

Cook County Nesting Season Bird Census
Chicago Audubon Society (see Chapter 15)
5801 N. Pulaski Road
Chicago, IL 60646
(773) 539-6793

River Rescue Day
Friends of the Chicago River (see Chapter 15)
407 S. Dearborn Street, Suite 1580
Chicago, IL 60605
(312) 939-0490

Build muscles as you join in the cleanup of stretches of the Chicago River and Skokie Lagoons.

Affie Elephant's Birthday Party
Brookfield Zoo (see Chapter 11)
1st Avenue and 31st Street
Brookfield, IL 60513
(708) 485-0263
(773) 242-2630

Free Fishing Days (no license required)
Urban Fisheries Program (see Chapter 13)
Illinois Department of Natural Resources
Division of Fisheries
9511 Harrison Street
Des Plaines, IL 60016
Contact:
Brenda Harris
Chicago Urban Program Coordinator
(847) 294-4134

Midnight Bicycle Ride
Friends of the Parks (see Chapter 15)
407 S. Dearborn Street
Chicago, IL 60603
(312) 922-3307

Meet at Buckingham Fountain and pedal through the night. Go north to Gompers Park, east along Foster Avenue, south along the lakefront, and end with breakfast at Buckingham Fountain.

Lockport Old Canal Days
Illinois and Michigan Canal Visitor Center (see Chapter 9)
Gaylord Building
200 W. 8th Street
Lockport, IL 60441
(815) 838-4830

Take a horse-drawn carriage ride and a museum tour, and see arts and crafts demonstrations as you celebrate the time when this town was the headquarters of the Illlinois and Michigan Canal. Go on a canal walk to look at this vital link in the Great Lakes/Mississippi River waterway that contributed to the settlement of the American West. See the first lock built on the canal, and the historic district, with buildings dating from the 1800s.

Long Grove Strawberry Festival
Contact:
Long Grove Merchants' Association and Tourist Center
Long Grove, IL 60047
(847) 634-0888

Getting there: Located in Long Grove, 32 miles northwest of Chicago. Take I-94 (Edens Expressway) north and exit west on Route 22. Drive west on Route 22 to Old McHenry Road. Turn south on Old McHenry Road to the town of Long Grove.

Rejoice in pies, jams, and other strawberry delights.

## July

The Annual Dog Wash
Anti-Cruelty Society (see Chapter 15)
157 W. Grand Avenue
Chicago, IL 60610
(312) 644-8338

Have your dog groomed (the fee depends on the size of your dog) and enjoy entertainment, photo opportunities, treats, and the gift of a beach towel.

Civil War Living History Days
The Grove National Historic Landmark (see Chapter 7)
1421 Milwaukee Avenue
Glenview, IL 60025
(847) 299-6096

On land that contains an old prairie grove, relive the time Chicagoans fought in the Civil War. See Union and Confederate troop encampments, Blue-Gray skirmishes, and military drills.

Zelebration
Brookfield Zoo (see Chapter 11)
1st Avenue and 31st Street
Brookfield, IL 60513
(708) 485-0263
(773) 242-2630

Attend the Animals in Action show with demonstrations of wild beasts' abilities. The spotlight is on native North American animals.

Pond Tour
Pond and Koi Society (see Chapter 15)
P.O. Box 1251
North Riverside, IL 60546
(630) 879-3717

Tour water gardens with wetland vegetation and *koi*, ornamental Japanese carp bred for color and patterns.

# August

Hosta Auction
Northern Illinois Hosta Society (see Chapter 15)
2959 Hobson Road
Downers Grove, IL 60517
Contact:
Laurie Skrzenta
(630) 969-1270

This is the time to bid on this perennial foliage plant. Choose from many of the eleven hundred varieties, including some that do well in partial shade.

Momence Gladiolus Festival
Momence, IL 60954
(800) 74-RIVER
(800) 747-4837

Getting there: Located in Momence, 60 miles southeast of Chicago. Take I-57 south to Route 17, exit 312. Turn east (left) on Route 17 and go 12 miles to the heart of Momence.

See flower-covered floats, antique cars, drum and bugle corps, and more.

Meteorite Showers in the Night Sky
Viewed from lakefront, parks, backyards
Telescope viewing
Adler Planetarium and Astronomy Museum (see Chapter 4)
1300 S. Lake Shore Drive
Chicago, IL 60605
(312) 322-0304

Prairie Days
The Natural Garden
38 W. 443 Highway 64
St. Charles, IL 60175
(708) 584-0150

Hear speakers on planning herbal and prairie gardens and look at display gardens with prairie plants, ornamental grasses, and perennial native plants.

Heirloom Garden Show
Garfield Farm Museum (see Chapter 12)
3 N016 Garfield Road
La Fox, IL 60147
(630) 584-8485

This heirloom garden show features an antique flower garden display; seeds of old varieties with members of the Seed Savers Exchange; and tastes of old varieties of vegetables and fruits.

Teddy Bear Picnic
Brookfield Zoo (see Chapter 11)
1st Avenue and 31st Street
Brookfield, IL 60513
(708) 485-0263
(773) 242-2630

Enter your teddy bear in a contest, and enjoy "bearious" other zoo activities.

## September

Sun Fest
Adler Planetarium and Astronomy Museum (see Chapter 4)
1300 S. Lake Shore Drive
Chicago, IL 60605
(312) 322-0304

Bring the family for this celebration of the autumnal equinox: the time when day and night are equal in length.

Archaeology Awareness Day
Sand Ridge Nature Center (see Chapter 7)
15890 Paxton Avenue
South Holland, Illinois 60473
(708) 868-0606

Investigate Illinois archaeology, with talks on Native American history, native foods, and interpretive walks.

Great Lakes Beach Sweep
Chicago lakefront
Cosponsors:
Lake Michigan Federation (see Chapter 15)
59 E. Van Buren Street, Suite 2215
Chicago, IL 60605
(312) 939-0838
Friends of the Parks (see Chapter 15)
407 S. Dearborn Street
Chicago, IL 60603
(312) 922-3307

Volunteer to clean up the beach and collect information on Lake Michigan. This event uncovers major polluters and gathers data on lakes, rivers, and oceans. Join in and be part of an international coastal cleanup that involves thirty states and seventy countries.

Family Fair
Morton Arboretum (see Chapter 10)
Route 53
Lisle, IL 60532
(630) 719-2465

See exhibits and play nature games in a setting with woody plants from all over the world.

Zoo Photo Contest Display
Brookfield Zoo (see Chapter 11)
1st Avenue and 31st Street
Brookfield, IL 60513
(708) 485-0263
(773) 242-2630

Catch special moments of acrobatic dolphins and awesome zoo elephants. View animal photography at its best.

HerPETological Weekend
Cosponsors:
Chicago Academy of Sciences (see Chapter 12)
North Pier
435 E. Illinois Street, 3rd Floor
Chicago, IL 60614
(773) 549-0606

Chicago Herpetological Society (see Chapter 15)
2060 N. Clark Street
Chicago, IL 60614
(773) 281-1800
(773) 508-0034 TDD or TTY

Become close to lizards, snakes, turtles, salamanders, and frogs and, perhaps, alligators. (Note: By mid-1998, the Chicago Academy of Sciences will be in a new building at Fullerton and Cannon Drive in Lincoln Park.)

Pow Wow
Forest Preserve District of Cook County
(312) 261-8400
(708) 366-9420
(800) 870-3666
(708) 771-1190 TDD

Native American music, dance, crafts, and wilderness skills demonstrations.

## October

The Grove Folk Fest
The Grove National Historic Landmark (see Chapter 7)
1421 Milwaukee Avenue
Glenview, IL 60025
(847) 299-6096

Hear folk music, take nature walks, and watch pioneer skill and craft demonstrations on what used to be the farm of a pioneer family.

Salamander Safari
Location: Camp Sagawau (see Chapter 3)
1255 W. 111th Street
Lemont, IL 60439
(630) 257-2045
Sponsor:
Chicago Herpetological Society
2060 N. Clark Street
Chicago, IL 60614
(773) 281-1800
(773) 508-0034 TDD or TTY

Take a different kind of census: count reptiles and amphibians. You will be surprised at the number of blue spotted and tiger salamanders; bullfrogs, green frogs, leopard frogs, and great tree frogs. You will also encounter fox snakes, brown snakes, queen snakes, hog-nosed snakes, and garter snakes.

Autumn Roadside Flower Sale
Chicago Botanic Garden (see Chapter 10)
1000 Lake Cook Road
P.O. Box 400
Glencoe, IL 60022-0400
(847) 835-5440

Purchase your favorites at this plant fair with wildflowers and other native plants and dried flower arrangements.

Fall Honey and Harvest Festival
River Trail Nature Center (see Chapter 7)
3120 N. Milwaukee Avenue
Northbrook, IL 60062
(847) 824-8360

Come for autumn color trail walks, bee-keeping demonstrations, crafts, and storytelling. Then quench your thirst with apple cider, munch on taffy apples, and buy honey, pumpkins, Indian corn, and maple syrup.

Chicago River Halloween Boat Float
Friends of the Chicago River (see Chapter 15)
407 S. Dearborn Street, Suite 1580
Chicago, IL 60605
(312) 939-0490

Halloween Walk
Chicago Botanic Garden (see Chapter 10)
1000 Lake Cook Road
P.O. Box 400
Glencoe, IL 60022-0400
(847) 835-5440

Take a walk in the dark where spider webs and scary figures hide among the greenery.

Haunted Forest
Forest Preserve District of Cook County
536 N. Harlem Avenue
River Forest, IL 60305
(312) 261-8400
(708) 366-9420
(800) 870-3666
(708) 771-1190 TDD

Shiver and scream with the ghosts and witches, and watch out for the
black cats that will cross your path in the forest.

Zoo Run Run
Brookfield Zoo (see Chapter 11)
1st Avenue and 31st Street
Brookfield, IL 60513
(708) 485-0263
(773) 242-2630

Run for the animals (proceeds support them in the zoo and in the
wild). Join in a three-kilometer walk, a five-kilometer run, or a half-
mile Fun Run (open to children age ten and under and to young adults
with physical disabilities). Registration required.

## November

Chrysanthemum Show
Lincoln Park Conservatory (see Chapter 10)
2400 N. Stockton Avenue
Chicago, IL 60614
(312) 294-4770

Delight in the magnificent mums—large and small blossoms in colors
that range from white and yellow to lavender and burgundy.

Chrysanthemum Flower Show
Garfield Park Conservatory and Gardens (see Chapter 10)
300 N. Central Park Boulevard
Chicago, IL 60624
(312) 746-5092

View seventy-five hundred spidery, round, and daisylike flowers, in
rainbow hues. Grown from cuttings, they come from plants around
the world.

Community and Corporate Tree Trim
Brookfield Zoo (see Chapter 11)
1st Avenue and 31st Street
Brookfield, IL 60513
(708) 485-0263
(773) 242-2630

Decorate balsam trees on the zoo's malls in preparation for the Holiday Magic Festival. Call to reserve a tree for your group.

Settler's Day
Sand Ridge Nature Center (see Chapter 7)
15890 Paxton Avenue
South Holland, IL 60473
(708) 868-0606

Volunteers from the Northwest Territorial Alliance take you back to the old days with a Revolutionary War encampment and people in costumes of the early 1800s. See demonstrations on pioneer living in the log cabins that stand on this site that was once an ancient beach ridge.

Thanksgiving Day Feast
Brookfield Zoo (see Chapter 11)
1st Avenue and 31st Street
Brookfield, IL 60513
(708) 485-0263
(773) 242-2630

Assist Children's Zookeepers as they feed the animals special Thanksgiving treats.

## December

Sun Fest
Adler Planetarium and Astronomy Museum (see Chapter 4)
1300 S. Lake Shore Drive
Chicago, IL 60605
(312) 322-0304

Bring the family for this celebration of the winter solstice: the time when the sun appears at its lowest point in the sky.

Winter Bird Count
The Chicago Ornithological Society (see Chapter 15)
559 Clinton Place
River Forest, IL 60305
(708) 366-2409

Join a team and count birds such as Canada geese, tundra swans, ducks, and sparrows that winter in the Chicago area. The information will be compiled with bird counts from all over the country to establish patterns and identify problems with populations.

Holiday Flower Show
Lincoln Park Conservatory (see Chapter 10)
2400 N. Stockton Avenue
Chicago, IL 60614
(312) 294-4770

Discover white, pink, and red poinsettias at this splendid December/January flower show.

Holiday Flower Show
Garfield Park Conservatory and Gardens (see Chapter 10)
300 N. Central Park Boulevard
Chicago, IL 60624
(312) 746-5092

Brightly colored ornamental pepper, Jerusalem cherry, and a poinsettia "tree" made of 250 single-stemmed poinsettia plants bring holiday cheer.

The Animal's Messiah
510 N. LaSalle Street
Chicago, IL 60610
Sponsor:
Anti-Cruelty Society (see Chapter 15)
157 W. Grand Avenue
Chicago, IL 60610
(312) 644-8338

Bring the kids and grandparents to this free concert. Listen to the music of a small orchestra accompanied by barking dogs and meowing cats. Then eat some treats at the volunteer bake sale.

Winter Solstice Festival
North Park Village Nature Center (see Chapter 7)
5801 N. Pulaski Road
Chicago, IL 60646
(773) 744-5472

Bring the whole family to roast chestnuts, learn how to predict the change of seasons with a stick, prepare edible ornaments for the animals, walk through the snowy nighttime trails, and view the winter stars.

Holiday Magic Festival
Brookfield Zoo (see Chapter 11)
1st Avenue and 31st Street
Brookfield, IL 60513
(708) 485-0263
(773) 242-2630

See wild animals and costumed characters while strolling along walkways lined with lights after dark. Listen to carolers and musical groups and hear celebrity storytellers tell holiday tales in the zoo.

Holiday Display and Plant Sale
Chicago Botanic Garden (see Chapter 10)
1000 Lake Cook Road
P.O. Box 400
Glencoe, IL 60022-0400
(847) 835-5440

See the display hall filled with Christmas trees artfully decorated by garden clubs. Then browse and buy poinsettia, wreaths, and dried arrangements.

Aurora Borealis (Northern Lights) in the night sky

For information, call the Adler Planetarium and Astronomy Museum, (312) 322-0304.

Winter Festivals and Games
The Field Museum (see Chapter 12)
Lake Shore Drive at Roosevelt Road
Chicago, IL 60605-2496
(312) 922-9410
(312) 341-9299 TDD

Celebrate Chicago's cultural diversity with Kwanzaa games, the dreidel game, jump rope, yo-yos, and tangrams. Listen to African-American drumming and Polish singing. Watch Philippine dancing and a Chinese-American Dragon Dance.

Volo Bog Winter Fest
Volo Bog State Natural Area (see Chapter 8)
28478 W. Brandenburg Road
Ingleside, IL 60041
(815) 344-1294

Come for the music, storytelling, scavenger hunts, snow sculpture, and other family entertainment.

Chicago Urban Annual Christmas Count
Chicago Audubon Society (see Chapter 15)
5801 N. Pulaski Road
Chicago, IL 60646
(773) 539-6793

Assist in a census of Chicago's resident birds.

Midwinter Owling
Heller Nature Center
2821 Ridge Road
Highland Park, IL 60093
(847) 433-6901

Bird Watching
Morton Arboretum (see Chapter 10)
Route 53
Lisle, IL 60532
(630) 719-2465

Birding for Beginners
Little Red School House Nature Center (see Chapter 7)
9800 S. Willow Springs Road
Willow Springs, IL 60480
(708) 839-6897

# Lakefront Festivals

Do you adore tasting food from Chicago's finest restaurants on picnic outdoors? Would you enjoy water shows and air shows and spectacular fireworks above Lake Michigan on Independence Day? Then come to Grant Park for spring and summer festivities, from Fourth of July celebrations to Taste of Chicago, Venetian Night, the Chicago Air and Water Show, and more. Call:

Chicago Park District
(312) 747-2200
(312) 747-2001 TDD

Mayor's Office of Special Events
(312) 744-3315

# Outdoor Concerts and Performances

Do you love to listen to music while relaxing on a meadow and looking up at the stars? Whether you like country, jazz, classical, blues, or rock, music sounds wonderful in natural settings. You can hear many outstanding musicians perform at bandshells along the lakefront.

Petrillo Music Shell
Grant Park
On the lakefront at Jackson and Columbus drives
Chicago, IL 60601

Enjoy free concerts Wednesday, Friday, Saturday, and Sunday during ten weeks of summer.

Ravinia Festival
Ravinia Park
301 Ravinia Park Road
Highland Park, IL 60035
(312) 728-4642
(847) 266-5000

For other outdoor happenings, call the Mayor's Office of Special Events, (312) 744-3315. For neighborhood festivals, call (312) 744-3370. In the suburbs, contact park and forest preserve districts.

# Wilderness Adventures

Still looking for adventures in the great outdoors? See the *Directory of Illinois Nature Preserves, Vol 1., Northeastern Illinois.* Illinois Department of Natural Resources, Division of Natural Heritage. Don McFall and Jean Karnes, Editors, 1995. This survey of nature preserves describes the main features of prairies, forests, and wetlands; indicates where rare plants and endangered animals are; and locates them by counties in the Chicago region.

## Additional sources:

Forest Preserve District of Cook County
536 N. Harlem Avenue
River Forest, IL 60305
(312) 261-8400
(708) 366-9420
(800) 870-3666
(708) 771-1190 TDD

Forest Preserve District of Kane County
719 Batavia Road
Geneva, IL 60134
(630) 232-5980

Forest Preserve District of Will County
22606 S. Cherry Hill Road
Joliet, IL 60433
(815) 727-8700

Lake County Forest Preserve District
2000 N. Milwaukee Avenue
Libertyville, IL 60048
(847) 367-6640
(847) 367-3675 TDD

Forest Preserve District of DuPage County
P.O. Box 2339
Glen Ellyn, IL 60138
(630) 790-4900
(800) 526-0857 TDD

Illinois Department of Natural Resources
524 S. 2nd Street
Lincoln Tower Plaza
Springfield, IL 62701-1787
(217) 782-6302

# 15

## *Nature Organizations*

"It is easy to live for others; everybody does."
—Ralph Waldo Emerson (1803–1882)

Do you like to bike through the forest? Are you thrilled to watch birds in a bog? Or does clearing brush from a prairie give you a sense of accomplishment? Your enthusiasm and talent will be welcomed by a variety of organizations. Join in the fun with wild beasts, wildflowers, and wilderness; and work to improve city rivers, parks, gardens, and Lake Michigan. You have unlimited opportunities to explore and restore nature in Chicago.

## Animal Organizations

Animal Welfare League
6224 S. Wabash Avenue
Chicago, IL 60637
(773) 667-0088
10305 Southwest Highway
Chicago Ridge, IL 60415
(708) 636-8586

Volunteers work in a shelter, grooming and socializing small animals. The Chicago shelter offers help in taking care of animals and receiving stray animals, weekdays 11 A.M. to 5 P.M. The Chicago Ridge shelter handles animal adoptions, animal rescue, cruelty investigations, and clinic services including spaying and neutering.

You may also assist with special events and programs like Humane Education, promoting kindness and care for animals; or Pet Therapy, bringing puppies and other animals to visit the elderly in nursing homes.

The Critter Club has monthly meetings where seven- to twelve-year-olds become acquainted with marine, endangered, farm, and native animals. The family calendar of events includes: April, photos with the Easter Bunny in pet stores; May, Be Kind to Animals Week, with programs on responsibility and humane care for animals; an autumn Dog Walk, and December Photos with Santa.

Anti-Cruelty Society
157 W. Grand Avenue
Chicago, IL 60610
(312) 644-8338

Help an organization that helps sixteen thousand animals a year. It also tries to reduce the number of homeless animals through its low-cost spay/neuter clinic and adoption of dogs and cats. Assist in animal rescue and cruelty investigations and a Humane Education program for clubs and for preschool through high school. As a volunteer, you may assist veterinarians; do washing and grooming before adoption; reunite lost pets with owners; or do pet therapy visits (cheer elderly people with animals) and special events.

In May, Bark in the Park takes place in Lincoln Park. Go on a five-kilometer run with your dog. The starting point is Montrose Harbor; you and your canine go through an obstacle course. You may also watch demonstrations on dog obedience or a performance by the Chicago Canine and Equine Police Unit. In July, the Annual Dog Wash provides dog grooming (the fee depends on the size of your dog), entertainment, photo opportunities, treats, and the gift of a beach towel. In December, the Animal's Messiah takes place at 510 N. LaSalle Street (Grand and LaSalle). Bring the family to this free concert performed by a small orchestra accompanied by barking dogs and meowing cats, and followed by a volunteer bake sale.

Chicago Audubon Society
5801 N. Pulaski Road
Chicago, IL 60646
(773) 539-6793

Participate in bird walks, monthly field trips, and activities during spring and autumn migration seasons.

Chicago Herpetological Society
2060 N. Clark Street
Chicago, IL 60614
(773) 281-1800
(773) 508-0034 TDD or TTY

Meet the last Wednesday of each month, 7:30 P.M., at the Field Museum. Hear experts such as museum curators and exotic animal veterinarians speak about the care, characteristics, and behavior of reptiles and amphibians. The group is also concerned about extinction in the wild and conservation issues. Members attend "behind the scenes" visits to zoos; and special events such as the March Annual Salamander Safari (census taking) at Camp Sagawau in Lemont; the May Live Reptile and Amphibian Show; and the September HerPETological Weekend at the Chicago Academy of Sciences Nature Museum.

The Chicago Ornithological Society
559 Clinton Place
River Forest, IL 60305
(708) 366-2409

Attend monthly meetings on birding topics at the Field Museum that include beginning birder workshops on identification, bird families and habitats, and conservation activities. Go on field trips to track native and migrating birds at the Chicago lakefront, Skokie Lagoons, Lake Calumet area, and other birding hotspots in Chicago and elsewhere. Also participate in the March owl census and the May and December bird counts.

Urban Fisheries Program
Illinois Department of Natural Resources
Division of Fisheries
9511 Harrison Street
Des Plaines, IL 60016
Contact:
Brenda Harris
Chicago Urban Program Coordinator
(847) 294-4134

Attend a fishing clinic or fishing derby (see Chapter 13).

## Environmental Action Groups

Boy Scouts of America
Chicago Area Council
1218 W. Adams Street
Chicago, IL 60607-2802
(312) 421-8800

Cub Scouts (first through fifth grade) go on outings to natural areas.
Boy Scouts (sixth grade to high school seniors) obtain merit badges
through nature studies, environmental studies, fishing, forestry, soil
and water conservation, insect study, botany, bird study, and landscape
design. Scouts perform many environmental service projects—such
as litter cleanup and prairie rehabilitation—that promote stewardship
of nature. Field trips are great fun, with day hikes and overnighters in
forest preserves and camping in state parks. High school freshmen to
seniors can join the High School Coeducational Explorer Post and
participate in year-long activities related to environmental themes. One-
to two-week summer camps offer many adventures in nature.

Chicago Environmental Network
Brookfield Zoo
Brookfield, IL 60513
(708) 485-0263, ext. 396

This networking organization has a large list of environmental groups
and a calendar of nature-related events.

Chicago Wilderness
Contact:
Chicagoland Environmental Network
(708) 485-0263, ext. 396

The ambitious goal of this first-of-its-kind partnership is to preserve, restore, and care for two hundred thousand acres of prairies, woodlands, oak savannas, wetlands, and waterways in the Chicago metropolitan area. It invites volunteers to help protect native species and unique habitats in the region that extends from Goose Lake Prairie (southwest of Joliet), through Cook, DuPage, Kane, Lake, McHenry, and Will counties (in and around Chicago), north to Chiwaukee Prairie in Wisconsin, and southeast along the shore of Lake Michigan to the Indiana Dunes.

Under the direction of the Chicago Region Biodiversity Council, it involves thirty-four organizations including Chicago-area zoos and museums, the Chicago Park District; the Forest Preserve District of Cook County; Illinois and federal agencies, and various environmental groups.

Calumet Environmental Resource Center
Chicago State University
Douglas Library, Room 303
9501 S. King Drive
Chicago, IL 60628-1598
(773) 995-2964

This center has information about environmental activities and groups that are trying to protect wetlands and bird refuges in the Calumet area.

Caretakers of the Environment International/USA
2216 Schiller Avenue
Wilmette, IL 60091
(847) 251-8935

This networking organization consists of high school students and teachers in more than fifty countries that think globally about environmental issues and work locally to solve them. International and local action projects include: Seeds of Biodiversity, river monitoring, litter cleanup, school beautification, and ecosystem restoration. At yearly meetings in different nations, member schools exhibit their projects, do hands-on investigations in the countryside, and discuss global environmental issues.

Center for Neighborhood Technology
2125 W. North Avenue
Chicago, IL 60647
(773) 278-4800

Become involved in promoting environmental reinvestment and re-building neighborhoods. This group builds solar greenhouses in low-income neighborhoods, promotes clean air and water, "greener cleaners" (environmentally friendly dry cleaning), urban agriculture, community planning, and energy justice. Its Campaign for Sustainable Chicago opposes big systems that drain resources from neighborhoods.

Chicago Green Alliance (an affiliate of Greens USA)
(312) 243-5619

This group publishes Chicago Green Calendar, holds monthly potluck meetings, participates in Earth Day, and hosts a Symposium on Sustainable Cities.

Citizens for Conservation
P.O. Box 435
Barrington, IL 60011
(847) 382-SAVE

Do prairie and savanna restoration, with controlled burns and winter brush removal. As a member, you will also collect prairie and wetland seeds; do bluebird monitoring; rescue native plants and wildflowers from construction sites and relocate them to Citizens for Conservation preserves. You can also participate in field trips, family walks at nature preserves, and an Earth Day celebration. The group offers brochures: *Natural Areas In and Around Barrington, Flint Creek Savanna,* and *The Natural Areas of Flint Creek.*

DuPage County Environmental Awareness Center
P.O. Box 3200
Lisle, IL 60532
(630) 719-2452

The center's brochures, *Three Rs: Reduce, Reuse, Recycle* and *Environmental Caretakers Resource Guide,* provide information on field trips, environmental shopping, water and energy use, speakers, starting an ecology club, and environmental restoration projects.

Friends of Downtown
6 N. Michigan Avenue, Suite 909
Chicago, IL 60602
(312) 726-4031

Voice your concerns about urban issues and downtown development planning at brown-bag lunches on the first Thursday of each month (at the Chicago Cultural Center). The group also has task forces that examine city space, planning for downtown, Miegs Field, Navy Pier, food and flower markets, and historic Michigan Avenue. As a member, you may also work with the Chicago Park District on the Cancer Survivors Garden and with other groups; give public testimony before the Chicago Plan Commission and the Landmarks Commission and City Council; or host a Summer Jazz Cruise.

Friends of the Chicago River
407 S. Dearborn Street, Suite 1580
Chicago, IL 60605
(312) 939-0490

Volunteer to do restoration along the Chicago River. Or participate in walking tours, canoe trips, and river cruises.

Friends of the Parks
407 S. Dearborn Street, Suite 1590
Chicago, IL 60605
(312) 922-3307

Improve Chicago's parks by assisting the Chicago Park District in an Earth Day cleanup and the September Beach Sweep (an international event). Attend the Osaka Garden Summer Festival in Jackson Park and the June Midnight Bicycle Ride.

Gaia Theater
6425 N. Francisco Street
Chicago, IL 60645
(773) 761-4233

If you have thespian aspirations, this professional company may be for you. The group performs at museums, zoos, nature centers and parks, and at environmental fairs and Earth Day celebrations. Its plays are about endangered species, recycling, water and rivers, and energy and water conservation, and its actors also teach theater and environmental science at elementary and junior high schools in Cook, Lake, DuPage, and King counties.

Girl Scouts of Chicago
222 S. Riverside Plaza, Suite 2120
Chicago, IL 60606
(312) 416-2500

Daisies (kindergarteners), Brownies (first to third graders), Juniors (fourth to sixth graders), Cadets (seventh to ninth graders) and Seniors (tenth to twelfth graders) work on badges and patches for each age level that deal with ecology, wildlife, and nature. They also have nature studies at summer camps in Wisconsin and Indiana.

Green Team
Chicago Parks
Chicago Park District
(312) 747-2121

Become an "ambassador" on in-line skates. Glide along the lakefront and report damage or emergencies in the park. Tell the people you meet about proper trash disposal, fire safety, and responsible use of the parks; and inform them about park attractions and cultural and educational programs.

Volunteer Illinois
Illinois Department of Natural Resources
524 S. 2nd Street
Springfield, IL 62701-1787
(217) 782-1274

Protect the natural heritage of Illinois by choosing from a variety of environmental tasks. Site associates maintain trails and facilities and do habitat improvement and prairie restoration. Site interpreters lead hikes, prepare exhibits, and teach about environmental topics. Campground hosts greet campers and report dangers. Other volunteers protect wildlife, forests, and fisheries.

Lake Michigan Federation
59 E. Van Buren Street, Suite 2215
Chicago, IL 60605
(312) 939-0838

The mission of this organization is to protect the lake and surrounding environment through citizen action. That is why volunteers participate in beach sweeps and work with the Canadian/U.S. International Joint Commission to protect the Great Lakes. You can work on special projects, such as the cleanup of contamination in Waukegan harbor, or landfills and munitions at Fort Sheridan. Or you can become involved in plans for developing 290 acres of Fort Sheridan's lakefront property that was donated to the Lake County Forest Preserve.

Nature Camera Club
Contact:
Velma Berry
(312) 944-1718

Show and discuss your photographs, go on camera safaris in natural areas, and enter photo competitions. Meetings take place the second Monday of the month, 7:30 P.M., at the west entrance of the Field Museum. Contests are based on themes such as: trees, landscapes, seascapes, wildflowers, animals, water in any form (rain, ice, etc.), and patterns of nature. (No picture may have a sign of a human being.)

The Nature Conservancy
8 S. Michigan Avenue, Suite 900
Chicago, IL 60603
(312) 346-8166

This national organization saves natural ecosystems, so members work on many cooperative programs. The Wild Garden Project begins with a workshop at Chicago Botanic Garden. Participants are given rare plants to put in their gardens, collect seeds, and return them to the group. Students and other volunteers who work on the North Branch Prairie Project do weed control, seed collecting, brush cutting, and

plantings in order to restore the forest preserve between Chicago and
Northbrook on the North Branch of the Chicago River. Other restora-
tion projects include Bunker Hill Prairie, Miami Woods Prairie, and
Harms Woods. The group also hosts an annual potluck dinner and an
August Family Prairie Day.

Volunteer Stewardship Network
The Nature Conservancy
8 S. Michigan Avenue, Suite 900
Chicago, IL 60603
(312) 346-8166, ext. 22

Join fifty-five hundred volunteers in northeastern Illinois who take care
of thirty-five thousand acres of rare prairie, woodland, and wetland
ecosystems. Work in an office, do plant propagation, artwork/photog-
raphy, ecosystem restoration, plant and animal monitoring, seed
collecting, research, environmental education, or lead nature walks.
Be part of a partnership that involves the Illinois Nature Preserves
Commission, land-owning public agencies, and many individuals.

Prairie University
The Nature Conservancy
8 S. Michigan Avenue, Suite 900
Chicago, IL 60603
(312) 346-8166, ext. 22

If you are a volunteer steward, you may participate in this environmental education program, which offers a tremendous variety of courses
in natural history and hands-on ecological projects.

Openlands Project
220 S. State Street, Suite 1880
Chicago, IL 60604-2103
(312) 427-4256

Become active in an organization that conserves open land and pro-
tects natural ecosystems. Major projects include the plan for the Joliet
Arsenal as the site of the Midewin National Tallgrass Prairie (see Chapter 5). The group also works with the Lake County Forest Preserve
District to improve the northern end of Fort Sheridan, a site with bluffs,
ravines, and threatened plant species on two miles of Lake Michigan
shoreline.

The Prairie Club
203 N. Wabash Street, Suite 1620
Chicago, IL 60601
(312) 899-1539

From the time it was established in 1908—when three hundred people at a time participated in nature hikes and worked to save the Indiana Sand Dunes—this club has fostered an appreciation of nature. Attend weekend hikes and trips in natural areas. Many activities take place at the fourteen-acre Spring Grove Camp, and at Camp Hazelhurst, which has six hundred feet of beachfront near Chesterton, Indiana.

The Sierra Club
1 N. LaSalle, Suite 4242
Chicago, IL 60602-4005
(312) 251-1680

Enjoy year-round activities such as prairie maintenance, wilderness hikes, cross-country skiing excursions, and canoe trips through natural areas. Take action on environmental concerns in the Great Lakes region, the United States, and other nations. Global issues are the focus of this national organization's political action agenda.

## Garden Groups

The Garden Clubs of Illinois, Inc.
1717 W. 31st Street, Suite A
Oakbrook, IL 60521
(630) 794-9625

Call Monday, Wednesday, and Thursday between 9 A.M. and 2 P.M. for information about joining or starting a garden club, and programs on gardening topics and environmental education. The *Garden Glories* publication lists garden walks and other events.

Note: For information about clubs that specialize in a particular flower (such as the rose, daylily, or daffodil), or to participate in bonsai, ikebana, and other garden organizations, contact:

Chicago Botanic Garden
(847) 835-5440

Morton Arboretum
(708) 968-0074

Herb Society of America, Northern Illinois Unit
1020 Grove Street
Evanston, IL 60201
Contact:
Beata Hayton
(847) 475-5912

If herbs are your passion, you can join discussions on cultivation, history, and the uses of herbs as flavoring agents, medicines, fragrances, and dyes. Meetings also cover topics such as herbs as radiation detectors and ornamentals; and herbs as sources of energy, rubber, and natural pesticides.

Gardeners of the North Shore
P.O. Box 704
Glenview, IL 60025
Contact:
Mort Ohren, President
(847) 998-0009

The first Tuesday of the month, find camaraderie among the many men and women who meet at the Chicago Botanic Garden. Bring cut flowers or potted plants for competition, listen to speakers on a range of horticultural topics, and participate in garden shows.

Midwest Daffodil Society
2959 Hobson Road
Downers Grove, IL 60517
Contact:
Laurie Skrzenta
(630) 969-1270

At meetings four times a year, find out about daffodil types and daffodil culture, exchange bulbs, and go on garden tours. Attend the Spring Daffodil Show at the Chicago Botanic Garden, where experts, novices, and juniors may enter single-stem daffodils for judging. Designs are entered by invitation, with prizes awarded by flower show judges. In early September, come for the Daffodil Bulb Sale at the Chicago Botanic Garden.

Northern Illinois Hosta Society
2959 Hobson Road
Downers Grove, IL 60517
Contact:
Laurie Skrzenta
(630) 969-1270

This club is devoted to the hosta, a perennial foliage plant native to Japan, Korea, and China. The plant is hardy in Illinois, and its eleven hundred registered varieties range in size from two inches tall to four feet tall and ten feet across. Speakers present ideas on growing hosta and gathering them from the wild during meetings. The society also hosts garden walks, displays, and workshops at gardening events. In January, the Winter Scientific Meeting has growers and speakers on propagating and raising hostas. In June, the Hosta Cut Leaf Show has leaves displayed in vases that are juried. In August there is a Hosta Auction.

Garden Club of Oak Park and River Forest
1117 Nichols Lane
Maywood, IL 60153
Contact:
Mrs. Beryl Garbrecht
(708) 343-8881

Come to monthly meetings and workshops on flower arranging and gardening. Members also work with the Oak Park Conservatory and do garden therapy at a nursing home. In May, there is a plant exchange; in June, a Garden Walk with ten gardens and plants for sale. The December holiday meeting invites professional florists to design floral arrangements and members present a mini–flower show and boutique.

Pond and Koi Society
P.O. Box 1251
North Riverside, IL 60546
(630) 879-3317

Water gardens and *koi*—ornamental Japanese carp bred for color and patterns—are the main interests of this organization. At meetings (on the third Friday of the month, 6:30 P.M. at Saw's Old Warsaw, 17th Avenue and Cermak Road, Broadview, Illinois) hear talks on topics such as vegetation choices, fish feeding regimens, how to winterize ponds, and other concerns. Special events include a May Trade Show with vendors of wetland and aquatic plants and fish; a July Pond Tour; and an August Koi and Goldfish Show, with speakers, seminars, and judging of fish.

Members set up ponds in their backyards with hardy and tropical water lilies, water papyrus, bamboos, cattail, and bog plants, some of which are fully submerged. Some of the ponds are stocked with koi or other fish, turtles, or tadpoles that mature into territorial frogs. These water gardens attract birds, butterflies, and dragonflies as well as salamanders and turtles.

University of Illinois Cooperative Extension Service
Cook/Chicago North Office
1000 N. Milwaukee, 4th Floor
Chicago, IL 60622
(773) 292-4444

Join the Master Gardeners Program for studies in botany and entomology (insect studies); and hands-on training with woody plants, annuals, perennials, vegetables, and lawns. This knowledge—plus team building and project planning skills—enable master gardeners to assist community and school groups with garden projects and food banks. Other programs cover integrated pest management, natural resources management, soil erosion, land preservation, home hazardous waste disposal, urban forestry, groundwater, reducing yard wastes, water conservation, rural-urban conflicts, nutrition, and food safety. Project VOLLY (Volunteer Leaders for Youth) promotes science activities in cooperation with the 4-H Program.

# Afterword

A re you a tourist? Or are you one of the three million people who
live in the largest urban ecosystem on Lake Michigan's southern
shore? Then you depend on nature for life support. You dwell in a
place that was drowned in a tropical sea, crushed by glaciers, then
covered by prairie and swamp. Although you are now surrounded by
streets and high-rise buildings, if you know where to look, you can find
a bit of the wild. You can glimpse the intricate web of nature that sustains us all.

Take time to do the really important things. Listen to waves lap
against the shore of Lake Michigan. Look at squirrels dashing across a
meadow. Smell the wildflowers in a wetland. Climb hills that were
made by glaciers. Revel in the rainbow of autumn forests. Feel winds
from the Arctic chill your skin. Watch birds fly over the cityscape. Rejoice with dawn, sunset, and clouds in the sky. Sense the natural wonders
of Chicago.

This city is much more than buildings, roads, and crowds of people.
It is also air and water and land and plants and animals. Everything is
interconnected and everything interacts in this urban environment.
But the city does not stand alone. It cannot exist without farms, forests, rivers, lakes, and wilderness. Chicago is in an intimate relationship

with the whole Earth and its nearest star. This is the true nature of Chicago. Celebrate it! And remember that nature needs nurture, so take care.

# Glossary

**alien invader:** A living thing that is not native to the area.

**bog:** A wetland with acidic water, where shrubs and trees grow on a floating mat of moss.

**coast:** The meeting place of land and water.

**constellation:** A star pattern.

**deciduous forest:** An ecosystem dominated by trees with broad flat leaves that turn color and fall in autumn and produce flowers that mature into fruits with seeds.

**ecosystem:** A community of plants and animals (including human beings) that interact with one another and with the physical environment.

**esker:** A snakelike ridge formed of sediments from a river that flowed deep inside a glacier.

**evergreen forest:** An ecosystem dominated by trees that have needle-like leaves that remain green all year and produce naked seeds on cones. Also called coniferous or gymnosperm forest.

**exotic species:** A living thing that is not native to the area.

**fen:** A wetland with plants adapted to alkaline water.

**glacier:** A lake of ice.

**gymnosperm:** A coniferous or evergreen tree. (*See* evergreen forest.)

**habitat:** A home or living space in nature with a particular set of physical and biological characteristics.

**humus:** Decayed plant material.

**kame** (pronounced "came"): A gravel hill formed by sediments that dropped out of a river flowing in a huge crack in a glacier.

**kettle:** A depression formed by a heavy glacier.

**lagoon:** A shallow pond.

**lake:** A body of fresh water surrounded by land.

**marl flat:** A flat level area, where water cannot flow out and plants are adapted to highly alkaline water.

**marsh:** A wetland dominated by grasses and reeds.

**moraine:** A long gravel hill made from the boulders and clay that fell out of a melting glacier.

**native species:** A plant, animal, or other organism that is adapted to the ecosystem.

**plankton:** Tiny plantlike algae and other single-celled organisms and small animals that drift on surface currents of lakes or oceans.

**pond:** A small lake.

**prairie:** A plant ecosystem dominated by grasses with many wildflowers. Mesic prairie is medium-dry prairie. Dry gravel prairie has plants adapted to dry and mineral-poor soil. Sand prairie has deep-rooted bunch grasses that resist the wind, and forbs with narrow small leaves and silvery hairs that conserve water. Virgin prairie is pristine prairie, intact since the time of the glaciers.

**reed:** A grasslike wetland plant with a rounded stem.

**salt springs:** Places where water that flows from underground limestone formations forcefully exits from the surface.

**sand dunes:** Hills of sand.

**savanna:** Scattered trees surrounded by prairie plants.

**sedge meadow:** An ecosystem dominated by sedges, grasslike plants with square stems, that grows where the water is rich in calcium and stays below the surface most of the year.

**seeps:** Places where water wells or oozes to the surface from underground limestone formations.

**shore or shoreline:** The border between land and water.

**succession:** A series of plant communities, each one adapted to a particular environment.

**swamp:** A wetland with scattered trees.

**tufa:** A light crumbly rock that is formed when calcium precipitates out of the water near alkaline seeps.

**tundra:** An ecosystem with low-growing plants and lichens adapted to severe winds, drought, and cold.

**urban ecosystem:** A community of plants and animals (including human beings), dominated by human-made structures but dependent on nature. A city.

**wetland:** The ecosystem at the meeting place of land and water, such as a marsh or swamp.

# Suggestions for Additional Reading

## Exploring Chicago

Bach, Ira J., and Susan Wolfson. *Chicago on Foot: Walking Tours of Chicago's Architecture.* Chicago: Chicago Review Press, 1987.

Mark, Norman. *Norman Mark's Chicago: Walking, Bicycling, and Driving Tours of the City.*

Chicago: Chicago Review Press, 1993.

Shaffer, Carolyn, and Erica Fielder. *City Safaris: A Sierra Club Explorer's Guide to Urban Adventures for Grownups and Kids.* San Francisco: Sierra Club Books, 1987.

## Chicago History

Balesi, Charles J. *The Time of the French in the Heart of North America.* Chicago: Alliance Francaise Chicago, 1992.

Burnham, Daniel H., and Edward H. Bennett. *Plan of Chicago.* New York: Da Capo Press, 1970.

Christensen, Daphne, ed. *Chicago Public Works: A History.* Chicago: Rand McNally and Co., 1973.

Cronan, William. *Nature's Metropolis: Chicago and the Great West.* New York: W. W. Norton and Co., 1991.

Kinzie, Mrs. John H. (Juliette Augusta McGill). *Wau-Bun, the Early Days in the Northwest.* New York: Derby and Jackson, 1856.

Moody, Walter D. *Wacker's Manual of the Plan of Chicago.* Chicago: Henneberry Company, 1911.

Pierce, Bessie Louise. *A History of Chicago: Volume II. From Town to City 1848–1871.* Chicago: University of Chicago Press, 1940.

Quaife, Milo M. *Checagou: From Indian Wigwam to Modern City, 1673–1835.* Chicago: University of Chicago Press, 1933.

Quaife, Milo M. *Chicago's Highways Old and New: From Indian Trail to Motor Road.* Chicago: D. F. Keller and Co., 1923.

## Ecology

Hare, Tony, ed. *Habitats.* New York: Macmillan Co., 1994.

Leopold, Aldo. *A Sand County Almanac.* New York: Ballantine Books, 1966.

Scott, Michael. *Ecology.* New York: Oxford University Press, 1995.

Storer, John H. *The Web of Life.* New York: New American Library, 1956.

"Urban Ecology: A Look at Chicago." *Current Energy and Ecology* Vol. 1 No. 3 (1978): 4–11.

Wilson, E. O., ed. *Biodiversity.* Washington, D.C.: National Academy Press, 1988.

## Nature Trails

Benton, Chris. *Chicagoland Nature Trails.* Chicago: Greatlakes Living Press for Contemporary Books, Inc., 1978.

Fisher, Alan. *Country Walks Near Chicago.* Baltimore, MD: Rambler Books, 1987.

*Illinois Visitors Guide.* Illinois Department of Commerce and Community Affairs, 1994.

Guides from Illinois Tourism Center, 1-800-526-0844.

Jeffords, Michael R., Susan L. Post, and Kenneth R. Robertson. *Illinois Wilds.* Urbana, IL: Phoenix Publishing, 1995.

McFall, Don, and Jean Karnes, eds. *A Directory of Illinois Nature Preserves: Volume 1–Northeastern Illinois.* Springfield, IL: Division of Natural Heritage, Illinois Department of Natural Resources, 1995.

Malo, John W. *Tranquil Trails*. Matteson, IL: Greatlakes Living Press, 1977.

Michaelson, Mike. *Chicago's Best-Kept Secrets*. Lincolnwood, IL: Passport Books, a division of NTC Publishing Group, 1991.

Watts, May Theilgaard. *Reading the Landscape*. New York: The Macmillan Co., 1957.

## Lake Michigan

Bailey, E. Stillman. *The Sand Dunes of Indiana: The Story of an American Wonderland Told by Camera and Pen*. Chicago: A. C. McClurg and Co., 1924.

Beecher, W. J. *Ancient Beaches and Dunes in Lincoln Park*. Chicago: Chicago Academy of Sciences.

_____. *Chicago's Ancient Coral Reefs*. Chicago: Chicago Academy of Sciences.

_____. *Lake Michigan's Ancient Beaches*. Chicago: Chicago Academy of Sciences.

_____. *The Indiana Dunes*. Chicago: Chicago Academy of Sciences.

Cantor, Michael. *The Great Lakes Guidebook: Lake Superior and Western Lake Michigan*. Ann Arbor, MI: University of Michigan Press, 1993.

Daniel, Glenda. *Dune Country: A Guide for Hikers and Naturalists*. Chicago: The Swallow Press, 1977.

Lake Michigan Federation Publications.

*Mobil 1994 Travel Guide: Great Lakes*. New York: Prentice Hall General Reference and Travel, a division of Simon and Schuster, 1994.

## Landforms

Adams, George F., and Jerome Wyckoff. *Landforms*. New York: Golden Press, 1971.

Conzen, Michael P., ed. *Geographical Excursions in the Chicago Region*. Washington, D.C.: Association of American Geographers and Contributors, 1995.

Nature Conservancy guides to Palos Restoration Project and Bluff Spring Fen.

## Skywatching

*New Concise Atlas of the Universe.* Chicago: Rand McNally and Co., 1978.

Peltier, Leslie. *Guideposts to the Stars: Exploring the Skies Throughout the Year.* New York: Macmillan Co., 1972.

Ridpath, Ian. *Atlas of Stars and Planets: A Beginner's Guide to the Universe.* New York: Facts on File, Inc., 1993.

## Prairies

Beecher, W. J. *The Chicagoland Prairie.* Chicago: Chicago Academy of Sciences.

Hirschi, Ron. *Save Our Prairies and Grasslands.* New York: Delacorte Press, 1994.

Korling, Torkel. *The Prairie: Swell and Swale.* Dundee, IL. 1972.

Pepoon, H. S. *Flora of the Chicago Region.* Chicago: The Lakeside Press, R. R. Donnelley and Sons Company, 1927.

Peterson, Roger Tory, and Margaret McKenny. *A Field Guide to Wildflowers of Northeastern and North-central North America.* Boston: Houghton Mifflin Co., 1968.

## Native Americans

Bierhorst, J., ed. *In the Trail of the Wind: American Indian Poems and Ritual Orations.* New York: Farrar, Straus, and Giroux, 1971.

Duel, Thorne. *American Indian Ways of Life.* Springfield, IL: Illinois State Museum, 1968.

*The Indians.* New York: Time-Life Books, 1973.

Lace, Edward J. *Prehistoric Indians of the Chicago Area.* Chicago: Chicago Academy of Sciences.

Wessler, Clark. *Indians of the United States.* New York: Doubleday, 1966.

## Forests

Beecher, W. J. *Chicagoland in the Coal Age.* Chicago: Chicago Academy of Sciences.

_____. *The Chicagoland Forest.* Chicago: Chicago Academy of Sciences.

Forest Preserve District of Cook County guides.

*Guide to Trees.* New York: Simon and Schuster, 1977.

Ketchum, Richard. *The Secret Life of the Forest.* New York: American Heritage Press, 1970.

## Wetlands

Beecher, W. J. *Chicagoland Pond Life.* Chicago: Chicago Academy of Sciences.

Ganeri, Anita. *Rivers, Ponds and Lakes.* New York: Dillon Press, 1991.

McCormick, Anita Louise. *Vanishing Wetlands.* San Diego, CA: Lucent Books, 1995.

*Pond Life.* New York: Golden Press, 1967.

## Rivers

Friends of the Chicago River guides.

Illinois and Michigan Canal National Heritage Corridor publications by the National Park Service.

Swanson, Leslie C. *Canals of Mid-America.* Moline, IL: 1984.

*The Chicago Portage.* Chicago: Chicago Historical Society.

## Parks and Gardens

Grese, Robert E. *Jens Jensen: Maker of Parks and Gardens.* Baltimore, MD: The John Hopkins University Press, 1992.

Johnston, Johanna. *Frederick Law Olmstead: Partner with Nature.* New York: Dodd, Mead and Co., 1975.

Lumsden, Sharon Lappin. *Green Byways: Garden Discoveries in the Great Lakes States.* Champaign, IL: Lime Tree Publications, 1993.

*Prairie in the City: Naturalism in Chicago's Parks, 1870–1940.* Chicago: Chicago Historical Society, 1991.

## Animals

Klein, Stanley. *The Encyclopedia of North American Wildlife.* New York: Facts on File, Inc., 1983.

Mlodinow, Steven. *Chicago Area Birds.* Chicago: Chicago Review Press, 1984.

Robbins, Chandler S., Bertel Bruun, and Herbert S. Zim. *Birds of North America: A Golden Field Guide.* New York: Golden Press, 1966.

Tinbergen, Niko. *Animal Behavior.* New York: Time Inc., 1965.

Zim, Herbert S., and George S. Fichter. *Zoo Animals.* New York: Golden Press, 1967.

# *Index*

Access to Fishing, Urban Fisheries
   Program, 195
Adler Planetarium and Astronomy
   Museum, 22, 29, 36, 64–66, 168, 173
   Aurora Borealis
      (Northern Lights), 227
   Meteorite Showers in
      the Night Sky, 219
   Sun Fests, 208, 215, 220, 225
Adventures in Nature Lecture Series,
   John G. Shedd Aquarium, 210
Affie Elephant's Birthday Party,
   Brookfield Zoo, 216
African-American drumming, 228
Air quality reports, 12
Alewives, 31
Alien invaders, 30–31, 106.
   *See also* Exotic animals
Alkaline groundwater, 49–50, 54, 70,
   110, 111
*American Buffalo* (Brown), 17
Anderson, Doug, 159
Animal organizations, 233–36
Animal Tracking, Hal Tyrrell Trailside
   Museum, 207
Animal Welfare League, 233–34
   Be Kind to Animals Week, 212
   Critter Club, 234
   Humane Education, 234
   Pet Therapy, 234
Animals, 157–82
Animal's Messiah, Anti-Cruelty
   Society, 226
Annual Cook County Owl Count,
   Chicago Audubon Society, 208
Annual Des Plaines River Canoe
   Marathon, Chicagoland Canoe Base,
   190, 192, 214

Annual Dog Wash, Anti-Cruelty
   Society, 218
Annual Spring Plant Sale, Chicago
   Botanic Garden, 213
Anti-Cruelty Society, 212, 234
   Animal's Messiah, 226, 234
   Annual Dog Wash, 218, 234
   Bark in the Park, 212, 234
Apparel Center, 122
Aquatic animals, 166–68
Arbor Day, Brookfield Zoo, 211
Arbor Day Plant Sale, Morton
   Arboretum, 212
Archaeology Awareness Day,
   Sand Ridge Nature Center, 220
Archaic Indians, 79
Archaic Period, 22
Arctic Blast, Lincoln Park Zoo, 206
Arctic tundra ecosystem, 51–52
Arrowhead Lake, 52
Art Institute of Chicago, 2, 25, 29, 174
Ashburn Prairie, 72
Asian trees, 90
Astronomy Museum. *See* Adler
   Planetarium
Atomic Age, 21, 26
Auburn Park, 106
August Family Prairie Day, Nature
   Conservancy, 241–42
August Koi and Goldfish Show,
   Pond and Koi Society, 246
Aurora Borealis (Northern Lights),
   Adler Planetarium and Astronomy
   Museum, 63, 227
Autumn Harvest Festival, 39
Autumn Roadside Flower Sale,
   Chicago Botanic Garden, 223
Aux Sable Aqueduct, 129, 130

Avondale Elementary School, 149
Azalea Flower Show
  Garfield Park Conservatory and
    Gardens, 207
  Lincoln Park Conservatory, 207

Bahai Temple to Baja Beach Club
  canoe trip, 191
Bailly de Messein, Honore Gratien
  Joseph, 44
Bailly/Chellberg Trail, 43–44
Baja Beach Club, 191
Bark in the Park, Lincoln Park, 212
Basalt plains, 71
Basketball, 183–84
Battle of Fallen Timbers, 23, 80, 118
Be Kind to Animals Week, Animal
  Welfare League, 212
Beach erosion, 29
Beach ridges, 9, 34–35, 73, 101, 135
Beaches, 36, 135
Beaubien Preserve, 126
Beebe, Charles William, 103
Belmont Harbor, 135, 188
Bennett, Edward H., 13–14, 26
Benson, Olaf, 135
Bergen Garden, 148
"Big Bang," 57
Biking, 129, 184–87
Biological control of pests, 154
Bird migration routes, 100
Bird Watching, Morton Arboretum, 228
Birding for Beginners, Little Red
  School House Nature Center, 228
Birds and birding, 73, 106, 112, 135,
  136, 158–63
Black Hawk, Chief, 24, 81
Black Partridge, Chief, 53
Black Partridge Woods Nature
  Preserve, 53
Blowouts, 42, 43
Blue Island, 34, 104, 125, 126
Bluff Springs Fen Nature Preserve,
  54–55, 70, 111

Boating, 187–94
Bogs, 45, 107–10
Bosons, 57
Botanical attractions, 133–56
Bottomland forest, 91
*Bowman, The* (Mestrovic, sculptor), 137
Boy Scouts of America, 236
Braidwood Dunes, 75
Brandon Road Dam, 193
Breeding Bird Census throughout
  Cook County, Chicago Audubon
  Society, 215
Briscoe Burial Mounds, 87
*Broken Symmetry* (sculpture), 56
Brookfield Zoo, 159, 165, 169–71, 198
  Arbor Day, 211
  Community and Corporate Tree
    Trim, 225
  Groundhog Day, 206
  Holiday Magic Festival, 227
  Memorial Day Weekend Festival, 213
  National Pig Day, 208
  Teddy Bear Picnic, 220
  Thanksgiving Day Feast, 225
  Zelebration, 218
  Zoo Photo Contest Display, 221
  Zoo Run Run, 224
Brown, Roger, *American Buffalo*
  (painting), 17
Buckingham Fountain, 36, 137
Buffalo, 10, 57
Buffalo Grove, 92
Buffalo Rock State Park, 86, 87,
  128, 130
Building codes, 19
Bunker Hill Prairie Project, Nature
  Conservancy, 241–42
Burial mounds, 22, 79, 87
Burnham, Daniel H. and Edward H.
  Bennett, *Plan of Chicago*, 13–14,
  26, 27
Burnham Harbor, 188, 203
Burnham Park, 36
Busse Woods Trail, 184

Calder, Alexander
  *Flamingo* (sculpture), 17
  *Universe* (sculpture), 18
Caldwell, Billy, 121
Calendar, sky, 59
Calendar of nature festivities, 205–28
Calumet area, 20
Calumet Beach, 79
Calumet beach level, 34
Calumet Division, Forest Preserve
  District of Cook County, 126
Calumet Environmental Resource
  Center, 237
Calumet Harbor, 28, 188
Calumet Park, 28
Calumet River, 115, 125–26
Calumet Woods, 126
Calumet-Sag Channel, 126
Camp Hazelhurst, Prairie Club, 243
Camp Logan, 46
Camp Sagawau, 52–53, 129, 199
  Ski-Fest, 206
Campaign for Sustainable Chicago,
  Center for Neighborhood
  Technology, 238
Camping, 194
Canal Bicycle Path, 129
Canoeing, 115, 190–94
Canopy of forest, 92
Cantigny Gardens, 156
Cap Sauers Holdings Nature
  Preserve, 55
Carboniferous forests, 22, 49
Caretakers of the Environment
  International/USA, 237–38
Carl Linneaus statue, 145
Carnivorous plants, 107–8
Carson Pirie Scott, 16
Caryn Center, 150
Catherine Chevalier Woods, 2
Centennial Trail, 129
Center for Neighborhood
  Technology, 238
Central business district, 15
Central Post Office, 14

*Ceres* (Storrs, sculptor), 18
Cernan Earth and Space Center, 66, 179
Chagall, Mark, *The Four Seasons*
  (sculpture), 17
Channahon State Park, 86, 87, 128
Chellberg Farm, 44
Chicago
  city panoramas, 21–22
  Department of Environment, 150
  as ecosystem, 7–8
  highway gardens of, 19–20
  incorporation of, 24
  the Loop, 15–18
  motto of (*Urbis in Horto*), 7
  Native American origin of name, 11
  nicknames of, 11
  population of, 24, 25
  port and industrial facilities, 36
  as railroad center, 25
  south side of, 20–21
  timeline of, 22–26
  underground, 50–51
  urban plan, 13–14
  weather in, 12–13, 16
Chicago Academy of Sciences, 161,
  174–75
Chicago Academy of Sciences and
  Chicago Herpetological Society,
  HerPETological Weekend, 221–22
Chicago Air and Water Show, Grant
  Park, 229
Chicago animal shelter, 233
Chicago Architecture Foundation, 131
*Chicago Area Birds* (Mlodinow), 158
Chicago Area Runners Association, 198
Chicago Audubon Society, 159, 235
  Annual Cook County Owl Count, 208
  Breeding Bird Census throughout
    Cook County, 215
  Chicago Urban Annual Christmas
    Count, 228
Chicago Avenue Pumping Station, 19
Chicago Bears, 185
*Chicago Bicycle Guidebook*
  (Palucki), 187

Chicago Blackhawks, 185
Chicago Board Options Exchange, 17
Chicago Board of Trade, 17–18, 72
Chicago Botanic Garden, 10, 83, 134,
    144–46, 165, 204, 243
    Annual Spring Plant Sale, 213
    Autumn Roadside Flower Sale, 223
    Holiday Display and Plant Sale, 227
    Plant Society Fair, 209
Chicago Bulls, 184, 185
Chicago Canine and Equine Police
    Unit, 212
Chicago Children's Museum, 176–77
Chicago Cubs, 185
Chicago Environmental Network, 236
Chicago Fire of 1871, 11, 18–19, 25, 50,
    104, 122, 133, 135
Chicago Fire Academy, 19
Chicago Flower and Garden Show,
    Navy Pier, 210
Chicago Green Alliance, 238
Chicago Herpetological Society,
    165, 235
    Live Reptile and Amphibian
    Show, 213
    Salamander Safari, 222–23
Chicago Herpetological Society and
    Chicago Academy of Sciences,
    HerPETological Weekend, 221–22
Chicago Historical Society, 175–76
Chicago Motor Club, 4
Chicago Ornithological Society, 159, 235
    Owl Census, 208
    Spring Bird Count and Bird
    Migration Field Trips, 213
    Winter Bird Count, 226
Chicago Park District, 26, 141, 143, 229
Chicago Park District Harbors, 188
Chicago Park Lagoons, 194
Chicago Peregrine Release and
    Restoration Project, 161
Chicago Picasso (sculpture), 16
Chicago Plain, 35
Chicago Portage: The Waterway West
    (Rebechini, sculptor), 117

Chicago Portage, 23, 24, 83, 116–17,
    118, 120, 127
Chicago Portage Canoe Trail, 85,
    192–93
Chicago Portage National Heritage Site,
    82, 125, 129
Chicago Region Biodiversity
    Council, 237
Chicago Ridge animal shelter, 233–34
Chicago River, 115
    in the city, 119–23
    floods on, 26, 31
    flow of, 25, 123
    main branch walk, 120–23
    See also Pollution
Chicago River Halloween Boat Float,
    Friends of the Chicago River, 223
Chicago River Lock, 121
Chicago skyline, 9
Chicago Sportfishing Association, 195
Chicago Transit Authority, 4
Chicago Urban Annual Christmas
    Count, Chicago Audubon Society, 228
Chicago Water Tower, 19, 33
Chicago Wilderness, 26, 237
Chicagoland Bicycle Federation, 184
Chicagoland Canoe Base
    Annual Des Plaines River Canoe
    Marathon, 214
    Mid-America Canoe Race, 216
Chicagoland Trails Northeastern Illinois
    Planning Commission, 184
Chinese-American Dragon Dance, 228
Chippewa tribe, 80, 81
Cholera, 31, 123
Chrysanthemum Flower Show, Garfield
    Park Conservatory and Gardens, 224
Chrysanthemum Show, Lincoln Park
    Conservatory, 224
Circadian rhythms, 60
Circle Interchange, 20
Cirrostratus clouds, 61
Cirrus clouds, 61
Cité, Lake Point Tower, 21
Citizens for Conservation, 238

City of Chicago Department of
Environment, 150
City in a Garden (*Ubis in Horto*), motto
of Chicago, 7, 134
City Hall, 104
City panoramas, 21–22
Civil War, 46, 72, 119
Civil War Living History Days,
Grove National Historic Landmark,
95–96, 218
Clark, George Rogers, 15
Clean Water Act, 124
Climax forests, 42, 90
Clouds, 61
Coal, 8, 49
Colored Sands Forest Preserve, 162–63
Columbia (statue), 21
Columbian Exposition of 1873, 21,
25, 138
Columbus Golf Course, 196
Columbus Park, 106
Comets, 64
Commonwealth Edison Nuclear Power
Plant and Power House, 46
Community and Corporate Tree Trim,
Brookfield Zoo, 225
Community gardens, 149–50
Compositae, sunflower family, 68
Concerts, outdoor, 229
Congress Circle, 14
Congress Plaza, 137
Congress Street, 14
Coniferous forest ecosystem, 51–52
Conservatories, 134
Cook County, establishment of, 24
Cook County Nesting Season Bird
Census, Chicago Audubon
Society, 216
Cook County Preserve Trails
(skiing), 200
Cook County's Wildlife Rehabilitation
Center, 99
Coral reefs, 32–33
Coral sea, 8
Cottonwood trees, 37, 38, 41, 42, 90

Cowles Bog Area, 45
Cowles, Henry, 38, 40, 45
Cowles Wetland, 105
Crabtree Lake, 98
Crabtree Nature Center, 97–98
Crabtree Nature Center, Migratory
Bird Day, 213
Cranberry Slough Nature Preserve, 112
Critter Club, Animal Welfare
League, 234
Cronon, William 7
Cross-country skiing, 53, 199–200
Cross-Country Slide and Glide Party, 53
Crosse Point Lighthouse, 47–48
Cubs Care Baseball Leagues, 202
Cumulonimbus clouds, 61
Cumulus clouds, 61
Cuneo Museum and Gardens, 155
Curie, Marie, 173

Daffodil Bulb Sale, Midwest Daffodil
Society, 244
Daley Plaza, 16
Daley, Richard, 16
Dan Ryan Expressway, 20
Dana, Charles A., 11
Days of week, 59
Dearborn Street Bridge, 122
Deciduous trees, 89, 93
Deep Tunnel, 124
Deer Grove Forest Preserve Trail, 186
Delaware tribe, 80
Deming Place Bridge, 35, 135
Des Plaines Conservation Area, 78
Des Plaines River, 34, 73, 115, 124–25
boating on, 190
dolomite rock on, 70
floods on, 28
flow of, 34
Native Americans on, 11
sewage in, 25
Des Plaines River Trail in Lake
County, 186
Des Plaines River Wetland
Demonstration Project, 111, 124

*Directory of Illinois Nature Preserves, Vol. 1, Northeastern Illinois,* 230
Dirkson Federal Building, 17
Disabled people. *See* Physically challenged people
Diversey Driving Range and Miniature Golf, 196
Diversey Harbor, 135, 188
Doane telescope, 65
Dolomite prairies, 70, 77
Dorothy Buell Memorial Visitor Center, 45
Douglas, Paul, 39
Douglas Park, 20, 106
Douglas Park Formal Garden, 141
Downers Grove, 92
Downtown area, 15
Drainage divide, 117–18
Dreidel game, 228
Dresden Bluffs, 73
Dresden Nuclear Power Plant, 73
Dress for hiking, 4
Du Sable, Jean Baptist Point, 23, 96, 120
Dubuffet, Jean, *Monument à la Bête Debout* (sculpture), 17
Dune lands, 37–48, 82
DuPage County Bikeways, 187
DuPage River Dam, 130

Early Woodland people, 22, 79
Eastern prairies, 71
Earth
  and the calendar, 59
  and the stars, 60
  and the weather, 61
Earth art, 87
Earth Day
  Grove National Historic Landmark, 95, 211
  Sand Ridge Nature Center, 100, 211
Earth fill, 104
Eastern deciduous forest ecosystem, 51–52

Ecology
  forest, 92
  succession principle, 38, 40, 42, 89–91
Ecosystems, 51–52
  Chicago as, 7–8, 62
  forest succession, 89–90
  of Lake Michigan, 27, 30, 31–32
  of prairies, 71
  restorations of, 242
  sand dune succession, 38, 40, 42
Edens Expressway, 19
Effigy tumuli, 87
Eiseley, Loren, 133
Eisenhower Expressway, 20
Elevated (El) trains, 15
Elgin/O'Hare Expressway, 20
Elmhurst College Arboretum, 153
Emerson, Ralph Waldo, 233
Endangered species, 81
Environmental action groups, 236–43
Environmental issues, 100
Environmentalists, 29
Equitable Building, 79, 120
Erie Canal, 24, 71
Eskers, 49, 55
Evans Field, 85
Evanston Art Center, 48
Evanston Lakefront, 47–48
Evergreen Cemetery, 87
Evergreen forests, 89
Exotic animals, 30–31. *See also* Alien invaders
Explorers, 10, 23, 68, 116
Eye of the bog, 109–10

Fall Honey and Harvest Festival, River Trail Nature Center, 223
Family Fair, Morton Arboretum, 221
Farms, 10, 70, 71–72, 156, 165
Feeding wildlife, 4
Fens, 45, 54, 70, 77, 110, 111
Fermilab, 10, 56–58
*Fermilab's Pursuit of the Fundamental* (film), 57
Festivals, lakefront, 229

Field Museum of Natural History, 10, 29, 36, 168, 177–78
Field Museum of Natural History, Winter Festivals and Games, 227–28
Fifty-Ninth Street Harbor, 188
*Fire* (Garner, sculptor), 144
Fire of 1871. *See* Chicago Fire of 1871
Fires
  designated sites for, 4
  and oak trees, 92
  and prairies, 71
First American Water Landmark, 19
First National Bank, 17
First-aid kits, 4
Fish in Lake Michigan, 30–31
Fisher Site, 87
Fishing, 106, 112, 165, 194, 203
Fishing Derby, 195
Fishing grounds, 83
Fishnet rapids, 193
*Flamingo* (Calder, sculptor), 17
Floods, 104
  on Chicago River, 26, 31, 50
  on Des Plaines River, 28
  prevention of, 124
Floor of forest, 92
Flower shows, 139
Flyways, 158
Food chain, 32
Food preservation, 82
Food for wildlife, 4
Forbs, 68, 75
Fords, 82
Foredunes, 40
Forest Preserve District of Cook County, 14, 26, 52, 102, 230
  Haunted Forest, 224
  Pow Wow, 222
Forest Preserve District of DuPage County, 102, 231
Forest Preserve District of Kane County, 230
Forest Preserve District of Will County, 102, 230
Forest preserve system, 14

Forest succession, 89–90
Forested bog, 110
Forests, 89–102
  Asian trees, 90
  locations of, 90–91
  and rain, 9
  in winter, 94
Fort Dearborn, 15, 24, 82, 85, 103, 118, 120, 121, 123
Fort Dearborn Massacre, 20
Fort St. Louis, 87
Fort Sheridan, 242
Fossil fuels, 8, 12
Foucault pendulum, 57, 179
*Four Seasons, The* (Chagall, sculptor), 17
Fourth of July celebrations, Grant Park, 229
Fox River Bike Trails, 187
Fox River Valley, 56
Fox tribe, 23, 80
Fraser, James Earle, 120
Free Fishing Days, Urban Fisheries Program, 216
French, Daniel Chester, *The Republic* (sculpture), 138
French voyageurs, 85–86, 179
Frese, Ralph, 190
Friends of the Chicago River, 130, 141
  Chicago River Halloween Boat Float, 223
  River Rescue Day, 216
Friends of the Parks, 211
  Midnight Bicycle Ride, 217
Friends of the Parks and Lake Michigan Federation, Great Lakes Beach Sweep, 221
Fruit Tree Grafting Seminar, Garfield Farm Museum, 209
Fuller Park, 134
Fulton Market, 21
Fur traders, 15, 23, 44, 85–86, 116, 119, 120

G.A.R. Woods, 99
Gaia Theater, 240

Garbage, 4
Garden Club of Evanston, 152
Garden Club of Oak Park and River
  Forest, 245
Garden Clubs of Illinois, Inc., 150, 243
  Spring Garden Walks, 214
Garden groups, 243–46
Garden Walk, Garden Club of Oak Park
  and River Forest, 245
Gardeners of the North Shore, 244
Gardening advice, 149
Gardens, 134
  community, 149–50
  school, 148–49
  suburban, 151–56
Garfield Farm Museum, 156, 181
  Fruit Tree Grafting Seminar, 209
  Heirloom Garden Show, 220
  Rare Breeds Livestock Show, 214
Garfield Park, 35, 106, 134
Garfield Park Conservatory and
  Gardens, 2, 134, 138–40
  Azalea Flower Show, 207
  Chrysanthemum Flower Show, 224
  Holiday Flower Show, 226
  Spring Flower Show, 209
Garner, Ted, *Fire* (sculpture), 144
Gebhard Woods State Park, 128
General Electric Midwest Fuel
  Recovery Plant, 73
Gensburg-Markham Prairie Nature
  Preserve, 73
"Getting there," 3–4
Gillson Park, 153
Ginkgo Organic Gardens, 150
Girl Scouts of Chicago, 240
Glacial Till, 44
Glaciers, 8–9, 22, 34, 49, 52, 53, 69.
  *See also* Ice Ages
Glenbrook North High School Prairie
  Nature Preserve, 74
Glencoe Gardens, 152
Glenwood beach level, 34
*Goat* (Peart, sculptor), 144
Golden Dome Fieldhouse, 139, 140

Golfing, 196
Gompers Park, 141
Gompers, Samuel, 141
Goose Island, 123
Goose Lake Prairie State Natural Area,
  2, 72–73, 129
Graceland Cemetery, 35, 81
Graminaeae, grass family, 68
Graminoid bog, 110
Grand Crossing Park, 143
Grant Creek Prairie Nature Preserve, 76
Grant Park, 14, 36, 133, 137, 200
  Chicago Air and Water Show, 229
  Fourth of July celebrations, 229
  Petrillo Music Shell, 229
  Taste of Chicago, 229
  Venetian Night, 229
Grass family, Graminaeae, 68
Grasslands, 9, 67–78
Gravel prairies, 70
Great divide, 117–18
Great Lakes
  formation of, 9
  waterway link to Mississippi River,
    23, 24, 116
Great Lakes Beach Sweep, Lake
  Michigan Federation and Friends of
  the Parks, 221
Great Lakes Fisheries Commission, 31
Great Western Bike Trails, 187
Green Bay Road, 36
Green Bay Trail, 84, 97
Green and Growing Fair, University of
  Illinois Cooperative Extension
  Service, 212
Green spaces, 14
Green Team, 240
Greens USA, 238
Groundhog Day, Brookfield Zoo, 206
Grove National Historic Landmark,
  95–96
  Civil War Living History Days, 218
  Grove Folk Fest, 222
Guided river tours, 130
Gurnee Ford, 84

Hal Tyrrell Trailside Museum, 99
Animal Tracking, 207
Halloween Walk, Chicago Botanic
Garden, 223
Ham Bone Lake, 52
Harbors, Chicago Park District, 188
Hardpan, 50
Hardwood trees, 90, 91
Harms Woods Project, Nature
Conservancy, 241–42
Haunted Forest, Forest Preserve
District of Cook County, 224
Havel, Vaclev, 59
Heald, Captain Nathan, 20, 85
Heat island, 12
Heat wave deaths, 26
Heidecke State Fish and Wildlife
Area, 129
Heirloom Garden Show, Garfield Farm
Museum, 220
Heller Nature Center, Midwinter
Owling, 228
Henry Crown Space Center, 179
Herb and Scented Plant Sale, Oak Park
Conservatory, 214
Herb Society of America, Northern
Illinois Unit, 244
Herbaceous plants, 68
Hering, Henry, 120
HerPETological Weekend, Chicago
Academy of Sciences and Chicago
Herpetological Society, 221–22
Hickory Creek, 87
High School Coeducational Explorer
Post, 236
Highway gardens, 19–20
Highway signs, 3
Highway system of Chicago, 13–14
Higinbotham Woods
Earthwork, 87
Hiking, 129, 197
dress for, 4
*Hiking and Biking in Cook County,
Illinois* (Hochgesang), 186, 187
Hill prairies, 70

Hochgesang, Jim, *Hiking and Biking in
Cook County, Illinois*, 186, 187
Hoffman, Malvina, 178
"Hog Butcher to the World," 11
Holiday Display and Plant Sale, Chicago
Botanic Garden, 227
Holiday Flower Show
Garfield Park Conservatory and
Gardens, 226
Lincoln Park Conservatory, 226
Holiday Magic Festival,
Brookfield Zoo, 227
Homeless people, 150
Hooked on Fishing, 195
Hoosier (Indiana) farmers, 15
Horseback riding, 198
Hosta Auction, Northern Illinois Hosta
Society, 219, 245
Hosta Cut Leaf Show, Northern Illinois
Hosta Society, 245
Hubbard, Gurdon S., 15
Hubbard's Trace, 16, 126
Hughes, Langston, 115
Humane Education, Animal Welfare
League, 234
Humboldt Park Flower Garden, 141
Hummocks, 110
Humus, 50
Hunting grounds, 83
Hurley Park, 106
Hurley Playlot, 143
Huron tribe, 80
Hyde Park, 21

"I Will City," 11, 19
Ice Ages, 8–9, 49. *See also* Glaciers
IDOT. *See* Illinois Department of
Transportation
Illinois
animals of, 163–66
boundaries of, 118–19
symbols of, 19, 51, 92, 101, 105, 163
Illinois Art Gallery, 17
Illinois Beach State Park, 36, 37, 46–47,
161, 194

Illinois Bikeways, 187
Illinois Central Railroad, 33
Illinois Department of Conservation, 106, 194
Illinois Department of Natural Resources, 194, 231
Illinois Department of Transportation (IDOT), 20
Illinois lakefront between Wisconsin and Indiana, 36
Illinois and Michigan Canal, 20, 24, 25, 33, 86, 118, 119, 123, 127–30
Illinois and Michigan Canal State Trail, 86, 128–30, 186, 194
Illinois and Michigan Canal Visitor Center, Lockport Old Canal Days, 217
Illinois and Michigan National Heritage Corridor, 74, 86–87, 125, 128–30, 131, 186, 190
Illinois National Guard, 46
Illinois Nature Preserves Commission, 242
Illinois Prairie Path Trail, 187
Illinois River, 34, 125
  flow of, 34, 123
  sewage in, 25
Illinois Territory, 23, 24, 118
  population of, 72
  and property rights, 81
Illinois Waterways, 127
Immigrant parks, 134
Immigrants, 68, 71, 123, 127, 134. *See also* Pioneers; Settlers
Indian Boundary Division of the Forest Preserve, 84–85
Indian Boundary Line, 52, 85, 126
Indian Boundary Park, 142
Indiana Dunes National Lakeshore, 36, 37, 38–45, 194
Indiana Dunes State Park, 46
Indians. *See* Native Americans
Industrial development, 39
Inland harbor, 28–29
Insect repellent, 4
International Cluster of Dog Shows, 210

International Kennel Club of Chicago, 210
Iroquois people, 80, 87
Isle à La Cache Museum, 85–86, 129, 179, 193
  Rendezvous: A French and Indian Trade Fair, 215

Jack pines, 41
Jackson Inner and Outer Harbors, 188
Jackson Park, 20, 21, 32, 36, 133, 138, 158, 160
Jackson Park Driving Range, 196
Jackson Park Golf Course, 196
James R. Thompson Center, 17
Jardine Water Filtration Plant, 36
Jean Baptist Point Du Sable High School (south), 148–49
Jefferson, Thomas, 67, 118, 120
Jensen, Jens, 48, 49, 133, 135, 152, 154
Jogging and running, 198
John G. Shedd Aquarium, 29, 36, 165, 167
  Adventures in Nature Lecture Series, 210
John Hancock Center, 21, 51
Joliet Arsenal, 78, 242
Joliet, Louis, 23, 82, 83, 85, 116, 117, 192
Joseph P. Kennedy, Jr. Foundation, 202
Judd Goldman Adaptive Program, 189, 203
July Inner City Games, 183
June Sand Volleyball Tournament, 202
*Jungle, The* (Sinclair), 21
Jurica Nature Museum, 181–82

Kames, 49, 54–55, 55
Kane County Bike Trails, 187
Kankakee marshes, 23
Kankakee River, 73, 125
Kankakee River State Park, 86, 128
Karnes, Jean, 230
Kaskaskia tribe, 80, 87
Kennedy Expressway, 19
Kennicott House, 95

Kettles, 49
Kinzie, John, 15, 85, 120
*Koi*, 134, 218, 245
Kruse's Hole, 97
Kwanzaa games, 228

La Salle, René-Robert Cavelier, Sieur de, 14, 23, 87, 118
Ladd Arboretum, 151, 191
Lagoons, 106–7
Lake Calumet, 28, 161
Lake Chicago, 9, 34, 35, 73, 100
Lake County Forest Preserve, 102, 111, 124, 230, 242
Lake Michigan, 27–48
    alien invaders in, 30–31
    beach erosion, 29
    boating on, 187–88
    drinking water from, 25, 27, 32
    ecosystem of, 27, 30, 31–32
    effects on weather, 12, 27
    fish in, 31
    formation of, 9
    measurements of, 33
    navigation on, 28
    pollution in, 31–32
    recreation on, 28
    turnovers in, 29, 31
    water levels of, 22, 23, 30
Lake Michigan Federation, 241
Lake Michigan Federation and Friends of the Parks, Great Lakes Beach Sweep, 221
Lake Michigan Shoreline ski trails, 200
Lake Point Tower, 21
Lake Renwick Heron Rookery Nature Preserve, 163
Lake Shore Drive, 29, 36
Lake Shore Road, 103
Lakefront festivals, 229
Lakefront park system, 14
Lakefront Ramble, 185
Lambert, Jacque H., 137
Land ownership, 81
Landfills, 124, 135

Landscape architects, 134
LaSalle Bank's Chicago Marathon, 198
Laughton Brothers Trading Post, 83, 117, 125
Laughton's Ford, 82
Le Rocher, 87
Lederman Science Education Center, 57
Leguminosae, pea family, 68
Leptons, 57
Lighthouse Beach, 48
Lighthouse Landing Park, 37, 39, 47–48
Lilacia Park, 154
Limestone, 8, 32–33, 49, 51
Lincoln, Abraham, 25, 135
Lincoln Park, 21, 25, 28, 35, 36, 133, 134, 135–36, 160
    Bark in the Park, 212
Lincoln Park Conservatory, 2, 134, 135, 136
    Azalea Flower Show, 207
    Chrysanthemum Show, 224
    Holiday Flower Show, 226
    Spring Flower Show, 208
Lincoln Park Zoo, 135, 136, 165, 168–69
    Arctic Blast, 206
Linnaeus, Carl, 145
Little Calumet River, 190
Little Red School House Nature Center, 98–99, 162, 165, 201
    Birding for Beginners, 228
Live Reptile and Amphibian Show, Chicago Herpetological Society, 213
Lizzadro Museum of Lapidary Art, 180
Lockport Old Canal Days, Illinois and Michigan Canal Visitor Center, 217
Lockport Prairie Nature Preserve, 77
Locks, 130
Logan Square Reef, 32
Logging, 90
Long Grove Strawberry Festival, Long Grove Merchants' Association and Tourist Center, 217
Loop tours, 15–18
Louisiana Purchase, 24, 118, 120
Low shrub bog, 110

Lower Fox River canoe trip, 193–94
Loyou, Jacque H., 137
Lumber interests, 81
Lunar cycle, 63
Lunar eclipse, 64

MacArthur Woods Nature
    Preserve, 162
McCormick Place, 29
McFall, Don, 230
McKinley Woods, 129
Magic Hedge Bird Sanctuary, 160
"Magnificent Mile," 14
Main Branch Walk on Chicago River,
    120–23
Main Ring accelerator, 57
Maple Syrup Festival, North Park
    Village Nature Center, 209
Maps, 4
Marathons, 198
Marl flats, 50, 54, 111
Marquette, Father Jacque, 23, 82, 83,
    85, 87, 116, 117, 192
Marquette Golf Course, 196
Marquette Park, 2, 106, 142
Marram grass, 37, 38, 39, 40, 42
Marshes, 54, 74, 75, 77, 105, 110
Mary Berkemeier Quinn Park of
    Trees, 142
Master Gardeners Program, 150
Material Service Corporation, 193
May Trade Show, Pond and
    Koi Society, 246
Mayor Daley's Fishing Derby, 195
Mayor's Office of Special Events,
    183, 229
Meat inspection laws, 21
Meigs Field, 29, 36
Memorial Day Weekend Festival,
    Brookfield Zoo, 213
Merchandise Mart, 122
Mercury Line, 131
Merrick Rose Garden, 151–52
Mesic black soil prairie, 54, 69–70,
    73, 74, 76

Mestrovic, Ivan
    *The Bowman* (sculpture), 137
    *The Spearman* (sculpture), 137
Meteorite Showers in the Night Sky,
    Adler Planetarium and Astronomy
    Museum, 219
Meteors, 64
Miami tribe, 80
Miami Woods Prairie Project, Nature
    Conservancy, 241–42
Michigan Avenue, 14, 25, 35
Michigan Avenue Bridge, 120
Mid-America Canoe Race, Chicagoland
    Canoe Base, 216
Midewin National Tallgrass Prairie,
    78, 242
Midnight Bicycle Ride, Friends of the
    Parks, 217
Midway Plaisance, 21
Midwest Daffodil Society, 244
Midwest Stock Exchange, 17
Midwest Volleyball Professionals, 201
Midwest's Largest Environmental
    Cleanup of Parks and Beaches, 211
Midwinter Owling, Heller Nature
    Center, 228
Migrating birds, 104
Migratory Bird Day, Crabtree Nature
    Center, 97, 213
Miller Woods Trail, 42–43
Mining interests, 81
Mississippi Flyway, 158
Mississippi River
    sewage in, 124
    waterway link to Great Lakes,
        23, 24, 116
Mississippi Valley, 8
Mississippian people, 23, 79–80
Mixed-grass prairies, 71
Mlodinow, Steven,
    *Chicago Area Birds*, 158
*Mobius Strip* (Wilson, sculptor), 57
Momence Gladiolus Festival, 219
Monadnock Building, 17
Monroe Harbor, 188

Monroe, James, 67
Montrose Harbor, 2, 21, 135, 188
Montrose Point, 21, 32
*Monument à la Bête Debout*
    (Dubuffet, sculptor), 17
Moon, 59, 63
Moore, Henry, *Nuclear Energy*
    (sculpture), 21
Moraines, 49, 52, 53, 55, 70, 74
Morton Arboretum, 2, 10, 72, 91, 134,
    146–48, 149, 244
    Arbor Day Plant Sale, 212
    Bird Watching, 228
    Family Fair, 221
    Winter Weekend of Trees, 207
Morton Grove, 92
Morton Salt Company, 147
Mount Forest Island, 34, 112
Mt. Baldy Trail, 44
Museum of Science and Industry, 21,
    36, 138, 178–79
Museums, 173–82
    suburban, 179–82
    urban, 173–79

Names
    of Chicago, 11
    of streets, 14–15
NASA. *See* National Aeronautics and
    Space Administration
National Aeronautics and Space
    Administration (NASA), 64
National Garden Week, 215
National Park Service, 86, 128
National Pig Day, Brookfield Zoo, 208
National Veterans Cemetery, 78
Native American Education Service, 87
Native American sites on the Illinois
    and Michigan Canal National
    Heritage Corridor, 86–87
Native Americans, 79–87, 116, 220, 222
    ancient sites, 129, 130
    and buffalo, 10, 71
    early tribes, 10–11
    as guides, 117

names from, 11, 15
    raids by, 80–81, 118
    and settlers, 80–81
    timeline of, 22–26
    trails of, 14, 15, 36, 44, 82, 84
    villages of, 81–82
Natural Garden, Prairie Days, 219
Natural resources, 8
Nature Artist Guild Exhibition, Morton
    Arboretum, 215
Nature Camera Club, 241
Nature Conservancy, The, 54, 241–42
Nature Ski, 53
Navigation on Lake Michigan, 28
Navy Pier, 22, 35–36, 128, 131
    Chicago Flower and Garden Show, 210
Nelson, Swain, 135
New France (Canada), 28
New Year's Day 5 K Run and Walk,
    198, 205
Niagaran dolomite, 53
Night sky, 62–63
Nimbostratus clouds, 61
Nippersink Advance, 35
Nordic Ski Program, 199
North Branch of the Chicago River, 185
North Branch of the Chicago River
    Project, Nature Conservancy, 241–42
North Branch Prairie Project, Nature
    Conservancy, 241–42
North Park College, 149
North Park Village Nature Center,
    94–95, 160
    Maple Syrup Festival, 209
    Owl Prowl, 206
    Winter Solstice Festival, 95, 227
North Pier, 191
North Pond, 35
North Pond Wildlife Preserve, 136
North suburban beaches, 200
Northerly Island, 36
Northern hardwood forest ecosystem,
    51–52
Northern Illinois Hosta Society, 245
    Hosta Auction, 219

Northern lights, 63
Northwest Expressway, 32
Northwest Indian Confederation, 80
Northwest Ordinance, 23
Northwest Territorial Alliance, 100, 225
Northwest Territory, 80
Northwestern train station, 122
Northwestern University, 36, 47, 152
*Nuclear Energy* (Moore, sculptor), 21
Nuclear reactions, 60

Oak forests, 22, 38, 90, 92, 94
Oak Park Conservatory, 154–55, 245
Oak Park spit, 34
Oak savannas, 54, 70, 71, 74
Oak Woods Cemetery, 143
Ogden Slip, 191
O'Hare Airport, 12, 50, 125
Ohio Street Beach, 36
Old Canal Days, 129
Old Geese tavern, 121
Old Kaskaskia Village, 87
Old Stone Gate, 20–21
O'Leary's barn, 18
Olive Park, 36
Olmstead, Frederick Law,
  133, 134–35
Olsen, Fritz, *Ripples* (sculpture), 144
Omnimax Theater, 179
Openlands Project, 242
Organizations, 233–46
Ottawa Trail Woods, 81, 83, 117
Ottawa tribe, 44, 80, 81
Outdoor concerts, 229
Outdoor recreation, 183–204
Owl Census, Chicago Ornithological
  Society, 208
Owl Prowl, North Park Village
  Nature Center, 206

Paleo-Indian hunters, 22, 79
Palm House, Garfield Park
  Conservatory, 139, 140
Palos Preserve, 98, 162
Palos Restoration Project, 74

Palucki, Michael, *Chicago Bicycle
  Guidebook*, 187
Pampas, 71
Park commissions.
  *See* Chicago Park District
Parking garages, 50
Parks
  Chicago, 133–44
  immigrant, 134
  suburban, 144–48
Passenger pigeons, 10, 18
Paul H. Douglas Center for
  Environmental Education, 38, 42–43
Paul H. Douglas Nature Sanctuary,
  2, 138, 160
Pea family, Leguminosae, 68
Peart, Jerry, *Goat* (sculpture), 144
Peat, 8
Peat moss, 107
Pedestrian arcades, 50
Peregrine Places, 151
Perennials, 68
Pesticides, 154
Pet Therapy, Animal Welfare
  League, 234
Petrillo Music Shell, Grant Park, 229
Philippine dancing, 228
Photosynthesis, 61–62
Physically challenged people, 189
  access for, 3
  sports for, 202–4
Picasso, Pablo, 157, 174
  *Chicago Picasso* (sculpture), 16
Pigeons, passenger, 10, 18
*Pillar of Fire* (Weiner, sculptor), 19
Pine forests, 22, 90
Pinhook Bog, 39
Pioneer cemeteries, 70, 72
Pioneer plants, 40, 41, 42
Pioneers, 14–15, 127. *See also*
  Immigrants; Settlers
*Plan of Chicago* (Burnham and
  Bennett), 13–14
Planets, 63
Plank roads, 103–4

Plant Society Fair, Chicago Botanic
Garden, 209
Plantlife Resources Project, 152
Plants, 133–56
and sunlight, 61
wetland, 104, 105
Plows, 10, 71
Polish singing, 228
Pollination, 68
Pollution, 12
and Calumet River, 126
in Chicago River, 106, 121–22, 123
and forests, 90
in Lake Michigan, 31–32, 121
prevention of, 124
of rivers, 115
and wetlands, 104
*See also* Sewage
Pond and Koi Society, 245–46
Pond Tour, 218
Pope, Nathaniel, 118–19
Port of Chicago, 36, 119, 191
Portages, river, 83
Potawatomi Pathways, 39
Potawatomi tribe, 11, 24, 44, 52, 53, 80,
81, 82, 83, 85, 87
Pow Wow, Forest Preserve District of
Cook County, 222
Powderhorn Lake, 126
Prairie Club, 243
Prairie Days, Natural Garden, 219
Prairie groves, 91–92
Prairie potholes, 71
Prairie territory, 9–10
Prairie University, Nature
Conservancy, 242
Prairies, 67–78
arrival of, 22
names of, 70, 71
Precipitation, 12–13
and Lake Michigan, 29–30
rain, 9
snow, 13
*See also* Weather
Private property, 4

Project VOLLY (Volunteer Leaders
for Youth), 246
Promontory Point, 21, 138
Property rights, 81
*Proton Pagoda* (sculpture), 57
Public wilderness, 81

Quaife, Milo, 11
Quaking bogs, 107, 108
Quarks, 57

Railroad rights-of-way, 70, 72, 165
Railroads, 16, 25, 72, 119, 127
Rainbow Fleet Program, 189
Ranching interests, 81
Rare Breeds Livestock Show, Garfield
Farm Museum, 214
Ravinia Festival, Ravinia Park, 229
Real estate interests, 81
Rebechini, *Chicago Portage:
The Waterway West* (sculpture), 117
Recreation, 183–204
on Lake Michigan, 28
therapeutic programs and sites,
202–4
Rendezvous: A French and Indian
Trade Fair, Isle à La Cache Museum,
86, 215
*Republic, The* (French, sculptor), 138
Republican National Convention, 25
Restoration of ecosystems, 242
Revolutionary War, 23, 80, 225
Rhizomes, 68
Ridge Park, 106
Riis Park, 34, 106
*Ripples* (Olsen, sculptor), 144
Riprap, 29
River North, 122
River portages, 83
River Rescue Day, Friends of the
Chicago River, 216
River Trail Nature Center, 96–97, 192
Fall Honey and Harvest
Festival, 223
Sugar Maple Festival, 210

Rivers, 115–31
  guided tours of, 130–31
  history of, 115–16
  trade on, 119
  urban, 115
Riverside Ford, 82
Robert A. Black Golf Course, 196
Robert R. McCormick Museum, 156
Robinson, Chief Alexander, 85, 121
Robinson Woods, 85
Rookery Building, 18
Roosevelt Road, 14
Rosehill Cemetery, 81
Running and jogging, 198
Rush Street Bridge, 120
Ryerson Nature Preserve, 192

Safety, 4
Saganashkee Slough, 189
Sailing, 135, 138, 189, 203
St. Augustine (Su Casa) Neighborhood
  Community Garden, 150
St. Lawrence Seaway, 28, 126
St. Louis, Missouri, 124
Saint-Gaudens, Augustus, *Seated
  Lincoln* (sculpture), 137
Salamander Safari, Chicago
  Herpetological Society, 53, 222–23
Salt Creek Canoe Trail, 193
Salt Creek Trail, 185
Salt springs, 33, 82
Sand Bluff Banding Station, 163
Sand Prairie Nature Preserve, 165
Sand prairies, 70, 73, 75, 77
Sand Ridge Nature Center, 100–102
  Archaeology Awareness Day, 220
  Earth Day, 211
  Settler's Day, 225
  Totally Trees, 207
Sandburg, Carl, 11, 37
Sanitary and Ship Canal, 25, 34, 124,
  125, 126, 193
Santa Fe Prairie: Palos Restoration
  Project, 74
Santa Fe Railroad, 34

Satellites, 64
Sauk tribe, 80
Savanna Nature Preserve, 75
Savannas, 92
School gardens, 148
Sears "Skate on State," 199, 205
Sears Tower, 18, 21, 51
Seasons, 2, 60
*Seated Lincoln* (Saint-Gaudens,
  sculptor), 137
"Second City," 11
Sedge prairies, 45, 54, 73, 75, 77,
  110, 111
Sediment pollution, 32
Seed Savers Exchange, 220
Seeps, 49, 111
Self-sustaining nuclear chain reaction, 21
Seneca Grain Elevator, 129
Sensory gardens, 204
Settlers, 10, 15, 23, 24, 33, 71–72, 80–
  81, 106, 116, 119. *See also*
  Immigrants; Pioneers
Settler's Day, Sand Ridge Nature
  Center, 225
Sewage, 25, 31, 106, 121, 123, 124.
  *See also* Pollution
Shabbona, Chief, 81, 83, 87
Shakespeare Garden, 152
Shawnee tribe, 80
Shedd Aquarium. *See* John G. Shedd
  Aquarium, 167
Shell Club, Field Museum of Natural
  History, 165
Sheridan Road, 36
Sheridan Road Trail, 186
Sherman Park, 106
Shoe Factory Road Prairie Nature
  Preserve, 55, 70
Shooting stars, 64
Short-grass prairies, 71
Shrub prairies, 70, 77
Sierra Club, 243
Silurian Sea, 8, 22, 32–33
Simonds, Ossian C., 134, 135
Sinclair, Upton, *The Jungle*, 21

Singing sands, 40
Skating, 199
Ski-Fest, Camp Sagawau, 53, 206–7
Skiing, 199–200
Skokie Lagoons, 106–7, 189, 190–91
Skokie Marsh, 83, 84
Skokie Northshore Sculpture Park, 144
Sky calendar, 59
Skyline of Chicago, 9
Sky-viewing sites, 62
Skywatch, 59–66
Slaughterhouses, 11, 21
Slavery, 23, 119
Sledge Hockey, 202
Smog, 12
Snowmobiling, 129
Sodbusting, 71
Soil erosion, 124
Solar eclipses, 64
Solar flares, 63
Solar winds, 63
Soldier Field, 29
Somme Prairie Nature Preserve, 72, 74
South Field House, 136
South Lagoon, 135
South Park, 25
South Pond, 136
South Shore Golf Course, 196
South side of Chicago, 20–21
Southwestern Plank Road, 103
*Spearman, The* (Mestrovic, sculptor), 137
Special Olympics, 202
Sphagnum moss, 107
Sports, 183–204
Spring Bird Count, Chicago
    Ornithological Society, 214–15
Spring Bird Count and Bird Migration
    Field Trips, Chicago Ornithological
    Society, 213
Spring Daffodil Show, Midwest Daffodil
    Society, 244
Spring Flower Show
    Garfield Park Conservatory and
        Gardens, 209
    Lincoln Park Conservatory, 208

Spring Garden Walks, Garden Clubs of
    Illinois, Inc., 214
Spring Grove Camp, Prairie Club, 243
Spring Hill Farm Fen, 70
Spring Lake Nature Preserve, 113
Spring Maple Sugar Time Festival,
    39, 95
Springs, 49, 111
Spruce forests, 22, 90
Stagecoach routes, 15
Stagg Field, 21
Stars, 59–66
Starved Rock, 80, 87
State of Illinois Center.
    *See* James R. Thompson Center
State symbols. *See* Illinois
Steppes, 71
Stevenson Expressway, 20
Stony Ford, 82
Stony Island, 33
Storrs, John, *Ceres* (sculpture), 18
Stratus clouds, 61
Street names, 14–15
Suburban birding, 161–63
Suburban boating, 189–90
Suburban gardens, 151–56
Suburban museums, 179–82
Suburban parks, 144–48
Subway train routes, 50
Succession
    bog, 110
    forest, 89–90
    sand dune, 38, 40, 42
Sugar Maple Festival, River Trail
    Nature Center, 210
Sullivan, Louis, 16, 18
Summit's Ford, 82
Sun, 60–63
Sun Fests, Adler Planetarium and
    Astronomy Museum, 208, 215,
    220, 225
Sunflower family, Compositae, 68
Sun-Times Building, 122
Supernovas, 60
Swallow Cliff Sports Area, 201

Swampland sites, 20, 105
Swells and swales, 69
Swimming, 138, 200
  for immigrants, 134
  and pollution, 31
  safety of, 4
Sydney R. Marovitz Golf Course, 196
Symposium on Sustainable Cities, 238

Taft, Loredo, 139
Tall shrub bog, 110
Tallgrass prairie ecosystem, 10, 23,
  51–52, 54, 58, 71, 72–73, 75
Tamarack (larch) trees, 89, 107, 110
Tarp and Reservoir Project, 124
Taste of Chicago, Grant Park, 229
Tecumseh, Shawnee Chief, 79
Teddy Bear Picnic, Brookfield Zoo, 220
Temperatures, 12. *See also* Weather
Tennis, 201
Tevatron, 57
Thanksgiving Day Feast, Brookfield
  Zoo, 225
Thatcher Woods, 85, 99
Therapeutic recreational programs and
  sites, 202–4
Thomas J. O'Brien Lock and Dam, 126
Thomas Jefferson Woods, 99
Thoreau, Henry David, 89
Thorn Creek, 33
Thornton-Lansing Road Nature
  Preserve, 114
Tides, 63
Timeline of Chicago, 22–26
Tinley Creek Bike Trail, 185
Tinley Creek Division of the Forest
  Preserve District of Cook County, 52
Tipis, 82
Tobogganing, 201
Tolleston beach level, 34, 35, 42
Totally Trees, Sand Ridge Nature
  Center, 207
Tours
  Loop, 15–18
  ratings of, 3

Toxic chemicals, 31
Trading posts, 15, 83, 120
Trail times, 5
Trail trees, 83
Transcontinental waterway, 117
Trappers. *See* Fur traders
Treaty of Chicago, 80
Treaty of Greenville, 23, 80
Treaty of Prairie du Chien, 84
"Tree Gang," 105
Tree graveyards, 42
Trembling wetlands, 107
Tribune Tower, 51
Triton College Botanical
  Garden, 155
Trout Park Nature Preserve, 56
True prairies, 71
Tufa, 50, 54, 111
Tunnels under Chicago, 26, 50–51,
  122, 124
Turnovers in Lake Michigan, 29, 31
Turtlehead Lake, 52
Tussock grasslands, 71
Typhoid, 31, 123

*Ubis in Horto* (City in a Garden),
  motto of Chicago, 7
Underground Chicago, 50–51
Understory of forest, 92, 94
Union prisoner of war camp, 46
Union Stockyards, 11, 13, 20–21, 25
*Universe* (Calder, sculptor), 18
University of Chicago, 21, 26, 36
University of Illinois Cooperative
  Extension Service, 149, 150, 246
  Green and Growing Fair, 212
Upland forest, 91, 110
Urban birding, 159–61
Urban Fisheries Program, 194, 195,
  203, 236
  Access to Fishing, 195
  Free Fishing Days, 216
Urban museums, 173–79
Urban national park, 39
Urban plan, 13–14

Urban Resources Partnership of the
U.S. Department of Agriculture, 141
*Urbis in Horto* (City in a Garden),
Chicago's motto, 7, 134

Valparaiso Moraine, 55
Veld, 71
Venetian Night, Grant Park, 187, 229
Vermillion River, 130
Vincennes Trace, 16, 82
Virgil L. Gilmand Bike Trails, 187
Volleyball, 201–2
Vollmer Road Wildlife Marsh, 52
Volo Bog State Natural Area, 108–10
Volo Bog Winter Fest, 228
Volunteer Illinois, 240–41
Volunteer Stewardship Network,
Nature Conservancy, 242
Von Steuben Metropolitan Science
Center, 149

Wabash River, 15, 16
War of 1812, 24, 84, 127
Ward, Aaron Montgomery, 25, 28
Washington Park, 20, 21, 106
Waste and sewage treatment plants, 124
Water canteens, 4
Water treatment plants, 29, 32
Waukegan Harbor, 32
Wayne, General Anthony, 23
Weather
in Chicago, 12–13, 16, 27, 61
and Lake Michigan, 29–30
of prairies, 71
*See also* Precipitation
Weather systems, 13, 60, 61
Weiner, Egon, *Pillar of Fire*
(sculpture), 19
Welland Canal, 30
Wentworth, Elijah, 121
West Beach Succession Trail, 40–42
West Park, 25
West Pullman Park, 143
Westrec Corporation, 189, 203
Wet prairies, 70, 74, 76, 77

Wetlands, 20, 54, 103–14, 124, 126
conservation of, 81
plants in, 104, 105
Wetlands Research, Inc., 111
Wheelchair access, 3.
*See also* Physically challenged people
Whistler's Woods, 81, 126
White Pines State Park, 90
Wigwams, 81–82
Wild Garden Project, Nature
Conservancy, 241–42
Wilder Conservatory, 153
Wilderness adventures, 230–31
Wildlife, 157–82
Wildlife Haven, 166
William G. Stratton State Park, 128, 129
William W. Powers Conservation
Area, 112
Willowbrook Forest Preserve and
Wildlife Haven, 166
Wilmette Wildflower Garden, 153
Wilmington Shrub Prairie Nature
Preserve, 77
Wilson, Robert, *Mobius Strip*
(sculpture), 57
Winds in Chicago, 12, 60, 61
"Windy City," 11
Winter
forests in, 94
temperatures in, 12
Winter Bird Count, Chicago
Ornithological Society, 226
Winter Canoe Ride, 191
Winter Festivals and Games, Field
Museum of Natural History, 227–28
Winter Fishing Clinic, 195
Winter Scientific Meeting, Northern
Illinois Hosta Society, 245
Winter Solstice Festival, North Park
Village Nature Center, 95, 227
Winter Weekend of Trees, Morton
Arboretum, 207
Winterbreak Chicago, 206
Wisconsin and Illinois boundaries,
118–19

Wolf Lake State Park and Conservation
    Area, 112, 126
Wolf Point, 121, 191
Wolf Road Prairie Nature Preserve, 75
Wooded Island, 160
Woodworth Prairie, 2, 76
World's fair. *See* Columbian Exposition
    of 1873
Worth Island, 34
Wrigley Building, 122

Yacht harbors, 36

Zelebration, Brookfield Zoo, 218
Zimmerman site, 87
Zoo Photo Contest Display, Brookfield
    Zoo, 221
Zoo Run Run, Brookfield Zoo, 198, 224